Kyd's Spanish Tragedy was perhaps the most famous play of Elizabeth's reign. Though there were many who jeered at its rhetoric and its emphatic passions, its influence on later plays, especially Hamlet, is known to every student of English drama.

This is the first major edition of the play for over 50 years, and it is more fully annotated than any previous edition.

The editor is senior lecturer in English in the University of Birmingham.

THE REVELS PLAYS

General Editor: Clifford Leech

THE SPANISH TRAGEDY

The Spanish Tragedie:
OR,
Hieronimo is mad againe.

Containing the lamentable end of *Don Horatio*, and
Belimperia ; with the pittifull death of *Hieronimo*.

Newly corrected, amended, and enlarged with new
Additions of the *Painters* part, and others, as
it hath of late been diuers times acted.

LONDON,
Printed by W. White, for I. White and T. Langley,
and are to be sold at their Shop ouer against the
Sarazens head without New-gate. 1615.

*Title page of
the 1615 edition*

The Spanish Tragedy

THOMAS KYD

EDITED BY

PHILIP EDWARDS

THE REVELS PLAYS

HARVARD UNIVERSITY PRESS
CAMBRIDGE, MASSACHUSETTS

This edition first published 1959

General Editor's Preface

The aim of this series is to apply to plays by Shakespeare's pre-decessors, contemporaries, and successors the methods that are now used in Shakespeare editing. It is indeed out of the success of the New Arden Shakespeare that the idea of the present series has emerged, and Professor Una Ellis-Fermor and Dr Harold F. Brooks have most generously given advice on its planning.

There is neither the hope nor the intention of making each volume in the series conform in every particular to one pattern. Each author, each individual play, is likely to present special prob-lems—of text, of density of collation and commentary, of critical and historical judgment. Moreover, any scholar engaged in the task of editing a sixteenth- or seventeenth-century play will recognize that wholly acceptable editorial principles are only gradually be-coming plain. There will, therefore, be no hesitation in modifying the practice of this series, either in the light of the peculiarities of any one play or in the light of growing editorial experience. Never-theless, in certain basic matters the plan of the series is likely to remain constant.

The introductions will include discussions of the provenance of the text, the play's stage-history and reputation, its significance as a contribution to dramatic literature, and its place within the work of its author. The text will be based on a fresh examination of the early editions. Modern spelling will be used, and the original punctuation will be modified where it is likely to cause obscurity; editorial stage-directions will be enclosed in square brackets. The collation will aim at making clear the grounds for an editor's choice in every instance where the original or a frequently accepted modern reading has been departed from. The annotations will attempt to explain difficult passages and to provide such comments and illustrations of usage as the editor considers desirable. Each volume will include either a glossary or an index to annotations: it is the hope of the editors that in this way the series will ultimately provide some assistance to lexicographers of sixteenth- and seventeenth-century English.

But the series will be inadequately performing its task if it proves acceptable only to readers. The special needs of actors and producers will be borne in mind, particularly in the comments on staging and stage-history. Moreover, in one matter a rigorous uniformity may be expected: no editorial indications of locality will be introduced into the scene-headings. This should emphasize the kind of staging for which the plays were originally intended, and may perhaps suggest the advantage of achieving in a modern theatre some approach to the fluidity of scene and the neutrality of acting-space that Shakespeare's fellows knew. In this connection, it will be observed that the indications of act- and scene-division, except where they derive from the copy-text, are given unobtrusively in square brackets.

A small innovation in line-numbering is being introduced. Stage-directions which occur on separate lines from the text are given the number of the immediately preceding line followed by a decimal point and 1, 2, 3, etc. Thus the line 163.5 indicates the fifth line of a stage-direction following line 163 of the scene. At the beginning of a scene the lines of a stage-direction are numbered 0.1, 0.2, etc.

'The Revels' was a general name for entertainments at court in the late sixteenth and seventeenth centuries, and it was from the Master of the Revels that a licence had to be obtained before any play could be performed in London. The plays to be included in this series therefore found their way to the Revels Office. For a body of dramatic literature that reached its fullest growth in the field of tragedy, the term 'Revels' may appear strange. But perhaps the actor at least will judge it fitting.

CLIFFORD LEECH

Durham, 1958

Contents

Preface

In the present edition, I have tried to give a reliable modernized text of *The Spanish Tragedy* and, in the Introduction and Commentary, I have done my best to solve the many problems posed by the play. Since it is impossible to perceive the movement of the original play in the expanded text of 1602, the 'Additions' are printed separately at the end of the main text. The Commentary is fuller than that of any previous edition, but I hope it will not be found burdened with unnecessary detail. The Introduction contains only light skirmishes with problems not central to the understanding of the play, such as the 'Ur-*Hamlet*' and the authorship of the 'Additions'. The date, the text, the original shape of the play, and the author's attitude to revenge have needed so full a treatment that I have had room for much less than I would have wished to say about the language of the play. Wolfgang Clemen's recent book on the language of pre-Shakespearian tragedy has put the study of Kyd's rhetoric on to a new plane, and a detailed study of *The Spanish Tragedy* on Clemen's lines would be welcome indeed.

I cannot here do more than record a general thanks to those who have answered queries and helped with problems during my preparation of this edition. But I wish to mention my particular gratitude to Richard Hosley of the University of Missouri, whose advice and encouragement have been invaluable to me. I have been helped over many stiles by my colleagues E. G. Stanley and D. R. Dudley; I am also much in the General Editor's debt for the sharpness of his eye and the mildness of his manner.

PHILIP EDWARDS

University of Birmingham
August, 1958.

Abbreviations

(excluding texts, for which see p. lxix)

Biesterfeldt	P. W. Biesterfeldt, *Die dramatische Technik Thomas Kyds. Studien zur inneren Struktur und szenischen Form des Elisabethanischen Dramas.* Göttingen, 1935; Halle (Saale), 1936.
Boas	Introduction to *The Works of Thomas Kyd*, edited by F. S. Boas. Oxford, 1901.
Bowers	F. T. Bowers, *Elizabethan Revenge Tragedy, 1587–1642.* Princeton, 1940.
Eliz. Stage	E. K. Chambers, *The Elizabethan Stage.* 4 vols. Oxford, 1923.
Franz	W. Franz, *Die Sprache Shakespeares.* Halle, 1939.
Green	H. Green, *Shakespeare and the Emblem Writers.* London, 1870.
Greg, *Bibl. E.P.D.*	W. W. Greg, *A Bibliography of the English Printed Drama to the Restoration.* 3 vols. London, 1939–57.
Henslowe's *Diary*	*Henslowe's Diary*, edited by W. W. Greg. 2 vols. London, 1904.
Jonson, *Works*	*Ben Jonson*, edited by C. H. Herford and P. and E. Simpson. 11 vols. Oxford, 1925–52.
M.S.R.	Malone Society Reprints.
MSR (1592)	Introduction to *The Spanish Tragedy (1592)*, edited by W. W. Greg and D. Nichol Smith. Malone Society Reprints, 1948 (1949).

MSR (1602)	Introduction to *The Spanish Tragedy with Additions, 1602*, edited by W. W. Greg in consultation with F. S. Boas. Malone Society Reprints, 1925.
Nashe, *Works*	*The Works of Thomas Nashe*, edited by R. B. McKerrow. 5 vols. London, 1904–10.
O.E.D.	Oxford English Dictionary.
Sarrazin	G. Sarrazin, *Thomas Kyd und sein Kreis: Eine litterarhistorische Untersuchung*. Berlin, 1892.
Schick[1]	Introduction to *The Spanish Tragedy*, edited by J. Schick. London, 1898 (*The Temple Dramatists*).
Schick[2]	Introduction to *Spanish Tragedy*, edited by J. Schick. Berlin, 1901 (*Litterarhistorische Forschungen*, Heft xix).
Schmidt	A. Schmidt, *Shakespeare-Lexicon*. 2 vols. 2nd edn, Berlin and London, 1886; 3rd edn (with revisions by G. Sarrazin), Berlin, 1902.
Schücking	L. L. Schücking, *Die Zusätze zur „Spanish Tragedy"*. Leipzig, 1938 (*Berichte über die Verhandlungen der Sächsischen Akademie der Wissenschaften zu Leipzig*. Band 90. Heft 2).
Tilley	M. P. Tilley, *A Dictionary of the Proverbs in England in the Sixteenth and Seventeenth Centuries*. Ann Arbor, 1950.

PERIODICALS

Archiv	*Archiv für das Studium der neueren Sprachen.*
J.E.G.P.	*Journal of English and Germanic Philology.*
M.L.N.	*Modern Language Notes.*
N. & Q.	*Notes and Queries.*
P.M.L.A.	*Publications of the Modern Language Association of America.*

P.Q.	*Philological Quarterly.*
R.E.S.	*Review of English Studies.*
Sh. Jahrbuch	*Shakespeare-Jahrbuch* (formerly *Jahrbuch der Deutschen Shakespeare-Gesellschaft*).
T.L.S.	*Times Literary Supplement.*

Quotations and line-numbers for Shakespeare from the Globe edition; for Seneca from the Loeb edition; for Marlowe from the Oxford edition (Tucker Brooke, 1910); for Marston's *Antonio* plays from the Malone Society Reprints; for Dekker from the Cambridge edition (Bowers, 1953+).

Introduction

I. AUTHORSHIP

The Spanish Tragedy was anonymous in its own day. No edition of the sixteenth or seventeenth century mentioned the author, and it was not until 1773 that Hawkins found, in Heywood's *Apology for Actors* (1612), its assignment to Thomas Kyd. Discussing tragedies sponsored by the Roman emperors, Heywood remarks:

> Therefore M. Kid, in his Spanish Tragedy, upon occasion presenting itselfe, thus writes.
>> Why, Nero thought it no disparagement,
>> And kings and emperours have tane delight
>> To make experience of their wits in playes.[1]

There is no other external evidence that Kyd wrote *The Spanish Tragedy*. But there is a peculiarly intimate relation between *The Spanish Tragedy* and Kyd's *Cornelia* (1594), translated from Garnier, and the only reasonable way of accounting for the relationship is to say that the same man was responsible for both works.[2] There is no cause for doubting Heywood's attribution.[3]

Apart from *The Spanish Tragedy* and *Cornelia* (a translation) no play which is certainly Kyd's is known. He is renowned for having written the lost play of *Hamlet* (pre-1589), which was the source of Shakespeare's play, but it cannot be proved that he wrote it; the evidence lies in a disputed interpretation of a passage from Nashe's Preface to *Menaphon* (see below, pp. xxii f.), and in similarities between *The Spanish Tragedy* and the later *Hamlet*, especially the first Quarto. The play *Soliman and Perseda* is attributed to Kyd chiefly because its plot is the same as that of the play-within-the-play in Act IV of *The Spanish Tragedy*; the stylistic resemblances are not

---

[1] Shakespeare Soc. Reprint (1841), p. 45. The excerpt is IV. i. 87–9.
[2] See Appendix C and notes to I. ii. 52–60 and III. vii. 8.
[3] The authorship of the Additions is discussed below in Section 6.

overwhelming. Arguments have been advanced, some with little cogency and others with less, for Kyd's authorship or part-authorship of *Arden of Feversham*, *King Leir*, *Titus Andronicus*, *Troublesome Reign of King John*, and other plays, even *The Rare Triumphs of Love and Fortune*. If the findings are usually questionable, the search is understandable, for Kyd was an established dramatist. Jonson refers in the First Folio to '*sporting* Kid' in company with Lyly and Marlowe as one of the dramatists whom Shakespeare has outshone. Meres put Kyd among 'our best for Tragedie' in his *Palladis Tamia* (1598). Heywood, in *Hierarchy of the Blessed Angels* (1635), refers to Kyd in the same tone as he refers to other well-known dramatists—'Famous *Kid* was call'd but *Tom*.' Dekker's reference to 'industrious Kyd' puts him among dramatists of rather less fame (see below, p. xxvi). Some of the plays which Kyd wrote may well be extant plays, either anonymous or wrongly attributed to another dramatist. But until more convincing evidence can be found, it is from *The Spanish Tragedy* alone that his qualities as a dramatist have to be assessed.[1]

A few facts concerning Kyd's life are known. The dramatist is usually identified with Thomas Kyd, son of Francis Kyd the scrivener. The baptismal register of St Mary Woolnoth in the City of London carries, for 6 November 1558, the entry, 'Thomas, son of Francis Kidd, Citizen and Writer of the Courte Letter of London' (Boas, p. xv). Francis Kyd was a citizen of some standing: he held high office in the Company of Scriveners,[2] he was a churchwarden of St Mary Woolnoth, and he appears as witness to the wills of men of substance. In October 1565 he entered his son Thomas at the recently founded Merchant Taylors' School, of which Mulcaster was headmaster and Spenser a senior schoolboy. The only other record of this Thomas Kyd tends to confirm his identity with the dramatist. On 30 December 1594, Anna Kyd, wife of Francis, made on behalf of her husband a formal and legal renunciation of the

---

[1] Of non-dramatic works, *The Householders Philosophie* (1588) by T. K. is probably Kyd's. There are some snatches of verse in *Englands Parnassus* (1600). A pamphlet, *The Murder of Iohn Brewen* (1592), is attributed to Kyd on the rather questionable evidence of his name being written in ink at the end of the one surviving copy; see Greg, *Sh. Jahrbuch*, xliv (1908), 155–6.

[2] B. M. Wagner, *N. & Q.*, 15 December 1928.

administration of the estate of her deceased son, Thomas, and of all title and interest in his goods—and his debts.[1] Boas calls this act a repudiation, and suggests that the clouded last days of Kyd were the 'divers causes and considerations' which led to the renouncement. This may seem fanciful: it was not uncommon to refuse to administer an estate; it may have been only the debts which shocked the parents. The importance of the deed is, first, that one would have conjectured that the dramatist, Kyd, died in 1594,[2] and, secondly, that it suggests Kyd had neither wife nor children, since his parents were apparently expected to administer his estate.

To return to the records of Kyd's life, there is no evidence that he went to either university. It has been suggested, chiefly on the evidence of Nashe's reference (see below, p. xxii) to a 'sort of shifting companions' who 'leave the trade of Noverint' in order to write plays, that he followed his father's calling of scrivener. Though it is indeed dubious whether Nashe is referring to Kyd at all, Greg (*English Literary Autographs*, Plate xv) thinks that Kyd's beautifully clear handwriting suggests a training as a scrivener, and others have found the frequency and accuracy of the legal terms in *The Spanish Tragedy* significant of Kyd's acquaintance with the law through his father's profession. But, frankly, Kyd's career as a young man is obscure. We are on firmer ground with Kyd's own words in his letter to Puckering, the Lord Keeper, the probable date of which is the summer of 1593.[3] Kyd wrote this letter to ask for help in being reinstated in the favour of his 'Lord', whom he does not name, whom he has served 'almost these six years now', that is, since about the end of 1587. Kyd does not say in what capacity he 'served', but he knew the 'form of divine prayers used duly in his lordship's house', and he contrasts his own relationship with that of Marlowe, who 'bore name to serve my Lord, although his lordship

---

[1] See Boas, p. lxxvi. The deed in the *Archdeaconry of London Probate and Administration Act Book* was discovered by Schick.

[2] There is a good deal of information about him in 1593, but silence afterwards; again, the dedication to *Cornelia* promises a translation of Garnier's *Porcie* in the summer, and so far as we know the promise was never fulfilled.

[3] There is a facsimile in Boas, and also a transcription (pp. cviii–cx), with an error of 'iij' for 'vj'.

never knew his service, but in writing for his players'. This last reference gives less help than it should in identifying the lord; possibly it was Lord Strange.[1]

Another gleaning from Kyd's letter is that about the year 1591 Kyd and Marlowe were sharing lodgings, or, to be exact, were 'writing in one chamber'. Kyd has recorded how extremely uncomfortable this proximity was for him[2] and it had dramatic consequences. On 12 May 1593, Kyd was in prison and a search of his lodgings had been carried out.[3] On the previous day the Privy Council had ordered urgent and severe measures to be taken to find and punish the author of 'late divers lewd and mutinous libels' (which have been identified with those attacking London's foreign artisans). Among Kyd's papers were found, not libels, but 'atheistical' disputations, which Kyd affirmed to be Marlowe's and which were a cause of Marlowe's being summoned before the Privy Council on 18 May. Kyd claims that he was put to the torture during his arrest (permission for the use of torture had been given in the Privy Council's decree). It is not known how long he was in custody, but he was apparently not found guilty of the libel or of atheism. His lord seems to have renounced him in his disgrace, however, and, 'utterly undone', Kyd wrote his letter to Puckering to ask for the favour of his interest, protesting his own innocence and his hatred of Marlowe (whom he refers to as dead).

The last record of Kyd is the translation *Cornelia* (before January 1594). The dedication to the Countess of Sussex is dark indeed.

> Hauing no leysure (most noble Lady) but such as euermore is traueld with th' afflictions of the minde, then which the world affoords no greater misery, it may bee wondred at by some, how I durst vndertake a matter of this moment: which both requireth cunning, rest and oportunity . . .
> . . . what grace that excellent GARNIER hath lost by my defaulte,

[1] So Tucker Brooke, *Life of Marlowe*, p. 47, and Boas, *Christopher Marlowe*, p. 242; but see also Boas' earlier suggestion of the Earl of Sussex, Kyd's *Works*, p. lxiv.

[2] In the memorandum concerning 'Marlowes monstruous opinions', discovered by F. K. Brown, *T.L.S.*, 2 June 1921.

[3] I give the briefest account of the famous story, since it is so fully covered in Boas and in all lives of Marlowe.

I shall beseech your Honour to repaire with the regarde of those so bitter times and priuie broken passions that I endured in the writing it.

This wretchedness is a lamentable end to Kyd's career, for he appears to have been innocent of the crimes in connexion with which he was arrested, and his disgrace was undeserved. If we accept the identification of Kyd with the son of Francis Kyd, he must have died before the late autumn of 1594.

2. DATE

The date of composition of *The Spanish Tragedy* is uncertain. Henslowe records in his *Diary* a performance of 'spanes comodye donne oracoe' on 23 February 1591/2 and of 'Jeronymo' on 14 March 1591/2 by Strange's Men at the Rose. There is no reason to doubt that 'Jeronymo' was *The Spanish Tragedy*, though it is customary to assume that 'spanes comodye donne oracoe' was not a variant title but a 'first part', or associated play, now lost (see Appendix A). The year 1592 as the upward limit for the date of the play is confirmed by the entry in the Stationers' Register on 6 October 1592 of 'the Spanishe tragedie of Don Horatio and Bellimpera' (see below, p. xxviii). The earlier limit of date is 1582. The opening of Act II, Scene i imitates Sonnet XLVII of Thomas Watson's *Hecatompathia* which (though published without date) was entered in the Stationers' Register on 31 March 1582, under the title of 'Watsons Passions'. Though Watson's images in the sonnet are commonplace (see note at II. i. 3–10) there is no doubt of Kyd's dependence on Watson, since he breaks the prosody of his blank verse to include Watson's rhyme-scheme.

In the Induction to Jonson's *Bartholomew Fair* (1614) occurs the following remark: 'Hee that will sweare, *Ieronimo*, or *Andronicus* are the best playes, yet, shall passe vnexcepted at, heere, as a man whose Iudgement shewes it is constant, and hath stood still, these fiue and twenty, or thirtie yeeres' (*Works*, VI, 16). This allusion gives us 1584–9, but one hesitates to take the dates literally. Jonson is clearly talking in round figures, and the bracket of 1582–92 is not much narrowed; Jonson was born in 1572, and can hardly be con-

sidered an authority on the dates of plays in the 1580's; thirdly, as
J. C. Maxwell remarks in the preface to the New Arden edition of
Titus Andronicus, Jonson was likely to exaggerate the antiquated-
ness of the plays.

But critics have found a point midway between Jonson's twenty-
five or thirty years, about 1586–7, an acceptable date in the light of
other evidence. The chief evidence is the renowned allusion to the
'Kid in *Æsop*' in the Preface which Nashe wrote to Greene's *Menaphon* (Stationers' Register, 23 August 1589). Nashe 'turns back' to
address 'a few of our triuiall translators'.

> It is a common practise now a dayes amongst a sort of shifting com-
> panions, that runne through euery Art and thriue by none, to
> leaue the trade of *Nouerint*, whereto they were borne, and busie
> themselues with the indeuours of Art, that could scarcely Latinize
> their neck verse if they should haue neede; yet English *Seneca* read
> by Candle-light yeelds many good sentences, as *Blood is a begger*,
> and so forth; and if you intreate him faire in a frostie morning, hee
> will affoord you whole Hamlets, I should say handfuls of Tragicall
> speeches. But O griefe! *Tempus edax rerum*, whats that will last
> alwayes? The Sea exhaled by droppes will in continuance bee drie,
> and *Seneca*, let blood line by line and page by page, at length must
> needes die to our Stage; which makes his famished followers to
> imitate the Kid in *Æsop*, who, enamoured with the Foxes new-
> fangles, forsooke all hopes of life to leape into a newe occupation;
> and these men, renouncing all possibilities of credite or estima-
> tion, to intermeddle with Italian Translations: Wherein how
> poorely they haue plodded, (as those that are neither prouenzall
> men, nor are able to distinguish of Articles,) let all indifferent
> Gentlemen that haue trauelled in that tongue discerne by their
> two-pennie Pamphlets. And no maruell though their home borne
> mediocritie bee such in this matter: for what can bee hoped of those
> that thrust *Elisium* into hell, and haue not learned, so long as they
> haue liued in the Spheres, the iust measure of the Horizon without
> an hexameter? Sufficeth them to bodge vp a blanke verse with ifs
> and ands, and otherwhile for recreation after their Candle-stuffe,
> hauing starched their beards most curiously, to make Peripateticall
> path into the inner parts of the Citie, and spend two or three
> howers in turning ouer French *Dowdie*, where they attract more
> infection in one minute, then they can do eloquence all daies of
> their life, by conuersing with any Authors of like argument.[1]

---

[1] Nashe, *Works*, III, 315–16.

Boas took the accepted view in supposing that one writer was being referred to, identified as Kyd by the references to the 'Kid in *Æsop*' and to *Nouerint* (that is, scrivener), and that Nashe, therefore, reveals Kyd as the author of the 'Ur-*Hamlet*'; that *The Spanish Tragedy* is alluded to in the phrase 'thrust *Elisium* into hell' (the description of the underworld in the first scene), in the phrase 'bodge vp a blanke verse with ifs and ands' (i.e., *What, villain, ifs and ands?* at II. i. 77), and in the phrase 'turning ouer French *Dowdie*' (i.e., the use of Garnier in the account of the battle in I. ii). This whole interpretation is admirably challenged by McKerrow (Nashe, IV, 449–52) and by G. I. Duthie (*The 'Bad' Quarto of Hamlet* (1941), pp. 55–76), who is able to review more recent contributions to the debate. It seems clear that Nashe is attacking several writers (a *sort* of companions—that is, a group) and not one alone; it needs also an extraordinary straining of the evidence to produce any allusion at all to *The Spanish Tragedy*. Kyd does not trip up over his Elysium (see note to I. i. 73); what Nashe means by bodging up a blank verse with ifs and ands is a very different thing from Kyd's inoffensive use of the phrase 'ifs and ands' itself; the reference to 'French *Dowdie*' is smut, an allusion to Garnier being most unlikely in the context. The question remains whether Kyd is or is not one of the group of writers whom Nashe is inveighing against—amongst whom is, apparently, the author of the first *Hamlet*. The matter is briefly discussed in Appendix B, since what matters in the present argument is that, there being no likely allusion to *The Spanish Tragedy* in the passage, the play is not required to be before 1589.

1587 has been favoured as a date because of the absence of any reference to the Armada in the play. In I. iv, the triumphs of English arms in the Iberian peninsula are celebrated in Hieronimo's pageant. The latest in date of these is John of Gaunt's expedition. Schick writes, in his Preface to the New Temple edition (p. xxiii):

> It is difficult to believe that these half-apocryphal stories should have been brought forward as a matter of satisfaction, in face of the real and tangible glories of the Armada. The enumeration of these old victories . . . was certainly more in place about 1585–87, when the great contest with Spain was only just brewing.

But the argument is poor.[1] Let us suppose that *The Spanish Tragedy* was written after the Armada; it surely would have been foolish for Kyd to have introduced an allusion to it in the pageant before his King of Spain, for such an allusion would have placed the play squarely in a contemporary setting, inviting an identification of the King with Philip II, and corresponding identifications of his leading characters and the events of the story. Historically speaking, his play is sheer fantasy, and it is in his interest to keep *his* Spain clear of association with the Spain of his own time. It is unfortunate that Schick attempted, in hunting after both source and date, to relate the affairs between Spain and Portugal in the play to the real clash between these countries which ended with Spain's annexation of her neighbour. It is true that there had been a bloody battle between Spain and Portugal in 1580 (Alcantara) in which Portugal was defeated; it is true that after the close of 1582 Portugal was governed, as in the play, by a viceroy; it is true that the last stage in the annexation of Portugal by Philip was the action over Terceira in 1583 (an action very well known to Englishmen) and that Terceira is mentioned in Kyd's play (I. iii. 82); it is true that Kyd refers (though most inaccurately) to Portugal's loss of her imperial position (see note to III. xiv. 6–7). But this 'late conflict' (I. i. 15) in Kyd's play is a war between Spain and its tributary Portugal, governed by a viceroy, arising from Portugal's refusal to pay its tribute. There was no war between Spain and Portugal after the institution of a viceroy by Philip, and since the viceroy was his own nephew, appointed by him to govern the country in his absence,[2] war between the two men is an absurd thought; and before the annexation there could be no question of tribute. It is equally ludicrous to suggest (cf. Schick, pp. xxiii–xxiv) that the projected marriage between Balthazar and Bel-imperia reflects a proposed marriage which was part of the negotiations between Philip and the Duke of Braganza *before* Alcantara.

If Kyd's play was based on real events, then the absence of any

---

[1] W. Bang suggested (*Englische Studien*, xxviii, 1900, 229–34) that Kyd's silence might simply imply that the intoxication over the victory was a thing of the past.

[2] H. V. Livermore, *History of Portugal* (1947), pp. 268–9.

reference to the Armada would be near to proof that the play was written before 1588. But the reflection of historical events is so trifling and tangential that the argument falls to the ground. One has only to look at a play which does deal with what really passed between Spain and Portugal, like *The Battle of Alcazar* (?1588), to realize that Kyd is innocent of contemporary allusions. Indeed, when we consider how much English dramatists (and their audiences) knew of the recent sad history of Portugal—of 'Sebastianism' for example—it seems, as I have suggested, that Kyd must have been trying to avoid verisimilitude. In *The Battle of Alcazar*, there is, besides a verifiable historical setting, the vein of English sympathy for Portugal's plight and the expected picture of Spain as the proud and perfidious papist kingdom, together with references to Spain's activities in the Low Countries. Here is an important silence in Kyd which has been strangely ignored. Even if *The Spanish Tragedy* had been written before the Armada, one would have expected something to show itself of English hostility to Spanish pride and Spanish religion, and to the campaigns in the Low Countries. Unless it be that Kyd deliberately eschewed 'local colour'—in which case the absence of any reference to the Armada ceases to be of any significance.

We must take it that Kyd was writing a revenge play, and that he wanted (or his source gave) war between two countries for its setting, and that he chose Spain and Portugal without much thought of the real Spain and the real Portugal. When he came to write Hieronimo's pageant, he was prepared for a moment to cater for English patriotic feeling, but he placed the English triumphs in a vague and inaccurate past, which has the needed effect of keeping his play at a distance from contemporary events and preserving the unhistorical flavour of his play. The absence of any reference to the Armada is of no consequence in dating the play.

An extremely early date, 1582–5, has been proposed by T. W. Baldwin.[1] He argues that from the time Kyd entered his unknown lord's service in 1587, he did not write plays. He believes that *The*

---

[1] 'On the Chronology of Thomas Kyd's Plays, *M.L.N.*, xl (1925), 343–9; 'Thomas Kyd's Early Company Connections', *P.Q.*, vi (1927), 311–13. Cf. Biesterfeldt, pp. 22–4.

Spanish Tragedy precedes *Soliman and Perseda*, which he dates
1584–6 on the basis that Death's compliment to Queen Elizabeth
refers to the Babington conspiracies. He also refers to Dekker's
A Knight's Conjuring (1607), which links 'learned Watson, industrious Kyd, ingenious Atchlow, inimitable Bentley', and he notes
that Dekker says that Bentley was 'moulded out of the pens' of Watson, Kyd and Atchlow. As Bentley died in August 1585, it is pre-
sumed that Kyd's works were written before that date. But it cannot be proved that *The Spanish Tragedy* did not follow *Soliman and
Perseda*, and it cannot be proved that *The Spanish Tragedy* was one
of the plays which moulded the forgotten Bentley. The most we can
say is that if it could be shown that Kyd wrote no plays after entering the service of his lord (who was a patron of players), then 1587
would be the latest date for the play.

The evidence from literary sources, apart from Watson, is nuga-
tory. It may well be that Kyd used the 1585 edition of Garnier's
tragedies for his borrowings from *Cornélie*, but he could have used
an earlier text. F. Bowers' suggestion that Kyd used a tract of 1584
in writing the Pedringano episode (see below, p. xlix) is persuasive,
but insufficient without support.

The only evidence which remains is in the agonizing battlefield
of verbal parallels with other works. A vast amount of work has been
done on parallel passages, mainly for the purpose of establishing
the canon of Kyd, but on the comparatively few occasions on which
the parallels seem significant, it is usually impossible to decide
which of the passages was written first. Five works seem to me to
have a really significant relation with *The Spanish Tragedy*: Marlowe's *Tamburlaine*, Part 2, and *The Jew of Malta*, Shakespeare's
King John and *3 Henry VI*, and Thomas Watson's English rendering of his own Latin elegy on Walsingham, *Melibœus*. The most
important of the relations is with Watson's work, discussed in
Appendix D; the elegy was published in 1590 (Walsingham died on
6 April): I tentatively suggest that Kyd borrowed from Watson.
The possible debt to *2 Tamburlaine* is described in Appendix C; the
play dates from about 1588 (published 1590). The parallels with
The Jew of Malta and *King John* are indecisive as respects precedence (see notes to III. xii. 71 and I. ii. 172). *3 Henry VI* (usually

dated 1590–1) appears to me to borrow from Kyd (see notes to I. iv. 140–57; II. v. 17; II. v. 51–2).

No reader will need to be warned of the entire absence of proof in these parallels; they are brought forward none the less, straws as they are, because the date they would hint at, namely 1590, seems to me not at all inappropriate to the style and manner of *The Spanish Tragedy*. I have tried to show that arguments used to place the play in the mid-1580's are not valid; it is time attention was turned to the possibility of a later date. The elaborately patterned rhetoric of the play perhaps conceals for some readers the 'modernity' of Kyd's handling of dialogue and character in many parts of his play; and the long stylized speeches themselves are used with a force and a cunning which puts them apart from their type. *The Spanish Tragedy* would be something of a miracle if it were written in the early 1580's. If the aptness of a date such as 1590 were granted, I think that new evidence would eventually be found, simply by redirecting the search. Meanwhile, on the basis of what firm evidence we have, the date for the play must remain as between 1582 and 1592; but one may express a firm preference for a date towards the upper limit.

3. TEXT

The one authoritative text of *The Spanish Tragedy* (excluding the Additions) is to be found in the edition printed by Edward Allde for Edward White, the only known copy of which is in the British Museum (C.34.d.7). The title-page is worded 'The Spanish Tragedie, Containing the lamentable end of Don Horatio, and Belimperia: with the pittifull death of olde Hieronimo. Newly corrected and amended of such grosse faults as passed in the first impression. At London Printed by Edward Allde, for Edward White.' The edition bears no date, but it is beyond reasonable doubt (as will be seen) that it was in print by the end of 1592, and it is most probable that it was printed during that year; for convenience, it is henceforward referred to as *1592*. Except for the text of the Additions, which were first printed in 1602, *1592* is the source of every other extant edition of the play; and it is, as it must be, the basis of the text in the present edition.

1592 has the appearance of a quarto (A–K⁴L²), but Allde printed it, as he did *Soliman and Perseda* (?1592), from some extra-large sheets, torn in half to give the normal working size, and it is customary to call the format so produced an 'octavo in fours'[1]; there is no other bibliographical irregularity of importance.[2] In the text itself, the general style of composition is uniform, and though there are variations in spelling and in the contraction of final -*ed*, the evidence does not show that more than one compositor was at work on the text (cf. below, p. xxxiii).

Although the Allde/Edward White edition is the earliest extant, it claims to have corrected 'the first impression'. Its predecessor would presumably be one published by Abel Jeffes, by whom the play was entered on the Register of the Stationers' Company on 6 October 1592:

> Abell Ieffes   Entred for his copie vnder thandes of mr Hartwell and mr Stirrop, a booke wche is called the Spanishe tragedie of Don Horatio and Bellimpera &c'.
>
> vjᵈ debt hoc[3]

On 18 December 1592, the full court of the Stationers' Company found that Edward White had 'offendyd' 'in havinge printed the spanishe tragedie belonging to Abell Ieffes'; White was fined ten shillings, and all the copies of his illegal edition were ordered to be confiscated and sold for the benefit of the poor of the Company.[4]

We want to know what was the nature of Jeffes' edition, and

---

[1] Cf. Greg, *Bibl. E.P.D.*, I, 109; F. T. Bowers, *Principles of Bibliographical Description* (1949), pp. 193–5. The technical description is not entirely satisfactory, but it will at least help the student to understand why the chain-lines are vertical, and not horizontal as in a quarto printed from normal-size paper. According to *MSR (1592)*, the edition of 1594 is also an octavo in fours.

[2] After the setting of Sheet A, which does not contain the usual headlines, two skeletons were used in the printing: one for each inner forme, and one for each outer forme. The running titles in both skeletons were slightly altered before the printing of Sheet C—the inner forme to correct *Tragedle*, the outer forme for no observable reason. There is no indication of an interruption in the printing. The four pages of sig. L were printed by half-sheet imposition, using the skeleton of the outer forme.

[3] Arber, II, 293; Greg, *Bibl. E.P.D.*, I, 8; *MSR (1592)*, p. vi.

[4] Greg and Boswell, *Records of the Court of the Stationers' Company, 1576–1602*, p. 44; *MSR (1592)*, pp. vii–xiii.

whether White's was a reprint of it or was set up independently from manuscript. It has been a common assumption that Jeffes' edition gave a defective and debased text, acquired and published without the authority of the theatre, while White's edition was 'an excellent version, perhaps supplied by the players with the express purpose of superseding the one already in print'.[1] Though I believe, for reasons later to be given, that this assumption is correct as respects Jeffes, the facts of publication alone do not give unwavering support to the theory. Abel Jeffes was in severe conflict with the authorities during the summer and autumn of 1592,[2] and it is most likely that he printed his edition of *The Spanish Tragedy* before the worst of his troubles began in August.[3] Provided he had licence from the ecclesiastical authorities, the publication would be quite regular, whether or not he had sanction from the theatre or the author; the fact of publication alone, without entry in the Register, would be sufficient to establish his copyright. He made his entry in the Register, nevertheless, on 6 October; perhaps to confirm his copyright when he learned that Edward White was bringing out an edition. (It will be understood that even if White were proposing to print from a new manuscript, there was still offence against copyright, which was invested in the work, and not in any particular form of it.[4]) White did not desist, however, and when Jeffes was sufficiently out of disgrace to lay his accusation against him, White countered with an accusation against Jeffes for having piratically printed his *Arden of Feversham*; Jeffes suffered exactly the same penalty as White. Interestingly enough, the third edition of the play (1594) was inscribed 'Printed by Abell Ieffes, and are to be sold by Edward White'. Though Jeffes' right in the play had been upheld by the Company, he was prepared to come to terms with White, and arrange a compromise whereby White had the subordinate role of bookseller in the publication (*MSR* (*1592*), p. xiii).

---

[1] Greg and Nichol Smith, *MSR* (*1592*), p. ix.
[2] For a sketch of his stormy career, see Kirschbaum, *Shakespeare and the Stationers*, 1955, pp. 300–1.
[3] He was ordered to be 'committed to ward' on 7 August; see Greg and Boswell, *op. cit.*, p. 42.
[4] Problems about copyright are discussed in Kirschbaum's *Shakespeare and the Stationers*.

White's title-page claim that he had 'corrected and amended' the 'gross faults' in the previous edition has to be taken with caution: many such claims were made when there was little or no justification for them. 'Perhaps,' says Kirschbaum,[1] 'White corrected the printing-house errors in Jeffes' edition; perhaps his claim was based on thin air.' But, we have to add, perhaps his claim was justified. The Second Quarto of *Romeo and Juliet* claims to be 'Newly corrected, augmented, and amended', and the claim is correct. White's claim may not necessarily mean that he put out a good text to supersede a bad, but the evidence cited by Kirschbaum does not necessarily mean that he did not. It would seem to be a strange piece of knavery in White to commit the worst crime in publishing (the contravention of copyright) by reprinting, line for line, a lawful edition and making the claim that he was supplying a corrected edition. Jeffes' willingness to come to terms with White over the 1594 edition suggests that White was not, in fact, such an audacious rogue.[2] But whatever significance one sees in the actions of the two men, there is little in the bare facts to help us to decide the provenance of the editions of Jeffes and White, and the relation between them. It is therefore necessary to try to establish the nature of the copy for *1592* from an examination of the text itself; but it will be seen that from this examination something about the nature of Jeffes' edition may be conjectured.

The Copy for 1592

1592 is carefully and neatly printed and an editor's problems are comparatively few. There are, however, certain oddities and anomalies, and, as most of these are to be found in the last quarter of the play, it is convenient to divide the play into two parts for the pur-

---

[1] 'Is *The Spanish Tragedy* a Leading Case?', *J.E.G.P.*, xxxvii (1938), 501–12.

[2] On the other hand, we do not need to think (cf. Greg, *The Library*, 4, vi (1926), 47–56) that Jeffes *had* to come to terms with White in order to reprint the 'good' text of 1592. Jeffes could cheerfully have gone ahead with White's text on his own, however bad his own previous effort had been; copyright, as we have said, inhered in the work, and not in good or bad versions of it. Similarly, the very fact that Jeffes chose *1592* as copy for *1594*, instead of his own edition, argues nothing: *1592* might simply have been a cleaner text to print from.

pose of discussion: (i) up to and including III. xiv (ll. 1–2349 in *MSR*), and (ii) III. xv to the end (ll. 2350–967).

(i) *I. i–III. xiv*

The evidence strongly suggests that the copy, whether directly or through Jeffes' edition, was an author's manuscript and a neat manuscript at that.[1] The stage-directions are full and elaborate, and are best explained as deriving from a dramatist with a good understanding of stage practice, who was anxious to note down in great detail the particular effects he wished to see produced on the stage; e.g., *She, in going in, lets fall her glove, which Horatio, coming out, takes up. . . Balthazar starts back. . . Hieronimo sets his breast unto his sword. . . Alexandro seems to entreat. . . He strives with the watch. . . She runs lunatic. . . He whispereth in her ear. . . He draweth out a bloody napkin. . . Bazulto remains till Hieronimo enters again, who, staring him in the face, speaks.* Several directions point to the dramatist's thinking of the 'real' environment of the story and forgetting the stage presentation; e.g., *Falls to the ground. . . Pedringano showeth all to the Prince and Lorenzo, placing them in secret. . . He diggeth with his dagger.*

The detail of some of the stage-directions might suggest that the book-keeper of the company had been through the manuscript and at least begun to prepare it for the stage. I do not think there are any unequivocal signs, however, of a theatrical 'layer' among the stage-directions. It is true that there are many indications for hand-properties (e.g., *Give him his chain. . . Enter Boy with the box.*) but on the other hand there is a lack of directions for flourishes and music.[2] In three places the evidence is debatable. (1) At III. ii. 25, there is the extraordinary direction *Red ink* at the side of the text of Bel-imperia's message written in her blood. It seems more likely that the author made a note that red ink was to be used for the letter than that the book-keeper was reminding himself to get such a letter written. (2) In II. ii, there is a direction for concealing Balthazar and Lorenzo which does not indicate the part of the stage where they

---

[1] Technically, 'foul papers'; one suspects, from the inferred neatness, that the MS. was not a first draft, but a fair copy.

[2] This double point was communicated by R. Hosley. Evidence for staging is discussed in detail by Biesterfeldt, Ch. 4.

are to be hidden. Before Balthazar speaks from his hiding-place, the direction *Balthazar above* occurs (II. ii. 17). I argue in the note to that passage that the latter direction would not be a satisfactory alteration for a book-keeper to make, but might well be an author's hasty addition to clarify the action on the stage. (3) At the end of II. v, there is some inconsistency in the directions for removing Horatio's body from the stage, and it might be argued (see note) that Hieronimo's Latin dirge was struck out by the theatre and a direction inserted to close the scene before the dirge. The directions are, in the last resort, actable, and the evidence for stage intervention is slight; there is, none the less, a difficulty here, and it is associated with others to be discussed shortly (see below, pp. xxxvi ff.).

There are, finally, several tell-tale authorial inconsistencies which must argue that even if the author's manuscript had been prepared for the stage, the preparation had not gone far. At III. i, we have *Enter Viceroy of Portingale, Nobles, Alexandro, Villuppo.* But Alexandro does not enter until l. 31, at which point an entry is provided for him. It seems impossible to explain this as a unique anticipatory entry in prompt-book style, or as a unique 'massed entry' heading in the style of some scribes. It seems to be an author's reminder of the characters he needed in the forthcoming scene. In I. iii, there is no provision for attendants to carry off Alexandro and, indeed, no exit is provided for him. There is some inconsistency in referring to characters. Balthazar is *Balthazar* or *Prince*. Castile is *The Duke of Castile, Castile, Don Cyprian, the Duke. Page* becomes *Boy.* In III. xiii, *an Old Man* enters, who is *Senex* in the speech-headings and is referred to in a stage-direction as *Bazulto*. These variations would hardly be tolerable in a prompt-book.

Though it may be tempting to attribute the absence of confusion in the text to the exceptionally clear handwriting of Kyd, there is no evidence of the spellings he favours in his autograph letters, such as (for example) *cold, wold, shold; don, donn; geue; breiflie; contynewd; teadious; toching; byn, wrytt; tyme; monstruous.* All these words are spelt differently in *1592*. Where spellings are the same, they are too orthodox to prove anything. On the other hand (assuming for the moment that *1592* is based upon manuscript) there is no reason to deny Kyd's hand because of the evidence of spelling. The careful spelling of *1592* has its origin in Allde's printing house, and it is possible to detect the same 'house-training' (if not the same compositor) in other works printed by Allde at this period; for example, *Rare Triumphs of Love and Fortune* (1589), *Famous History of Palladine of England* (1588), Perkins' *A Golden Chain* (1592), *Massacre at Paris* (1594 ?).[1] Kyd's spellings may well have been ironed out by a compositor with his own views on spelling. I do not enter on the difficult ground of whether the variation in spelling is more likely to imply a printing from a manuscript than from a printed text.[2]

So far as the first part of the play is concerned (by far the larger part) it is reasonable to say that the copy, either directly or through a previous edition, was an author's manuscript, probably not yet edited for stage use.

(ii) *III. xv—the end*

What has been said of the first part of the play applies to the second part, but the second part contains four features which are irregular and demand special attention. I shall outline all the problems before attempting any solutions, because the reader may well think he needs a frontier between fact and fancy.

(i) III. xv is a short scene of fifty lines, one of the 'chorus' scenes between Andrea and Revenge which close every act. The text is extremely corrupt and in marked contrast with the rest of the play. In several lines, no convincing emendations can be suggested (e.g., 3–7, 11). Where there is no demonstrable corruption, the syntax is often awkward, and the verse crabbed. There is an inane repetition of 'Awake!': 'Awake *Erictha, Cerberus* awake,' (1), '*Reuenge* awake. —Awake, for why?—Awake *Reuenge*, for thou art . . .' (8–10), 'Awake *Reuenge*,' (13), 'Awake *Reuenge*' (17), 'Awake *Reuenge*' (29). For the dumb-show, in striking contrast with the elaborate detail given for Hieronimo's pageant (I. iv. 137) and the fullness of the stage-directions generally, there is only the bare direction, 'Enter a dumme shew'. Finally, the initial and the concluding directions, 'Enter *Ghoast* and *Reuenge*.', and '*Exeunt*.', are palpable

[1] A brief code of the spellings is: *freend*; *-nes, -les*, etc.; *heere*; *goe*; *he, be*, etc.

[2] Cf. A. Walker, *Studies in Bibliography*, vii (1955), 7–8.

C

mistakes, since it is obvious not only from the previous 'choruses' but also from the present ('I will sit to see the rest') that Andrea and Revenge remain on the stage during the whole of the play (cf. Biesterfeldt, pp. 86–7).

(ii) IV. i, from the entry of Lorenzo and Balthazar at l. 52 to the end, shows great irregularity in the metre. Though editorial adjustment can make a few improvements, it is not a question of mislineation but of writing which (prosodically speaking) is thoroughly uneven. Yet the language does not lack vitality and clarity, as in III. xv. This part of the scene is devoted to the arrangement of the play-within-the-play.

(iii) At IV. i. 172–8, Hieronimo suddenly remarks that his play is to be given in 'unknown languages', one player is to speak in Latin, one in Greek, one in Italian, one in French. The 'actors' protest that this will mean 'mere confusion', but Hieronimo reassures them that he will 'make the matter known' in an oration at the end. At the close of the playlet, we have this:

> *King*. But now what follows for Hieronimo?
> *Hier*. Marry, this follows for Hieronimo:
>   Here break we off our sundry languages
>   And thus conclude I in our vulgar tongue.
>   Haply you think . . . etc.

But the playlet is of course given in English, and immediately before it stands the following note:

> *Gentlemen, this play of* Hieronimo *in sundrie Languages, was*
> *thought good to be set downe in English more largely,*
> *for the easier vnderstanding to euery*
> *publique Reader.*

The presence of the note, and the contradiction between the promised and the actual language of the play argue that there is a problem to be solved concerning the unity of the copy.

(iv) At the end of the lethal play-within-the-play, Hieronimo makes a long speech (during which he shows Horatio's body), giving a full account of the murder of his son and the revenge which he has taken on the murderers by means of the play. In spite of this explanation, the King, having prevented Hieronimo's attempt at suicide, says, 'Now I have thee I will make thee speak: / Why hast thou done this undeserving deed?' He is echoed by Castile and the Viceroy. Hieronimo gives a brief reply, but the King goes on, 'Why speak'st thou not?' But Hieronimo swears silence: 'I may not, nor I will not tell thee.' And even with the threat of torture, he says,

> Never shalt thou force me to reveal
> The thing which I have vow'd inviolate.

He then bites out his tongue. But there is nothing which Hieronimo has vowed inviolate, and nothing which he has not told the King in his long speech. That the King should be violently moved and strangely bewildered is only to be expected, but that his passion should take the form of insisting on information which he already has is almost as odd as Hieronimo's vowing to conceal what he has already told.

Besides containing so marked a contradiction, the scene is crude aesthetically and (to some extent) textually. The crudity of the speeches and the action speak for themselves in a reading of the passage, but there is also an inner inconsistency in the fact that even in stressing his new role of saying nothing, Hieronimo twice avows that Lorenzo murdered his son. Textually, the passage is not verbally corrupt like III. xv, but, in contrast with the earlier part of the play, it is remarkably deficient in stage-directions (two are supplied in the present text from later editions). The breaking in of the guard (if they do break in), the arrest of Hieronimo, the biting out of the tongue, and the final letting of blood are accompanied by two directions only, found at the end of the violent action, and appearing thus in *1592*:

> *King.* And if in this he satisfie vs not,
> We will deuise the'xtreamest kinde of death,
> That euer was inuented for a wretch.
>
> Then he makes signes for a knife to mend his pen.
> *Cas.* O he would haue a knife to mend his Pen.
> *Vice.* Heere, and aduise thee that thou write the troth,
> Looke to my brother, saue *Hieronimo.*
>
> He with a knife stabs the Duke and himselfe.
> *King.* What age hath euer heard such monstrous deeds?

The first direction is interesting: it appears to take words from the text which follows; the *he* is vague in its reference; *Then* is used in a narrative fashion, to be contrasted with its use to indicate part of a sequence of stage-business at I. iv. 137.2. (The passage is also corrupt in that the line 'Looke to my brother . . .' is mis-ascribed; but mis-ascription of speeches is found elsewhere.) It may also be noted that the stage-direction at the end of this last scene of the play proper contains a slight irregularity: the Viceroy goes out *'bearing the body of his son'*, though he directed Don Pedro in the preceding speech to take the body up. The final chorus opens with a repetition of the erroneous *'Enter'* for Andrea and Revenge.

The irregularities suggest the possibility (*a*) that *The Spanish Tragedy* was at some stage revised to make it shorter and more suitable for the public stage, and (*b*) that the copy for *1592* contained a portion of alien and inferior copy.

Hieronimo's silence will seem less queer if we suppose with Schücking that in IV. iv. 153–201 we have, not confusion, but an alternative ending to the play. The *1592* text of *The Spanish Tragedy* is rather long for an Elizabethan play of its period (cf. Schücking, p. 6, and Hart, *Shakespeare and the Homilies*, especially pp. 81–3), and abridgement may well have been needed. Hieronimo's long speech of explanation tells the audience what they already know. To cut this speech after Horatio's body has been revealed (Schücking, p. 71) and to substitute vows of silence for the long elucidation—perhaps even to add the biting out of the tongue —would shorten the play, and it is possible that someone thought it would add to the piquancy of the ending. Both versions would end with the murder of Castile and Hieronimo's suicide, but the original would not have been without the grandeur which the existing text completely lacks. Secondly, the contradiction between the promise of foreign languages for the play-within-the-play and the English text which is in fact given can be understood if we postulate a revision for the sake of shortening and sharpening the play. There are, of course, other ways of accounting for the inconsistency. (*a*) The printer might have secured a translation for a play in 'sundry languages' and hence the note before the play is to be taken literally. But that would argue extraordinary complaisance in the printer, and no less complaisance among the audience if, in the theatre, they had been asked to endure sixty lines in languages they could not understand. (*b*) The text might be as performed in the theatre; foreign languages are promised but, since an unlettered audience could not accept them, the play is, in fact, given in English. But this course would be entirely pointless: there is not the least need for foreign languages to be mentioned at all. It is much more likely that the mention of foreign tongues represents one version and the English text of the playlet represents another. But which is the earlier and which is the later? It could be argued that in the original version Kyd promised, and wrote, the Soliman and Perseda episode in 'sundry languages', but that the stage objected more strongly than did Lorenzo and Balthazar that this would be 'mere confusion', and so Kyd decided to provide a translated version. Though this may seem a very reasonable procedure, it is more likely that the modification was in the other direction. For Hieronimo's suggestion that they should speak in different languages is very much of an afterthought (IV. i. 169ff.) and can be explained as a later addition, and the reference to the 'sundry languages' at the close of the play-within-the-play (IV. iv. 74–5) is indeed a 'detachable' couplet. And, if abridgement is in question, the text of Hieronimo's play can very well be cut. As Biesterfeldt pointed out (p. 45), the audience has already been given, at IV. i. 108–26, a detailed plot of the play, one-third as long as the playlet itself. I take it that Kyd originally intended the play to be in English, but that, when abridgement of an over-long play was required, a mime was substituted, a mime accompanied, for the sake of 'drama', with a few well-chosen lines in gibberish or 'sundry languages', and references to these languages were inserted before and after the mime.[1]

---

[1] My view of how the playlet was given on the stage agrees very closely with that put forward by Biesterfeldt in 1935 (p. 45), though the grounds of his argument were quite different. 'Es war wahrscheinlich eine Pantomime mit sehr knappem Begleittext, der ruhig fremdsprachlich und zum Teil unverständlich sein konnte, da die „Handlung", das Vorgangmässige des Spieles, eingehend vorbereitet war.' Biesterfeldt thought it significant that the printer's note says that the play is set down 'in English more largely', for the *more largely* implies that the stage-version was shorter.

But it will immediately be asked how elements of two versions still stand in the text, and how it was that the printer was so puzzled by inconsistencies in his copy that he had to provide the note to the 'public reader'. (And, of course, how two versions of the ending come to be present in *1592*.) It is possible that in Kyd's manuscript cancelled versions were not properly deleted, and that the printer included part of what should have been erased or it is possible that the copy for the printer contained only the *beginnings* of a revision which was completed in another manuscript; the problem of the stage-directions at the end of II. v (see above, p. xxxii) might support a theory of inchoate revision. But this latter problem is small and isolated; there is nothing else in the first two-thirds of the play to suggest that any revision had taken place or even been started. And surely it is the early part of the play, with the long accounts of the battle, which would certainly have been marked for revision. There is, I think, a simpler explanation than that contradictory versions stood side by side in the 'foul papers'.

The inadequacies in III. xv (the scene between Andrea and Revenge discussed above, p. xxxiii), inadequacies in textual quality, in stage-directions, and in the style of the language, suggest very strongly that the copy for this scene was different in kind from the copy used up to that point, and inferior to it. Although some of the difficulties could be explained by supposing that on one particular page of the manuscript the writing was very hard to read, illegibility would hardly account for the *errors* of the initial and final stage-directions, nor for the repetition of 'Awake!' nor for the general weakness of the verse (see also note on III. xv. 24). I incline to the view that we have, not an illegible text, but a debased text. How, then, does it come to be present ? Let us suppose that a leaf, or even a single page, of the copy is damaged or defective. The printer might quite naturally turn to a text of the play which is already in print—Jeffes' edition. If this supposition is correct, then it seems that Jeffes' text was indeed 'bad'—that is to say, reported or assembled by 'unauthorized' persons (cf. above, p. xxix). Let us suppose again that, Jeffes' text being in the printing house, it is used again during the printing of the remainder of the play, either for convenience, or to supply further defective parts of the manuscript.[1] A reported text would naturally give the version of the play which was acted, including (according to the hypothesis which I have advanced) the 'vow of silence' ending, and the mime instead of the English-language play-within-the-play. It is easy to imagine that, in setting-up Hieronimo's long speech of explanation from the manuscript copy, the printer could not see that it conflicted with what he then set from printed copy, although earlier he had seen that the English text of the play-within-the-play (missing, naturally, from Jeffes) conflicted with a promise of foreign languages in the printed copy, and he had therefore supplied the ingenious note to the 'public reader'.

The evidence that Allde used both manuscript copy and 'bad' printed copy in the last act of the play does not rest alone on the presence of contradictory versions of the play-within-the-play and the ending. My suggestion has been that the reference to the 'unknown languages' at IV. i. 172–8 was not in the play as Kyd originally wrote it, and not in the manuscript copy which Allde was using, but derived from Jeffes' text. The reference occurs in the passage of irregular verse discussed under (iv) above (p. xxxiv); the irregularity is quite unlike the general standard of prosody in the play, and it supports the view that inferior copy was being used. Similarly, it was noted that the passage dealing with Hieronimo's silence (which also, I believe, derives from Jeffes) is surprisingly deficient in stage-directions, in comparison with the wealth of detail provided in other parts of the play. It is extremely hard to establish the 'badness' of a text without the control of a parallel 'good' text, but if one had to choose from *The Spanish Tragedy* one stage-direction which seemed to belong to a 'reported' text, it would be that odd direction, 'Then he makes signs for a knife to mend his pen.'

Since, without Jeffes' edition, there is no way of proving that *1592* was contaminated in three places by inferior copy (III. xv, IV. i. 52–199, IV. iv. 153–201), I have not admitted into my text what the editorial implications of the theory would dictate. In editing a 'bad' text, one can often allow sheer nonsense and irregular

---

[1] Such things happened. See, for example, Hosley's demonstration that Q2 of *Romeo and Juliet* used both the 'bad' Q1 and a distinct MS. as copy. *Studies in Bibliography*, ix (1957), 129–41.

verse-lining to stand, and, at the other extreme, one can often permit oneself unusual licence in emendation. I have, however, treated the suspect passages as though they were parts of Kyd's MS. (cf. my notes to III. xv. 4–7 and IV. i. 105).

To sum up: *1592* is a good text, deriving from a manuscript of the dramatist which had probably not been worked over for the stage. There is some corruption, irregularity, and inconsistency in the last act and the last scene of the third act, though the 'affected area' is small. The inconsistency in the action, which relates to the play-within-the-play and to Hieronimo's behaviour just before his death, may suggest that the text contains elements of a revised and abridged version of the play. The presence of one unusually corrupt scene (III. xv) may suggest the use of inferior copy. If Jeffes' edition, which preceded White's, did indeed contain an 'unauthorized' text, the inconsistencies and the corruptions could be explained on the ground that the printer of *1592* used Jeffes' text as copy to supply defective parts of his manuscript copy.

Subsequent editions

The edition printed by Jeffes in 1594 (to be sold by Edward White) is known in a single copy only, which is in the University Library at Göttingen. It is an untidy and careless reprint of *1592*, though the punctuation is sometimes improved. Well over 100 new readings are introduced. Most of these are careless errors: misreadings, omissions, transpositions, insertions; 21 words misprinted in *1592* receive the obvious corrections, though three misprints are erroneously corrected (e.g., *made* for *mad*, II. ii. 9—read *may*). Nineteen of the new readings are hardly to be attributed to a compositor, and suggest that the copy of *1592* used in the printing house had been cursorily 'edited'—probably in the printing house. (*a*) Two wrong attributions of speeches have been corrected; (*b*) a half-hearted attack on the corrupt Latin has produced seven corrections. These corrections in the Latin cannot be from an authoritative source, since so much nonsense is allowed to stand, but they cannot (on the other hand) be from the compositor, because if he had known enough Latin to correct *poplito* into *poplite*, he could not have perverted *1592*'s *nulla* into *nalla*. (*c*) A rather pedantic 'im-

provement' of grammar is here and there noticeable, the most justi-
fiable being *darkt* for *darke* at I. ii. 54. (*d*) Five readings remain:
Shew no brighter is an easy enough correction of *Shew brighter* (III.
xiv. 102); *Which God amend that made Hieronimo* (IV. iv. 120) is a
beautiful example of the obtuseness of printing-house corrections
(*1592* reads *With God amend that mad* Hieronimo, sc. 'With "God
amend that mad Hieronimo".'); *when* for *what* (III. x. 99) is a similar
attempt to remove fancied corruption; *hale* for *hall* (IV. iv. 213) may
not be a new reading but a compositor's normalizing of spelling (see
note); there is, finally, this new reading at III. xii. 46:

> *1592* To knit a sure inexecrable band
> *1594* To knit a sure inexplicable band

1592's enigmatic word *inexecrable* is found in two other places
where its meaning is not clear (*Merchant of Venice*, IV. i. 128, and
Constable, *Diana*, viii, Sonnet 1). No meaning which ingenuity
might suggest for the word will satisfactorily fit the context of *1592*.
The nearest one can come would be something like 'that cannot be
cursed away'. There is a very good case for saying that *inexecrable* is
a corrupt reading; the only edition to preserve it is Prouty's. Many
modern editors since Hawkins have read *inextricable*; but both *inextricable* and *inexplicable* would be understood by an Elizabethan
as denoting the firmness of a bond (in the context, a link which
could not be unfastened), and there would seem to be good reason
for preferring *inexplicable*, the reading adopted in several recent
American editions of the play. For *inexplicable* is a more daring
emendation than any other in *1594*. We have to remember when we
are dealing with unique copies (as we are with the first three extant
texts of *The Spanish Tragedy*) that we have no means of telling what
press-corrections occurred in the printing of the edition; we do not
know if, in the copy we possess, some formes have been corrected
and others not; we do not know if the succeeding reprint was set up
from copies containing different arrangements of corrected and un-
corrected formes. New readings in *1594* may have derived from
corrected formes of *1592* which do not appear in the British
Museum copy. Every single variant in *1594* has to be scrutinized
with this possibility in mind, but it seems either impossible or un-

necessary to posit a now-lost corrected forme except for the inner
forme of Sheet G, for the reading *inexplicable*. Press-correction was
a capricious business, and the fact that the forme contains no other
corrections need not be a stumbling-block. There can be no proof,
but there seems a good chance that *inexplicable* is an authoritative
reading, coming from a corrected forme of *1592* which is not in the
one surviving copy; the soundness of the reading, and the good
chance it has of being authoritative, argue most strongly for its
adoption in preference to *inexecrable* or *inextricable*.

On 13 August 1599, Jeffes assigned his rights in *The Spanish
Tragedy* to William White, who brought out an edition in that year.
1599 is a straightforward reprint of *1594*, and entirely dependent on
it.[1] The printing is more refined than that of the two preceding editions, proper names and stage-directions are carefully italicized,
open parentheses are closed, much new punctuation is added (not
always happily). It is nevertheless an unintelligent reprint: some
obvious corrections are made but lapses of *1594* are often repeated
(*wroth* for *worth*, for example) or corrupted still more deeply; the
confusion in foreign tongues is further confounded. There are
erroneous corrections of misprints, and several needless and foolish
'improvements'—*euer-killing* for *neuer-killing*, for example (I. i.
69). The general quality of the reprint is such that it is impossible to
pay respect to one variant reading accepted in every edition which
I have seen, sc. *hate* for *heat* at III. i. 4 (see note). Since the original
reading is sound, *hate* must be a misreading of copy.

By 14 August 1600, the copyright in the play had passed to
Thomas Pavier, who brought out in 1602 an edition printed by W.
White, 'Newly corrected, amended, and enlarged with new additions of the Painters part, and others, as it hath of late been diuers
times acted'. *1602* provides us with the sole authoritative text of the
famous Additions, but it is most important to notice that, apart
from the Additions, *1602* is a poor and slavish reprint of *1599*. It is
true that four stage-directions are added: *Draw his sword*. and *Offer*

---

[1] Except that *1599* repeats *1592*'s erroneous *poplito* (I. ii. 13) which had
been corrected by *1594* to *poplite*. Since there is no other evidence that a
copy of *1592* was used in the printing of *1599*, the repetition of the error
would seem to be a coincidence.

to kill him. [C3r], *They breake in, and hold* Hieronimo. [L4v], *He bites out his tongue.* (M1r); that an important reordering of misplaced lines occurs at IV. i. 185–6; that some of *1594*'s corruptions of *1592* are put right. But all these improvements could easily be made without reference to a manuscript or to *1592*, and the bovine way in which *1602* repeats the errors of *1599*, and perpetrates errors of its own, does not encourage us to think that *1602* was (except for the Additions) based on anything other than a copy of *1599* which had received some meagre and desultory 'editing'. (Concerning the copy for the Additions, see below, pp. lxii–lxv.)

The remaining editions of the seventeenth century need not detain us (1603, 1610–11, 1615, 1618, 1623, 1633). They are described in Greg's *Bibliography*, the Malone Society's edition of *1602*, and Schick's second redaction. Each edition was based on its predecessor, except that *1610–11* was based chiefly on *1602*.[1] To set against the expected textual degeneration, there was some gain over the years and several received readings were established; these are indicated in the textual apparatus, but it will be understood that they do not have any greater authority than emendations made by a modern editor. The quarto of 1615 is often known as the first 'Illustrated' edition, because of its famous woodcut of the murder of Horatio; the title now runs *The Spanish Tragedie: or, Hieronimo is mad againe.* (See Frontispiece.)

Modern editions begin with Dodsley, who printed the play in the second volume of his *Select Collection of Old Plays* (1744); he knew only the quarto of 1633. The credit of being the first editor in any real sense goes to T. Hawkins, who, in the second volume of *The Origin of the English Drama* (1773), produced a text based on *1592*; many of his emendations have stood the test of time. The reissues of Dodsley, by Reed (1780), Collier (1825), Hazlitt (1874), mark a continued improvement, but, although Hazlitt went back to *1592* for himself, there is no basic change in editorial approach from that of

[1] Schick's confident claim that *1603* stands outside the main line of transmission is belied by his own collation. He claimed that *1610–11* went back to *1602* and ignored the unique readings of *1603*. But, as MSR (*1602*) points out, six substantial readings of *1603* are incorporated in *1610–11*, and, moreover, *1615* independently adopts some more of *1603*'s. The bibliographical position is curious.

Hawkins. In 1897, J. M. Manly (in vol. II of his *Specimens of the Pre-Shaksperean Drama*) made the first attempt to provide a critical 'old-spelling' edition; it profits from some conjectural readings by Kittredge, and Manly's very conservative policy did much to re-establish the readings of *1592*; unfortunately, the critical apparatus contains some bewildering ghost-readings from *1592*. Manly's edition appeared too late for J. Schick to make use of it in his excellent modernized edition of 1898 for *The Temple Dramatists*.

In 1901, by one of those common coincidences of scholarship, there appeared two editions of distinction: F. S. Boas', in the standard edition of Kyd's works, and Schick's second and fuller edition. It is a great pity that Boas (who does not seem to have known of Manly's edition) should not have been able to incorporate Schick's findings in his own work, for Schick's edition (published as vol. XIX of *Litterarhistorische Forschungen*) is now little known and rare. Both editions preserve *1592*'s spellings, though punctuation is much altered. Schick's edition is a careful piece of scholarship, and its account of the early texts, in the Introduction and in the Collation, is to be given very high praise, though it is not perfect. Boas also collates all the early editions, though there are some omissions and errors; his literary commentary is much more full than that of Schick. Any editor of *The Spanish Tragedy* is bound to acknowledge his great indebtedness to Schick and Boas.

There have been many editions of *The Spanish Tragedy* in anthologies of Elizabethan drama, particularly in the United States. Some are entirely derivative, some have gone back to the original text. I have found the edition by C. F. Tucker Brooke and N. B. Paradise in *English Drama, 1580–1642* (1933) extremely sound and sensible. Mention may also be made of A. K. McIlwraith's edition for the *World's Classics* volume, *Five Elizabethan Tragedies* (1938), and C. T. Prouty's for the *Crofts Classics* (1951).

Reprints of the two authoritative texts of 1592 and 1602 have appeared in the Malone Society's publications. That of 1602 was prepared under the direction of W. W. Greg in consultation with F. S. Boas in 1925; that of 1592 by Greg and D. Nichol Smith in 1949. The introduction to the *1592* edition is sounder as regards the history of the publication of the play. The List of Irregular, Doubtful, and Variant Readings is not complete, but in spite of this, and of a ghost-reading in the *1592* reprint (see my note to III. x. 75), these two reprints are invaluable.

There is also a concordance to the works of Kyd, compiled by C. Crawford, and published as volume 15 of Bang's *Materialien*.

The Present Edition

In accordance with the practice in this series, the spelling in the present edition is modern. A few archaic forms will be found, the general rule being that such a form should be distinct from the Elizabethan form which eventually produced our modern form. A few examples are *leese*, *welding* (wielding, see note to I. iv. 35), *wan* (won), *holp*, *scinder'd* (sundered), *strond*. I have tried to excise forms which are mere spelling variants, but sentiment has triumphed on one or two occasions: for example, *recompt*, *quire*, and *fauchon*. *murder* and *murther* are both found in the copy-text; I have regularized to *murder*. Though the practice can hardly be called modernization, I have abbreviated the unstressed final syllable of the past forms of weak verbs into -*'d*, whether the contraction is made in the copy-text or not; where the metre demands the accented -*ed*, and *1592* prints the contracted form, I give the expanded form and note the original reading in the Textual Notes.

There is a good deal in the original of what appears to our eyes to be irregularity in agreement between subject and verb. I have not modernized Elizabethan syntax nor attempted to improve Kyd's English. Only on the very rare occasions when I could not relate a false concord to Elizabethan practice or to a confused sentence have I emended; such emendations are, of course, recorded. Kyd's occasional use of the third person singular form for second person singular in the present tense has been allowed to stand without comment (e.g., II. v. 31, III. viii. 14, III. ix. 6, IV. i. 2, IV. ii. 33). Mislineation has been corrected (and the correction noted) but no attempt has been made to force certain passages of irregular verse into pentameters (e.g., in IV. i).

The stage-directions of the original have been preserved, some very few modifications and minor additions being made for the sake of absolute clarity (e.g., I. ii. 131, I. iii. 90, II. ii. 6 and 17, IV. ii. 38).

A few stage-directions from *1602*, offering some evidence of near-contemporary staging, are added. These, and all other departures from *1592*, are clearly indicated by the use of square brackets. Preservation of the original Entrances is at the cost of a little inconsistency in the naming of characters; there is no chance of uncertainty, and all speech-headings are normalized throughout; the Dramatis Personae gives all the names given to each character. The rather unusual division of the play into four acts only has been maintained (see note at head of III. viii). Scene-numbers are given in square brackets at the beginning of each scene, but no 'places' are indicated: *1592* is not divided into scenes.

Though it may seem paradoxical to say so, the punctuation in this edition is a complete re-punctuation based on the pointing of *1592*. I do not believe that Elizabethan punctuation goes well with a modernized text; it is illogical to discard spellings which are interesting and give the reader little trouble, and preserve a punctuation which can be highly misleading and which is (in any given play) rarely loyal to any one principle of pointing. To preserve the original punctuation in an old-spelling text is a different matter, but with modern spelling the reader's attention is lulled, or directed away from the old conventions, and he constantly trips up. An editor's first duty is to present a clear and readable text, and piety towards the sense of the original is more important than piety towards a difficult punctuation, the source of which may be obscure. Yet a big problem remains. For very often there are traces of what appears to be 'rhetorical' or histrionic pointing, which at least suggests the actors' patterns of delivery; one is reluctant to remove these traces, and one is also quite certain that it will be disastrous to the flow of the verse to chop up the lines into grammatical units on a principle of pointing which is now perhaps obsolescent. In respect of *The Spanish Tragedy*, a decision to re-punctuate to some extent is unavoidable; the punctuation of *1592* is inconsistent, arbitrary, and often absurd. One has a strong impression that there is a blend of two men's punctuation: the one, deriving from the copy, being extremely light, but often rhetorically interesting; the other, deriving from the compositor, heavy, cumbersome, and unintelligent. Perhaps one would not go far wrong in saying that medial punctuation comes from the copy, whereas the compositor is responsible for punctuation at the ends of lines. In re-punctuating, I have steered a middle course between Elizabethan standards and a too-strict grammatical punctuation. I have corrected obviously erroneous punctuation; I have preserved the original where there is no danger of misunderstanding; I have modernized, on as light a system of pointing as possible, where there is ambiguity, or a possibility of misunderstanding. What has been done may seem too modern to some readers; but I hope that it will be found faithful to the sense and rhythm of the verse.

In the critical apparatus I have tried to give significant information only, and to give it rapidly and clearly. The purpose of the textual notes is to record (i) all substantial departures from *1592*; (ii) important emendations and alternative readings which I have not accepted. There are thus two kinds of standard note:

> (i)   A   B   C   D
> *oblivia*] *Hawkins; oblimia 1592*
> writ]   *Manly;* write *1592*

in which A = reading of present text, B = source of reading, C = reading of (D) *1592*.

> (ii)   A   B   C   D
> Nor ferried] *1592;* O'er-ferried *Schick*
> reveng'd]   *1592;*   reuenge   *1623*

in which A = reading of present text, B = a note that this is the reading of the original text, C = a rejected emendation, D = source of rejected emendation.

Additional citation in either of these standard forms should not present difficulty, e.g.:

> inexplicable] *1594;* inexecrable *1592;* inextricable *Hawkins.*

in which the last item is a rejected alternative to the emendation accepted.

New readings are marked *this ed.*; readings suggested but not inserted into a text by the originator are marked *conj.* (conjectured). Readings from the text are occasionally given without source, e.g.:

> cited] scited *1592*

Attention is here called to the form of the original in a reading substantially the same. It is occasionally necessary to cite original spelling:

haul] hall *1592;* hale *1594*

A few 'plain language' entries should not cause difficulty. Changes in punctuation are only recorded when the new punctuation alters the sense of the original. Obvious misprints in *1592* are not recorded (e.g., *wodres* for *wordes*).

No attempt is made in the collation to provide either the history of the text or something which looks like the history of the text. The material is available elsewhere, and I cannot think that any reader will regret the absence of a jungle of worthless readings from the early editions (after *1592*) and bright and unnecessary normalizations from the eighteenth-century editions. No attempt is made to name the editors who have supported or rejected any particular emendation (except for the originator, of course). This counting of heads, as though there were a democratic election in progress, serves no purpose. If a particular editor's support or rejection of a reading is important, the information will be found in the note discussing the passage. The main purpose of the textual apparatus in the present edition is to make clear the relation of the text to the text of *1592*, and to record the source of all substantial departures from *1592*.

4. SOURCES

No source for *The Spanish Tragedy* has been found. Attempts have been made, however, to identify the sources of different parts of the play. The plot of the play-within-the-play is taken (though the conclusion is much altered) from H. Wotton's *Courtlie Controversie of Cupids Cautels* (1578), or from Wotton through the anonymous *Soliman and Perseda*; see note to IV. i. 108. I have already argued that it is most unlikely that the 'political' background of the play is based upon the relations between Spain and Portugal ca. 1580 (see above, p. xxiv). Lorenzo's treatment of Pedringano seemed to R. S. Forsythe[1] to echo a section of Greene's *Planetomachia*

[1] *P.Q.,* v (1926), 78–84.

(1585) but the stories are not at all close. F. Bowers has brought forward many analogues to Lorenzo's behaviour to his accomplice, Pedringano.[1] One of these may well be a source. *The Copie of a Leter . . . Concerning . . . some proceedings of the Erle of Leycester* (1584—by R. Parsons?) accuses Leicester of ridding himself of accomplices to his nefarious activities. It is told how one Gates was imprisoned and appealed to Leicester, who sent him good assurances while hastening his death. Gates threatens to reveal his master's secrets; he is hanged. Bowers points out that 'Leycesters Ghost' (of unknown date), appended to *Leycesters Commonwealth* (1641), which reprints *The Copie of a Leter*, is a retelling of Gates's story which seems to make a definite link between Lorenzo and Leicester, e.g., 'For his reprivall (like a crafty Fox) / I sent no pardon, but an empty Box.'

But, while little has been found to indicate how much of his plot Kyd borrowed, we have much evidence of incidental borrowings for various purposes. Kyd's debt to Seneca needs no documentation here.[2] It ranges from tags and sentences to the machinery of a ghost, lusting for revenge—and, indeed, much of the atmosphere of revenge; Andrea's Prologue is thoroughly Senecan and so are the more lurid horrors (reported in Seneca, of course); it may well be because of Seneca's example (especially in the *Hyppolitus*) that Kyd was able to create the character of a bold passionate woman like Bel-imperia. Robert Garnier, himself influenced by Seneca, was another from whom Kyd borrowed much, both generally and verbally; it was *Cornélie* which seems to have impressed Kyd most. Virgil gave Kyd his account of the underworld (though it was well established as a literary convention) and scraps of his Latin compositions. Other borrowings are recorded in the commentary. But on the whole Kyd does not seem to have been an excessively derivative writer; if a source for his main plot turns up, it may well appear that Kyd's originality in ordering his material is more remarkable than his powers as a copyist.

[1] *Harvard Studies and Notes*, xiii (1931), 241–9.
[2] See, e.g., H. B. Charlton in *Works of Sir William Alexander* (1921); J. W. Cunliffe, *The Influence of Seneca on Elizabethan Tragedy* (1893). An unsuccessful attempt to deny Senecan influence is Howard Baker's *Induction to Tragedy* (1939).

D

5. THEME AND STRUCTURE

One of the most popular and influential of plays in its own day, *The Spanish Tragedy* became the object of affectionate derision in the succeeding generations—or of derision without affection, as with Jonson. Such elements of the play as Hieronimo's outcries and the sallies of his madness, the elaborately patterned verse, Andrea's sombre prologue, were constantly parodied and guyed by Jacobean and Caroline dramatists.[1] This attention to the play, however scornful, shows the hold which Kyd's work had; a hold demonstrated by the successive editions of the play, and the desire to keep it fresh by adding new scenes.[2] It was looked on as an extravagant and crude work, and yet a bold work, holding a special position as the best that could be done in an age which had not learned to produce a polished play. And it may be said that the attitude has stuck, and still prevails. Once the play had sunk into oblivion, after the mid-seventeenth century, it was not rehabilitated in the Romantic period, as so many other 'forgotten' plays were. Lamb (1808) was interested only in the Additions: he gave the 'Painter's Scene' in his *Specimens of English Dramatic Poets* and remarked that these scenes were 'the very salt of the old play (which without them is but a caput mortuum, such another piece of flatness as Locrine)'. With the growth of evolutionary criticism, historians of drama found the play a seminal work in tragedy and the revenge play, in spite of the crudity which they did not gloss over. Mild merits of various kinds were proposed by various critics, chiefly skill in maintaining suspense and in working out a complicated plot. There have been wide differences of opinion on Kyd's powers of characterization. But although there has been general recognition of Kyd's unusual ability in contriving a theatrically effective play, no one has made a serious claim that Kyd has much to offer as a poet or tragic dramatist. It is significant that the most exhaustive and sympathetic study

---

[1] Some imitations and parodies are cited in the Notes. See Boas, pp. xci–xcix, for a representative collection.

[2] Not to speak of the anecdote told by Braithwaite in 1631 and retold by Prynne (see Schick[1], p. xxix) of the unregenerate old woman who, on her deathbed, kept crying out, 'Hieronimo, Hieronimo, O let me see Hieronimo acted!'

of *The Spanish Tragedy*, the monograph by Biesterfeldt published in 1936, is a study in structure (*Die dramatische Technik Thomas Kyds*). A standard view of Kyd is Gregory Smith's summing-up in *The Cambridge History of English Literature* (vol. v, 1910, p. 163):

> The interest of Kyd's work is almost exclusively historical. Like Marlowe's, it takes its place in the development of English tragedy by revealing new possibilities and offering a model in technique; unlike Marlowe's, it does not make a second claim upon us as great literature. The historical interest lies in the advance which Kyd's plays show in construction, in the manipulation of plot, and in effective situation. Kyd is the first to discover the bearing of episode and of the 'movement' of the story on characterisation, and the first to give the audience and reader the hint of the development of character which follows from this interaction. In other words, he is the first English dramatist who writes dramatically.

The historical position of Kyd has been the chief concern of criticism, and that is one reason why the brief account of the play which follows avoids questions of what Kyd borrowed and what he gave to others. Another reason is that our uncertainty about the date of the play makes it extremely difficult to mark Kyd's place in a fast-moving development of the drama. Was Lorenzo the first great Machiavellian villain? Did Kyd invent the Elizabethan revenge play? Yet Kyd's play is a most ingenious and successful blending of the old and the new in drama, and the fact that a comparative method is not followed here will not, I hope, obscure the obvious point that no good verdict can be made on Kyd's achievement which does not take into account what was achieved in plays written or performed at the same period.

The Spanish Tragedy is a play about the passion for retribution, and vengeance shapes the entire action. Revenge himself appears as a character near the beginning of the play, a servant of the spiritual powers, indicating what a man may find in the patterns of existence which are woven for him. Retribution is not only the demand of divine justice but also a condescension to human wants. Andrea seeks blood for his own blood; though he died in war, Balthazar killed him in a cowardly and dishonourable fashion, and not in fair fight (I. iv. 19–26, 72–5; I. ii. 73). The gods look with favour on Andrea and are prepared, by destroying his destroyer, to bring him peace. When all is completed, he exults : 'Ay, now my hopes have end in their effects, / When blood and sorrow finish my desires ... Ay, these were spectacles to please my soul!' Men lust for retribution, and the gods, assenting to this idea of satisfaction as only justice, can and will grant it. Marlowe never wrote a less Christian play than *The Spanish Tragedy*: the hate of a wronged man can speak out without check of mercy or reason; when a sin is committed, no-one talks of forgiveness; the word 'mercy' does not occur in the play.

Once Proserpine has granted that Balthazar shall die (I. i. 81–9), everything that happens in the play serves to fulfil her promise. To bring about what they have decreed, the gods use the desires and strivings of men. Hieronimo and Bel-imperia and Lorenzo, as they struggle and plot to bring about their own happiness, are only the tools of destiny. The sense of a fore-ordained end is strongly conveyed by Kyd by his constant use of dramatic irony. The characters always have mistaken notions about what their actions are leading them towards. Bel-imperia believes that 'second love will further her revenge', but only, it turns out, through the murder of her second love. As Horatio and Bel-imperia speak of consummating their love, they are overheard by those who are plotting to destroy it. And as the unwitting lovers go off the stage, the King enters (II. iii) complacently planning the marriage of Bel-imperia with Balthazar. By the very means he chooses to make his crime secret, the liquidating of his accomplices, Lorenzo betrays the crime to Hieronimo. Pedringano is secure in his belief in the master who is about to have him killed. The King and the court applaud the acting in a play in which the deaths are real. And there are very many other examples. In a way, the play is built upon irony, upon the ignorance of the characters that they are being used to fulfil the decree of the gods.

The play seems to move in a rather leisurely way from the entry of Andrea's Ghost to the killing of Horatio, the deed which opens the play's chief interest, Hieronimo's revenge. There is the description of the underworld by Andrea, two long reports of the battle in which Andrea was killed (one by the General to the King, and one by Horatio to Bel-imperia), Hieronimo's 'masque', and the introduction of the sub-plot concerning Villuppo's traducement of Alexandro at the Portuguese court. These prolix early scenes should not be dismissed without taking into account Kyd's use of the long speech in general throughout the play. Two recent and most interesting brief studies of the play's language have put Kyd's 'antiquated technique' in a new light. Both Moody E. Prior and Wolfgang Clemen[1] demonstrate how Kyd converts the techniques and conventions of an academic and literary drama with considerable skill to new dramatic ends: the long speech becomes more dramatic in itself and is used more dramatically. A good example used by both critics is that the most elaborately stylized rhetoric issues from the mouth of Balthazar, and these studied exercises in self-pity are used as a means of characterization; the more practical people, like Lorenzo and Bel-imperia, are impatient of his roundabout utterance (e.g., I. iv. 90–8, II. i. 29, II. i. 134). Clemen has particularly valuable things to say about how Kyd controls the tempo of the play through his use of the long speech, and how purposefully he knits together (each mode serving its own function) the long speech and dialogue; a long speech, for example, will introduce, or sum up, issues which are to be or have been set out in dialogue. But although Clemen (pp. 94–5), like Biesterfeldt before him (pp. 65–6), can find the early scenes in some measure artistically justified, and an improvement on what Kyd's predecessors achieved in long 'reports',[2] it is the very absence of that artistry which Kyd shows in his handling of the long speech in the later parts of the play which makes the early scenes seem so laboured. And, long speeches apart, it is very hard to justify the sub-plot. The Portuguese court could have been introduced more economically and the relevance of theme is very slight. Few readers of *The Spanish Tragedy* resent the clamant appeals and laments of Hieronimo and the rest once the play is under way, but few readers fail to find the early scenes tedious, and I think the common reaction is justified. It is as though Kyd began to write a literary Senecan play, and, even as he wrote, learned to handle his material in more dextrous and dramatic fashion.

[1] *The Language of Tragedy* (1947), pp. 46–59; *Die Tragödie vor Shakespeare* (1955), pp. 91–102, 238–47.

[2] For example, what seems to be the tiresome quadruple repetition of Balthazar's role in the battle is in fact the attempt to present the same event through different eyes. I am uncertain that Kyd intended this effect.

But the opening of the play will seem far more dilatory than it really is to those who take it that the real action starts only with the death of Horatio.[1] It is Balthazar's killing of Andrea which begins the action—the news being given by the ghost of the victim. The avenging of Andrea is, as we have seen, the supernatural cause of all that follows; but in terms of plot, too, or of direct, human causes, all flows from Andrea's death. For Andrea's mistress wishes to revenge herself on the slayer of her lover. Bel-imperia is a woman of strong will, independent spirit, and not a little courage (witness her superb treatment of her brother after her release, first furious and then sardonic, making Lorenzo acknowledge defeat; III. x. 24–105); she is also libidinous. Kyd has successfully man-œuvred round a ticklish necessity of the plot (that Bel-imperia and Horatio should be lovers) by making Bel-imperia a certain kind of woman; what *has* to be done, is credibly done, naturally done. There is no question about her relations with Andrea (see I. i. 10, II. i. 47, III. x. 54–5, III. xiv. 111–12); and, with Horatio, she does not appear to be planning an early wedding; the two are entering upon an illicit sexual relationship, and it is Bel-imperia who is the wooer (II. i. 85, II. ii. 32–52).

But, not to anticipate, Bel-imperia, while wishing to avenge Andrea, finds herself conceiving a passion for Horatio (I. iv. 60–1). She is momentarily ashamed of her lightness and tries to rationalize her affection as being a sign of her love for Andrea (62–3); then she repents and decides that revenge must come before she is off with the old love and on with the new (64–5) and then (triumphant ingenuity!) realizes that to love Horatio will in fact help her revenge against Balthazar, since it will slight the prince, who is a suitor for her love (66–8). So character and plot are married, and the action drives forward on its twin pistons of love and revenge.

Bel-imperia's scheme brings about her lover's death. Balthazar has new cause to hate the man who took him prisoner, but his hate would be nothing were it not given power by the hate of Lorenzo, whose fierce pride has twice been wounded by the lowly-born Horatio: once over the capturing of Balthazar, and now in his

---

[1] E.g., Bowers, pp. 66–8, 71; W. Farnham, *Medieval Heritage of Eliza-bethan Tragedy*, pp. 393–4; but cf. Biesterfeldt, especially pp. 50–60.

sister's preferring Horatio to his royal friend. Bel-imperia's re-
vengeful defiance brings about the simple reaction of counter-
revenge—the murder of Horatio in the bower. Horatio is hanged
and the *fourth* of the interlocked revenge-schemes begins:
Andrea's the first, then Bel-imperia's, then Lorenzo's and Balthazar's, and finally Hieronimo's. Kyd may seem to take some time
to reach this most important of his revenge-schemes, but he chose
to set layer within layer, wheels within wheels, revenge within
revenge. The action is a unity (the Portuguese scenes excepted), and
in engineering the deaths of Balthazar and Lorenzo, Hieronimo
satisfies not only himself, in respect of Horatio, but Bel-imperia in
respect of Horatio and Andrea, and Andrea in respect of himself.
And Hieronimo's efforts to avenge his dead son are the means by
which the gods avenge Andrea. The presence of the Ghost of
Andrea and Revenge upon the stage throughout the play, with
their speeches in the Choruses, continually reminds us of this fact,
which is indeed so central to the meaning of the play that it is
astonishing that it is occasionally overlooked.

Hieronimo's motives for revenge are several. (i) Revenge will
bring him emotional relief; (ii) it is a duty; (iii) a life for a life is the
law of nature, and (iv) is, in society, the legal penalty for murder.

Hieronimo's first remark about revenge is to tell Isabella that if
only he knew the murderer, his grief would diminish, 'For in
revenge my heart would find relief.' The therapeutic virtues of
homicide may seem doubtful, but Hieronimo insists:

> Then will I joy amidst my discontent,
> Till then my sorrow never shall be spent.   (II. v. 55–6)

Closely associated with this odd and selfish cue for revenge is the
idea of revenge as an obligation. We are to imagine (because it is
hardly stated explicitly) that Horatio's peace in the world beyond
depends, like Andrea's, upon his obtaining the life of his murderer
as a recompense for, and a cancellation of, his own death. For
Hieronimo to assume the duty of securing this price is a tribute to
his son and a measure of his love:

> Dear was the life of my beloved son,
> And of his death behoves me be reveng'd.   (III. ii. 44–5)

Hieronimo takes a vow to avenge Horatio and, of course, the notion of a vow to be fulfilled, with the bloody napkin as a symbol of it, provides a good deal of the play's dramatic force, particularly as regards Hieronimo's sense of insufficiency, failure, or delay. But, it may be noted, delay itself is not an issue in the play.[1] That Hieronimo's conscience should accuse him for being tardy (III. xiii. 135) is a measure only of the stress he is under and the difficulties he faces, and of the depth of his obligation; that Bel-imperia and Isabella should speak of delay (III. ix and IV. ii. 30) is a measure only of their understandable impatience and does not mean that Hieronimo *could* have acted more quickly. It is the sense of delay which is real, and not delay itself. Hieronimo does everything possible as quickly as possible.

The idea of revenge as a personal satisfaction for wrongs endured is enlarged into the idea of revenge as punishment, a universal moral satisfaction for crime committed, or the demands of divine justice. Though Hieronimo's wrongs are personal, he sees his claims for satisfaction as the claims of the Order of Things. The mythology chosen to represent the governance of the world is rather muddled in *The Spanish Tragedy*; paganism sits uneasily with—something else; but the gods (whoever they are) hate murder and will, through human agents, punish the murderer. There is morality among the gods, or so Hieronimo (somewhat anxiously) trusts:

> The heavens are just, murder cannot be hid. (II. v. 57)

> If this incomparable murder thus
> Of mine, but now no more my son,
> Shall unreveal'd and unrevenged pass,
> How should we term your dealings to be just,
> If you unjustly deal with those that in your justice trust?
> (III. ii. 7–11)

> Murder, O bloody monster—God forbid
> A fault so foul should scape unpunished. (III. vi. 95–6)

---

[1] Janet Spens (*Elizabethan Drama*, pp. 70–1) thinks it is, and that Hieronimo, 'being very old, lacks the virile courage and fears death'; the play shows how he overcomes his weakness. Boas (p. xxxv), claiming that delay is *the theme* of the later acts, believes that Kyd's cardinal weakness is failure to provide 'an adequate psychological analysis of the Marshal's motives for this delay'.

When things go wrong with Hieronimo, he pictures himself beating at the windows of the brightest heavens, soliciting for justice
and revenge (III. vii. 13–14). When things go well, he has the sense
of divine support. But the nexus between Hieronimo's plans for
revenge and the workings of providence is a somewhat controversial
matter, and must be discussed with other facts in mind.

Punishment of murder is the course of human law, and Hieronimo's revenge is to be within the framework of law. Yet he goes
about to discover the murderer in a manner curious to modern eyes.
He sees it as his personal duty to find the criminal, and he conceals
the crime. But this is no usurpation of the law; there is no C.I.D. to
call in and he must act himself.[1] The secrecy is to be explained by
Hieronimo's fear that someone is contriving against his family so
that it behoves him to move warily. Bel-imperia's letter seems to
confirm his suspicions; nothing could be less credible than its news,
and, should there be a plot against his family, what more suitable
means to entrap him than to get him to lay an accusation for murder
against the King's own nephew (III. ii. 34–43)? He will find out
more, still keeping his mission secret (III. ii. 48–52). Confirming
evidence comes via Pedringano, and Pedringano's arrest and punishment are an important accompaniment of Hieronimo's vendetta.
For here is an orthodox piece of police-work, as it were. Pedringano
commits murder, he is arrested *flagrante delicto* by the watch, tried
by a court, and executed. There is law in Spain, and, once a murderer is known, he can be brought to account by due process of law.
Hieronimo's anguish at the trial of Pedringano is not because for
him justice has to be secured by different means, but because the
course of justice which is available cannot be started since he, the
very judge, cannot name the murderer of his son. It is not the least
part of Hieronimo's design to indulge in Bacon's 'wild justice'; it
does not enter his head to 'put the law out of office'.

But, now that Hieronimo has Pedringano's letter and the clinch-
ing evidence which he needed, he may proceed to call in the aid of
law and get justice. To lay an accusation, however, proves to be the
heaviest of Hieronimo's difficulties. The protracted battle of wits

---

[1] See Bowers, pp. 7–8, for the necessity at this time for the nearest relative of the victim to lay an appeal or file an indictment.

between Hieronimo and Lorenzo (so excellently handled by Kyd
and so unfortunately obscured in the Additions) comes to a head,
and, more powerful obstacle still, just as Hieronimo is ready to call
down punishment on the criminals, the strain on his mind begins to
tell, and his madness begins. The unsettling of Hieronimo's mind
is well done; it has been prepared for long ago, in Hieronimo's
excessive pride in his son when he was alive, and it is made more
acceptable in that Isabella ('psychologically' unimportant as a
character) has already been shown to be going out of her mind with
grief. Hieronimo's frenzy makes Lorenzo's task of keeping him
from the King easy; Hieronimo really prevents himself from securing justice. Thwarted, he plots to be his own avenger.[1]

At this point, we may bring in again the question of divine justice.
Momentarily, and most awkwardly, Jehovah assumes a role in the
play; Hieronimo remembers that the Lord says, 'Vengeance is
mine, I will repay' (III. xiii. 1 and note). He acknowledges that
'mortal men may not appoint their time' (l. 5). But since 'justice is
exiled from the earth' he persuades himself that private vengeance
is justified. Bowers (pp. 71 and 77–82) is of the opinion that the
play condemns Hieronimo for taking it upon himself to be the
executioner instead of waiting for God's will to be done, and that
'Kyd is deliberately veering his audience against Hieronimo.' The
problem is far from simple. It has been seen that the gods of the
play like revenge. More important, after the *Vindicta mihi* speech,
Hieronimo is convinced that his private course is congruent with
the morality of heaven. When he is joined by Bel-imperia, he interprets his good fortune as a sign of the approval of the gods, and feels
that he is a minister of providence:

> Why then, I see that heaven applies our drift,
> And all the saints do sit soliciting
> For vengeance on those cursed murderers.   (IV. i. 32–4)

Moody Prior (*Language of Tragedy*, p. 57) sees this outcry as a
turning point in the drama. 'Private vengeance is now identified

---

[1] The ignorance of the King about the disappearance of Horatio is best
not inquired into. The plot demands it and the play shall have it. But, by
this stage in the play, everyone else seems to know what has happened, from
Hieronimo's Deputy (III. vi. 13–14) to the Duke of Castile (III. xiv. 88).

with the justice of heaven, and the torment of his mind is over. In the episodes which follow, he is calculating and self-possessed.' This seems a most sensible view, but the question must be asked, Is Hieronimo deluding himself in supposing he now has divine support? To answer 'yes' to this question must suggest that there is a clash in the play between the dominant pagan morality and a Christian morality. The only overt introduction of the Christian morality on revenge is in the brief allusion to St Paul; where, in other parts of the play, the mythology for Providence seems to be Christian— as in the passage just quoted, with its reference to heaven and saints—we almost certainly are faced with inconsistency and confusion on Kyd's part and not a dualism. We could, indeed, make no sense out of a dualism which meant that every reference to powers below was a reference to evil and every reference to powers above a reference to good. The clash, if it exists, must be between the ideas which Hieronimo has and ideas not expressed in the play, except in the *Vindicta mihi* speech. In other words, the argument must be that Hieronimo is condemned because the Elizabethans condemned revenge, however strongly the play's gods support him.

But what an Elizabethan might think of Hieronimo's actions in real life may be irrelevant to the meaning of *The Spanish Tragedy*. Hieronimo may still be a sympathetic hero in spite of Elizabethan indignation against private revenge. The cry of *Vindicta mihi*, and the pause it gives Hieronimo may be more of a dramatic than a moral point. Hieronimo, robbed of the law's support, rocks for a moment in indecision before determining that at all costs the murderers must die. The indecision, and then the determination, are dramatically most important and effective; but the cause of the indecision (the inappropriate promptings of Christian ethics) is not important. Kyd has won sympathy for Hieronimo in his sufferings; there is no sign, at the end of the third and the beginning of the fourth Act, that Kyd now wishes the audience to change their sympathetic attitude, even though orthodoxy would condemn the private executioner. Kyd creates, and successfully sustains, his own world of revenge, and attitudes are sanctioned which might well be deplored in real life. The moral world of the play is a make-believe world; the gods are make-believe gods. In this make-believe world, the private executioner may be sympathetically portrayed and his Senecan gods may countenance his actions. And all this may be, however strongly Kyd himself disapproved of private vengeance. I remarked that *The Spanish Tragedy* was an un-Christian play, and so it is. But it is not written to advocate a system of ethics, or to oppose one. If its moral attitudes are mistaken for the 'real life' attitudes of the dramatist, then the play has an appalling message. But if the play is seen as a thing of great—and skilful—artificiality, with standards of values which we accept while we are in the theatre, there is no problem at all about sympathizing with the hero. The play had power enough to lull an Elizabethan conscience while it was being performed.

It could well be said, however, that it is a poor play which depends on the audience suspending its belief in law and mercy. And yet a swingeing revenge-play has its own emotional satisfaction for the audience. Vengeance is exacted from evil-doers by a man whose wrongs invoke pity; in enabling an audience to forget their daily docility and to share in Hieronimo's violent triumph, it may be that Kyd has justified himself as an artist more than he would have done in providing a sermon on how irreligious it is to be vindictive.

It would be foolish to gloss over the difficulty of siding with Hieronimo to the very end, after the punishment of the criminals. As Bowers points out, he seems in the final scene little more than a dangerous and bloodthirsty maniac. Although I have suggested (see above, p. xxxvi) that the crudities of Hieronimo's departure from life might have been much less apparent in Kyd's original version of the play, no theory of revision can explain away what seems to be the pointless savagery of the murder of the unoffending Castile. It may be that Kyd was trying to give a Senecan touch of the curse upon the house, but there are other considerations which make *condemnation* of Hieronimo rather irrelevant. In the first place, Castile was Andrea's enemy (see II. i. 46–7 and III. xiv. 111–13) and Hieronimo is the agent of destiny employed to avenge Andrea; Castile's death appears to make Andrea's peace perfect. Revenge is satisfied, and we had best try not to worry about the bloodthirstiness of it all.

Much more important, however, is the reflection that *The Spanish Tragedy* is, after all, a tragedy of sorts. Hieronimo has gone mad with grief, with the stress of observing his vow, and with the long war between himself and Lorenzo. As Castile falls, horror is mingled with pity that this should be the end of Hieronimo's life. If we cannot take Senecan revenge very seriously, or the somewhat contrived idea of destiny, we can take Lorenzo's machinations and Hieronimo's sufferings without embarrassment. *The Spanish Tragedy* has most merit in its study of the hero's grief and final distraction, and, when at the end the innocent man suffers at the hands of the hero whose innocence was not in question, it is probable that an audience feels a more complex emotion than revulsion against extra-legal revenge.

6. THE ADDITIONS OF 1602

Pavier's edition of 1602 introduced into the play five additional passages, some 320 lines in all. In the present edition they will be found separated from the original text, on pp. 122–35.

The first, second, and last of the Additions have little to commend them; their literary quality is slight and they do much damage to Kyd's careful unfolding of plot and character. The third Addition is an imaginative piece of rhetoric which does not distort the original play; the fourth is the famous 'Painter scene' and stands head and shoulders above the rest—as good a scene of madness as anything in Elizabethan drama outside *Hamlet* or *King Lear*.

Concerning the source of these Additions, there are two important entries in Henslowe's *Diary* (1, 149, 168):

Lent vnto m^r alleyn the 25 of septmber 1601 to lend vnto Bengemen Johnson vpon his writtinge of his adicians in geronymo the some of xxxx^s

Lent vnto bengemy Johnsone at the a poyntment of E Allyen & w^m birde the 22 of Iune 1602 in earneste of a Boocke called Richard crockbacke & for new adicyons for Jeronymo the some of x^{ll}

There are difficulties in accepting the printed Additions as those mentioned by Henslowe. First, there is a general feeling that the style of the Additions is not in the least like anything Jonson could or would write.[1] Secondly, Henslowe has paid a large sum, £2 and a portion of £10, for his additions, and it is hard to think that all he was getting for his money was three-hundred-odd lines. Thirdly, it is a question whether the Additions could have been composed such a short time before they were published: 'there is an initial improbability that important additions to the acting version should have been allowed to reach the press so soon after composition' (*MSR* (*1602*), pp. xviii–xix). Fourthly, there is the enigmatic reference by Jonson himself in the Induction to *Cynthia's Revels* in 1600 (printed 1601), which seems to suggest that *The Spanish Tragedy* had already been recast. A foolish playgoer is made to swear '*that the old Hieronimo*, (as it was first acted) *was the onely best, and iudiciously pend play of Europe*' (*Works*, IV, 42). Fifthly, Schücking and H. Levin[2] have pointed out parodies of the Painter Scene in Marston's *Antonio and Mellida*, which is usually dated 1599, two years before Jonson was paid for his work.

In view of these objections, there has been a tendency to push back the extant Additions to a date which would sympathize with Henslowe's (now erased) *ne* against a revival of *The Spanish Tragedy* in 1597,[3] and to look for an author other than Jonson. Lamb fancied Webster, Coleridge fancied Shakespeare; Shakespeare has perhaps been the favourite in the continuing search, though a case has been made out for Dekker.[4]

But there are questions about the Additions which must be answered before one starts hunting for an author. What kind of copy does the text of the Additions suggest? How far does the revised play as printed bear relation to the revised play as acted?

Schücking (pp. 38–9), considering the extreme metrical deficiencies of the Additions, thought that they could not be as they were written by the author; in some places, indeed, the text seemed to him so corrupt that it could not be restored. Greg and Nichol

---

[1] E.g., Lamb, *Specimens* (Bohn, 1897), p. 11; Coleridge, *Table Talk* (Bohn, 1888), p. 203; Herford and Simpson, Jonson's *Works*, II, 237–45. But see J. A. Symonds, *Ben Jonson* (1886), p. 15.

[2] Schücking, pp. 33–5; Levin, *M.L.N.*, lxiv (1949), 297–302.

[3] *Diary*, I, 50 and 223.

[4] By H. W. Crundell and R. G. Howarth, *N. & Q.*, 4 March 1933, 7 April, 4 August 1934, 4 January 1941.

Smith (*MSR (1592)*, p. xv) suggested that, if the 1602 Additions 'were supplied by a reporter relying on his memory', we might have the explanation of their scantiness as compared with the large sum paid to Jonson. 'The hypothesis of reporting,' they go on, 'also, of course, meets the objection that the Admiral's men would have been unlikely to release the additions for publication so soon after the revival.' The authors agree, however, that it is still difficult to reconcile the style of the Additions with Jonson.

Metrically, the Additions are indeed very rough—or the verse is very free: see, for example, the latter part of Hieronimo's speech in the Third Addition. The verse of the famous Painter Scene is often impossible to scan on any recognized principle: the scene is full of short lines and long lines, and irregularly printed lines which cannot be pulled into decasyllabic shape. From the Painter's entry at l. 78, it is very hard to know whether prose or verse is the correct basis; all editions print as prose from l. 113, and some (as in this edition) from l. 107, but the quarto continues to give the appearance of verse throughout the scene, and certainly there are many blank-verse phrases in the prose. But apart from this disorder in the verse, there seems to me little evidence of the corruption of a reported version. While one might agree with Schücking (pp. 38–9) that something appears to have gone wrong with Hieronimo's speeches and exchanges with Isabella at ll. 42–72 of the Fourth Addition, the language of that Addition as a whole seems quite free from the muddle, weakness, and repetitions to be expected from a memorial report. On the face of it, it would seem that a careless and hurried transcript could be responsible for the shortcomings of the text.

But what are these Additions? It is most unlikely that the text of *1602* gives us *The Spanish Tragedy* in a form that was ever acted. Schücking rightly argues that the old play *plus* the Additions gives a text far too long for acting. He thinks that the purpose of the Additions was, not to pander to the audience's demand for new scenes of Hieronimo's lunacy, but to modernize the antiquated style of the play; the Additions are not additions, but replacements. The Painter Scene, with its bereaved father Bazardo, is to be substituted for that part of III. xiii which shows the bereaved father Bazulto seeking for justice. So far, this seems only reasonable, but Schücking's ingenious suggestions about what other parts of the old play were to disappear in favour of the new material are much less convincing. The general theory, however, is surely sound: that we have in *1602*, 'ein Nebeneinander von dem, was die Bretter nur als Nacheinander gekannt haben' (p. 78); a text in which new material is inappropriately added side by side with old material which had been erased for the stage. The bibliographical evidence, already submitted, would seem to support this: *1602* was not printed from new copy, but is a reprint of the last edition (and therefore eventually going back to Kyd's foul papers) with the additional material inserted. Admittedly, the 'joins' are quite neat, especially in the First and at the end of the Fourth Additions, but Schücking expresses strong doubts about the fitness of place of the Third Addition: the dialogue with the Portingales is awkwardly broken, and the reference to Balthazar (l. 39) seems too mild for the stage of the plot which has been reached. It seems just as likely that the working in of the new material was a piece of editorial patching and seaming as it is that it represents an author's dovetailing of material to make a new acting text.

The train of events which seems to me most fitting to explain the relation between the Additions which we have and the new-furbished play as acted is as follows. A fairly extensive revision of *The Spanish Tragedy* was undertaken. This involved (i) the writing of new scenes to take the place of similar scenes in the old play, as with the Painter Scene; (ii) the excision of 'dead' material to provide space for new scenes of Hieronimo's madness like the First Addition; (iii) the reworking of unsatisfactory scenes, such as the ending, in which old material is incorporated with the new; (iv) the incidental enlivening of the dialogue, as in the Second Addition. When this revised version was acted, Pavier obtained *some* of the new material, but what he obtained has roughness enough to make us suspect that he got it surreptitiously—perhaps by transcript, but conceivably through the actors.[1] He was able to fit his material with reasonable ease into the printed text which he had of the old play (*1599*), but

---

[1] It is quite impossible that a 'reporter' in the audience should have known the old play so well that he would be able to spot that the brief Second Addition *was* an addition.

the new play which he thus created is an unwieldy thing not at all like the new *Spanish Tragedy* which was acted.

What can be surmised about the condition of the text does not really strengthen the case for Jonson. There is support for Greg and Nichol Smith's view that it is no longer an argument that the Additions are too thin for the payment given, or that they were released for publication too early. But there is nothing new in favour of Jonson's having written them. It is not an attractive theory that *The Spanish Tragedy* twice underwent revision, first by an unknown dramatist and then by Jonson, but the problem of style is acute. The possibly unauthorized transmission of the Additions cannot have transmuted the style, and the search for traces of Jonson's known style is hopeless. Yet it is important not to return a flat 'impossible' to Jonson. The principle of decorum has to be remembered: it is no use comparing the Additions with what Jonson writes in *Volpone* or *Sejanus* or *Cynthia's Revels*; we need to try to imagine what Jonson would have written for *The Spanish Tragedy*.[1] Must he not have indulged a more romantic vein, with its own type of language (something not allowed to emerge in plays for which he was wholly responsible), when he tried to fit scenes to an old 'romantic' play? Would anything that is truly Jonsonian have done? The first and last of the Additions are perfunctory hack-work which Jonson could have managed in his sleep. He may have despised the passions he created.

But there is still the question of date. The reference in *Cynthia's Revels* may be too ambiguous to build an argument on, but the Marston parodies are a different matter (see Appendix E). The accepted conjectural date of Marston's plays is 1599.[2] If we accept the possibility, however, that the parodies of the Painter Scene were added later, then it is conceivable that Jonson is Marston's butt. Jonson's first payment for his work is 25 September 1601; Marston's plays were entered in the Stationers' Register on 24 October 1601 and published together in 1602. It is something of a strained conjecture that Jonson's revised play was on the stage early enough, and that Marston thought it worth while to tinker with his play in

---

[1] Cf. Max Priess, *Englische Studien*, lxxiv, 341.
[2] See *Eliz. Stage*, III, 429–30; Levin, *op. cit.*

E

order to parody the new material, but it is not beyond the bounds of possibility.

And in that awkward state of affairs it is necessary to leave the matter. It cannot be disproved that the Additions of *1602* are the relics of those for which Jonson was paid, but one is not at all happy in accepting them as such. If a really convincing case had been made out for another dramatist, and an earlier date, one would readily accept it.

7. STAGE HISTORY

The first recorded performances of *The Spanish Tragedy* were, as we have seen, in the early months of 1592 at the Rose on Bankside. The company was called Lord Strange's Men by Henslowe but was an amalgamation of Strange's and the Admiral's Men (*Eliz. Stage*, II, 120). The play (or the play and its putative first part) was given twenty times in that season, and was played three times in the short season of December–January 1592–3 (see Appendix A). Thereafter, there is no record in Henslowe's Diary until the Admiral's Men's season at the Rose beginning 25 November 1596. '*Jeronimo*' was played first on 7 January 1597, and against the entry Henslowe placed his enigmatic *ne*, since erased from the document. Twelve performances are recorded between January and July, and in the joint season of the Admiral's and Pembroke's Men which followed, '*Jeronimo*' was the opening performance on 11 October 1597. That performance is the last recorded by Henslowe, and the last datable professional performance in England. Henslowe's only other references are to the payments to Jonson for additions in 1601 and 1602.

One would expect *The Spanish Tragedy* to have been played in the provinces in the 1590's, and Dekker's *Satiromastix* (1602) taunts Jonson ('Horace') with having played Hieronimo in a company of strolling players.

> Thou hast forgot how thou amblest (in leather pilch) by a play-wagon, in the high way, and took'st mad Ieronimoes part, to get seruice among the Mimickes.   (IV. i. 130–2)

> I ha seene thy shoulders lapt in a Plaiers old cast Cloake, like a Slie knaue as thou art: and when thou ranst mad for the death of Horatio, thou borrowedst a gowne of *Roscius* the Stager, (that

honest Nicodemus) and sentst it home lowsie, didst not?

(I. ii. 354-8)

The date suggested by Herford and Simpson for this episode is July 1597 (*Works*, I, 12).

That *The Spanish Tragedy* in its revised form (whatever the authorship and date) continued to be acted with success in the first fifteen years of the seventeenth century can easily be inferred, though specific evidence is lacking. The title page of *1602* refers to the enlarged play 'as it hath of late been diuers times acted', and the very publication of the Additions, probably unauthorized, bears witness to popularity, as does Marston's parody. In 1615, J. Tomkis' play, *Albumazar*, was presented before the King at Cambridge and one of the characters talks of using 'complements drawn from the plaies I see at the Fortune and Red Bull', and then speaks a parody of the notorious 'O eyes, no eyes,' speech. It was at the Fortune rather than the Red Bull that revivals of the play could be seen, since it was there that the Admiral's Men (continuing under the name of Prince Henry's and later of the Palsgrave's Men) were accustomed to play (*Eliz. Stage*, II, 441). There is some question whether the Admiral's Men and their successors remained the sole proprietors of the play; the matter is discussed in Appendix F. In 1615, also, appears the edition of the play which bears on its title-page the woodcut of the crucial arbour-scene—Horatio hanging, Hieronimo in his night-shirt, Bel-imperia calling for help and being pulled away by Lorenzo in disguise (sc. with a blackened face). It seems quite possible that the artist took his ideas from stage-performances of the time.

References to and parodies of the play are innumerable in the earlier seventeenth century, but their existence does not depend upon a live theatrical tradition; but the successive editions of 1610, 1615, 1618, 1623, and 1633 seem to speak of more than a literary interest. Boas (p. xcvii) quotes an interesting exchange from Thomas May's *The Heir* of 1620:

Roscio. Has not your lordship seen
       A player personate *Hieronimo*?
Polymetes. By th' mass 'tis true. I have seen the knave paint grief
       In such a lively colour that for false

> And acted passion he has drawn true tears
> From the spectators. Ladies in the boxes
> Kept time with sighs and tears to his sad accents,
> As he had truly been the man he seemed.

In Rawlins' play, *The Rebellion* (?1638–9), however, the acting of Hieronimo by 'wide-mouth'd Fowler'—who was one of the pillars of the Fortune in those years—inspires only contempt (Bentley, *Jacobean and Caroline Stage*, v, 996).

For the English stage, there is little else to record. Schick and Boas give full accounts of the adventures of *The Spanish Tragedy* abroad. A band of English actors took the play to Germany and a performance is recorded at Frankfurt in 1601. Boas gives the text of a German adaptation made by Jacob Ayrer before 1605. Versions of the play were acted at Dresden in 1626 (by English actors), at Prague in 1651, and Lüneburg in 1660; Creizenach cites a play, *Der tolle marschalk aus Spanien*, from an early eighteenth-century play list (see Boas, pp. xcix–c). In Holland, an adaptation by Adriaen van den Bergh was published in 1621, and a later anonymous version was regularly reprinted until 1729.

In the present century, as is only to be expected with a play occupying a key position in the histories of Elizabethan drama, *The Spanish Tragedy* has been several times revived by university dramatic societies. Birkbeck College twice produced the play, in December 1921 and December 1931. It was played in the library at Christ Church, Oxford, in a production by John Izon, in March 1932. There was another production at Oxford, at St John's, in 1951. August 1951 saw the play performed at the Edinburgh Festival by the Edinburgh University Dramatic Society. The producer was Roy Smith and Hieronimo was taken by Alexander Grant. The play was given with the Additions, but with some of the original play cut; *The Times* (25 August) spoke favourably of Kyd's dramatic skill, and particularly of the effectiveness of the Ghost and Revenge. A photograph of the final scene of the play (*The Times*, 27 August) shows the Ghost and Revenge on an upper stage while (quite properly) Hieronimo addresses his captive audience on the main stage.

It is a pity that there is not more to record from the professional stage; the play is worth the trial.

Editions Cited in the Notes

(See Introduction, pp. xl–xlv)

Schick[2]   *Spanish Tragedy*, ed. J. Schick, 1901 (*Litterarhistor-*
                 ische Forschungen, Heft xix).
                 [*Note: Schick* = agreement of these two editions.]

Boas   *Works of Thomas Kyd*, 1901.

Brooke   *English Drama 1580–1642*, ed. C. F. Tucker Brooke
                 and N. B. Paradise, 1933.

McIlwraith   *Five Elizabethan Tragedies*, ed. A. K. McIlwraith,
                 1938.

Prouty   *The Spanish Tragedy*, ed. C. T. Prouty, 1951 (The
                 Crofts Classics).

THE SPANISH TRAGEDY

Ghost of ANDREA.
REVENGE.

KING of Spain ('Spanish King').
CYPRIAN, Duke of Castile ('Castile', 'Duke'), *his brother.*
LORENZO, *the Duke's son.*
BEL-IMPERIA, *Lorenzo's sister.*
GENERAL *of the Spanish Army.*

VICEROY of Portugal ('King').
PEDRO, *his brother.*
BALTHAZAR ('Prince'), *his son.*
ALEXANDRO, } *noblemen at the Portuguese court.*
VILLUPPO, }
AMBASSADOR *of Portugal to the Spanish court.*

HIERONIMO, *Knight Marshal of Spain.*
ISABELLA, *his wife.*
HORATIO, *his son.*

PEDRINGANO, *servant to Bel-imperia.*
SERBERINE, *servant to Balthazar.*
CHRISTOPHIL, *servant to Lorenzo.*
Page ('Boy') *to Lorenzo.*
Three Watchmen.
Messenger.
Deputy.
Hangman.
Maid *to Isabella.*
Two Portuguese.
Servant.
Three Citizens.
An Old Man, BAZULTO ('Senex').

DRAMATIS PERSONAE] First given by Dodsley (1744) and expanded by Schick, Boas, and *M.S.R.* Alternative names are given in parentheses.

Portuguese Nobles, Soldiers, Officers, Attendants, Halberdiers.

Three Knights, Three Kings, a Drummer *in the first Dumb-show.*
Hymen, Two Torch-bearers *in the second Dumb-show.*

In HIERONIMO's play:

SOLIMAN, Sultan of Turkey (BALTHAZAR).
ERASTO ('Erastus'), Knight of Rhodes (LORENZO).
Bashaw (HIERONIMO).
PERSEDA (BEL-IMPERIA).

In the Additions:

PEDRO ⎫
JAQUES ⎬ *servants to Hieronimo.*
A Painter, BAZARDO.]

The Spanish Tragedy

CONTAINING THE LAMENTABLE END OF DON
HORATIO AND BEL-IMPERIA: WITH THE
PITIFUL DEATH OF OLD HIERONIMO.

Act I

[I. i]

Enter the Ghost *of* ANDREA, *and with him* REVENGE.

Andrea. When this eternal substance of my soul
    Did live imprison'd in my wanton flesh,
    Each in their function serving other's need,
    I was a courtier in the Spanish court.
    My name was Don Andrea, my descent,   5
    Though not ignoble, yet inferior far
    To gracious fortunes of my tender youth:
    For there in prime and pride of all my years,
    By duteous service and deserving love,
    In secret I possess'd a worthy dame,   10
    Which hight sweet Bel-imperia by name.
    But in the harvest of my summer joys
    Death's winter nipp'd the blossoms of my bliss,
    Forcing divorce betwixt my love and me.

Act I] ACTVS PRIMVS. *1592.*   1. *Andrea.*] *Ghoast. 1592.*

   1ff.] Of the many parodies of the opening of the play, the best-known is in
The Knight of the Burning Pestle, V. i: 'When I was mortal, this my costive
corpse / Did lap up figs and raisins in the Strand.'
   8. *prime*] The line is cited in *O.E.D.* (s.v. *prime, sb.*[1], 8) to illustrate the
meaning 'the spring-time of human life, the time of early manhood . . . from
about 21–28 years of age'.
   10. *In secret*] For further details about this clandestine relation and its
consequences, see II. i. 45–8, III. x. 54–5, III. xiv. 111–12.

4

For in the late conflict with Portingale   15
My valour drew me into danger's mouth,
Till life to death made passage through my wounds.
When I was slain, my soul descended straight
To pass the flowing stream of Acheron:
But churlish Charon, only boatman there,   20
Said that my rites of burial not perform'd,
I might not sit amongst his passengers.
Ere Sol had slept three nights in Thetis' lap
And slak'd his smoking chariot in her flood,
By Don Horatio, our Knight Marshal's son,   25
My funerals and obsequies were done.
Then was the ferryman of hell content
To pass me over to the slimy strond
That leads to fell Avernus' ugly waves:
There pleasing Cerberus with honey'd speech,   30
I pass'd the perils of the foremost porch.
Not far from hence, amidst ten thousand souls,
Sat Minos, Aeacus, and Rhadamanth,
To whom no sooner gan I make approach,
To crave a passport for my wand'ring ghost,   35
But Minos, in graven leaves of lottery,

---

15. *the late conflict*] See Introduction, p. xxiv.

Portingale] Portugal; a quite usual form during the 16th and preceding centuries.

18ff.] The description of the underworld is based upon the *Aeneid*, Bk VI. See note to l. 73.

25. *Knight Marshal*] or Marshal of the King's House. A law officer whose authority was exercised in the English royal household, in hearing and determining all pleas of the crown, and suits between those of the king's house and others within the verge (sc. within a radius of twelve miles), and in punishing transgressions committed within his area. (See Jacob's *Law Dict.*, s.v. *Marshal*.) The office was abolished in 1846.

28. *strond*] strand, shore.

33. *Minos, Aeacus, and Rhadamanth*] appointed judges in the underworld because of the justice and integrity of their lives. Minos had the casting vote, as in ll. 50–3.

36. *graven leaves of lottery*] Virgil says that the dead are assigned to their dwellings 'not without lot, or judgement; Minos, who presides, shakes the urn . . .' (*Aen.*, VI, 431–2). But here Minos is consulting the graven leaves

Drew forth the manner of my life and death.
'This knight,' quoth he, 'both liv'd and died in love,
And for his love tried fortune of the wars,
And by war's fortune lost both love and life.'   40
'Why then,' said Aeacus, 'convey him hence,
To walk with lovers in our fields of love,
And spend the course of everlasting time
Under green myrtle trees and cypress shades.'
'No, no,' said Rhadamanth, 'it were not well   45
With loving souls to place a martialist,
He died in war, and must to martial fields,
Where wounded Hector lives in lasting pain,
And Achilles' Myrmidons do scour the plain.'
Then Minos, mildest censor of the three,   50
Made this device to end the difference.
'Send him,' quoth he, 'to our infernal king,
To doom him as best seems his majesty.'
To this effect my passport straight was drawn.
In keeping on my way to Pluto's court,   55
Through dreadful shades of ever-glooming night,
I saw more sights than thousand tongues can tell,
Or pens can write, or mortal hearts can think.
Three ways there were: that on the right-hand side
Was ready way unto the foresaid fields,   60
Where lovers live, and bloody martialists,
But either sort contain'd within his bounds.
The left-hand path, declining fearfully,

---

for an account of Andrea's past; there might, therefore, be some support for
Brooke's gloss, 'book of fate'; *lottery* would presumably mean 'what is
allotted to one', i.e., destiny (cf. *Merchant of Venice*, II. i. 15; *Antony &
Cleopatra*, II. ii. 248). But *drew forth* (l. 37) is best interpreted literally and
we must suppose that Minos draws from his urn the lottery slip on which
was engraved the manner of life which Andrea has by now fulfilled, i.e.,
what has been his lot.

38–40.] The figure of repetition in these lines (anadiplosis) is a favourite
with Kyd; cf. I. iii. 33ff.; II. i. 119ff.

46. *martialist*] used by Kyd again in *Cornelia*, IV. ii. 46.

53. *doom*] give judgement on.

Was ready downfall to the deepest hell,
Where bloody furies shakes their whips of steel,   65
And poor Ixion turns an endless wheel:
Where usurers are chok'd with melting gold,
And wantons are embrac'd with ugly snakes,
And murderers groan with never-killing wounds,
And perjur'd wights scalded in boiling lead,   70
And all foul sins with torments overwhelm'd.
'Twixt these two ways, I trod the middle path,
Which brought me to the fair Elysian green,
In midst whereof there stands a stately tower,
The walls of brass, the gates of adamant.   75
Here finding Pluto with his Proserpine,
I show'd my passport humbled on my knee:
Whereat fair Proserpine began to smile,
And begg'd that only she might give my doom.
Pluto was pleas'd and seal'd it with a kiss.   80
Forthwith, Revenge, she rounded thee in th' ear,
And bade thee lead me through the gates of horn,
Where dreams have passage in the silent night.
No sooner had she spoke but we were here,

69. groan] grone *1592;* greeue *1594.*   82. horn] *Hawkins;* Hor: *1592;*
Horror *1599.*

---

64. *downfall*] a sudden descent.
65. *shakes*] For this form of the plural, see Franz, §155.
73. *Elysian green*] See Introduction, p. xxiii, for the relation between
Kyd's description and Nashe's sneer, 'What can be hoped of those that
thrust Elysium into hell?' Virgil's Elysium is in the netherworld, and Kyd
does not confuse the 'fair green' of the blessed with the 'deepest hell' of the
damned. But he does take some liberties with Virgil's picture: the adamant
gates and the tower of Pluto's court (ll. 74–5) belong to the abode of the
damned in Virgil (*Aen.,* VI, 552–4); there are not 'three ways' in Virgil
(l. 59) but two, the fields of lovers and martialists having been already
passed by Aeneas. Did Kyd anticipate Dryden's error in supposing that
corripiunt spatium medium (*Aen.,* VI, 634) meant *trod the middle path*
(l. 72)?
79. *doom*] sentence.
81. *rounded*] whispered.
82. *gates of horn*] Cf. *Aeneid,* VI, 893–6; there are twin gates of sleep: from
those of horn true visions emerge, from those of ivory, false visions.

I wot not how, in twinkling of an eye.   85

Revenge. Then know, Andrea, that thou art arriv'd
Where thou shalt see the author of thy death,
Don Balthazar the prince of Portingale,
Depriv'd of life by Bel-imperia:
Here sit we down to see the mystery,   90
And serve for Chorus in this tragedy.

[I. ii]

Enter Spanish KING, GENERAL, CASTILE, HIERONIMO.

King. Now say Lord General, how fares our camp?

Gen. All well, my sovereign liege, except some few
That are deceas'd by fortune of the war.

King. But what portends thy cheerful countenance,
And posting to our presence thus in haste?   5
Speak man, hath fortune given us victory?

Gen. Victory my liege, and that with little loss.

King. Our Portingals will pay us tribute then?

Gen. Tribute and wonted homage therewithal.

King. Then blest be heaven, and guider of the heavens,   10
From whose fair influence such justice flows.

Cast. O multum dilecte Deo, tibi militat aether,
Et conjuratae curvato poplite gentes

I. ii. 8. then?] *1615;* then. *1592.*   13. *poplite*] *1594; poplito 1592.*

---

89. *Depriv'd of life*] a fairly common phrase; see, e.g., *1 Henry IV*, IV. iii.
91 and *Soliman and Perseda,* I. vi. 28.

90. *mystery*] events with a secret meaning. An unusual sense, repeated at
III. xv. 29; it is more usual to use the word for the secret meaning than for
the events or for the story, and so Kyd uses it at I. iv. 139 (cf. *O.E.D.,* 7).
There is possibly a suggestion here of the sense 'secret rites'—usually in
a religious connexion. It is only a coincidence that each time Kyd uses the
word, it is in the context of a stage presentation; the word *mystery* for the
old biblical plays is much later.

I. ii. 1. *camp*] army; properly, army on a campaign (*O.E.D., sb.²,* 2). Doll
Common uses this opening line to greet Face: *Alchemist,* III. iii. 33.

12–14.] 'O man much loved of God, for you the heavens fight, and the
conspiring peoples fall on bended knee; victory is the sister of just rights.'
An address deriving from Claudian.

Succumbunt: recti soror est victoria juris.

King. Thanks to my loving brother of Castile.   15
      But General, unfold in brief discourse
      Your form of battle and your war's success,
      That adding all the pleasure of thy news
      Unto the height of former happiness,
      With deeper wage and greater dignity   20
      We may reward thy blissful chivalry.

Gen. Where Spain and Portingale do jointly knit
      Their frontiers, leaning on each other's bound,
      There met our armies in their proud array,
      Both furnish'd well, both full of hope and fear,   25
      Both menacing alike with daring shows,
      Both vaunting sundry colours of device,
      Both cheerly sounding trumpets, drums and fifes,
      Both raising dreadful clamours to the sky,
      That valleys, hills, and rivers made rebound,   30
      And heaven itself was frighted with the sound.
      Our battles both were pitch'd in squadron form,
      Each corner strongly fenc'd with wings of shot:
      But ere we join'd and came to push of pike,
      I brought a squadron of our readiest shot   35
      From out our rearward to begin the fight:
      They brought another wing to encounter us.
      Meanwhile our ordnance play'd on either side,
      And captains strove to have their valours tried.

38. ordnance] *1623;* ordinance *1592.*

---

20. *wage*] reward ('wages').
21. *chivalry*] skill in arms.
22ff.] Massinger caricatures this speech in *The Picture* (1629), II. i. 111ff.
27. *colours of device*] heraldic standards or banners.
32. *battles*] formations of soldiers, battalions.
squadron form] form of a square.
33. *shot*] troops equipped with firearms (*O.E.D., sb.*[1], 21a).
34. *push of pike*] close in-fighting. The phrase is common; cf. Massinger, *Maid of Honour,* I. i. 59: 'When, at push of pike, I am to enter / A breach...' *push* has a special sense of the thrust of a weapon (*O.E.D., sb.*[1], 2).

Don Pedro, their chief horsemen's colonel,   40
Did with his cornet bravely make attempt
To break the order of our battle ranks.
But Don Rogero, worthy man of war,
March'd forth against him with our musketeers,
And stopp'd the malice of his fell approach.   45
While they maintain hot skirmish to and fro,
Both battles join and fall to handy blows,
Their violent shot resembling th' ocean's rage,
When, roaring loud and with a swelling tide,
It beats upon the rampiers of huge rocks,   50
And gapes to swallow neighbour-bounding lands.
Now while Bellona rageth here and there,
Thick storms of bullets rain like winter's hail,
And shiver'd lances dark the troubled air.

>   *Pede pes et cuspide cuspis,*   55
> *Arma sonant armis, vir petiturque viro.*

---

40. colonel] Colonell *1594;* Corlonell *1592;* Coronell *1602.*   53. rain]
Collier; ran *1592;* run *conj. Manly.*   54. dark] darke *1592;* darkt *1594.*
56. *Arma*] *1633; Anni 1592.   armis] 1633; annis 1592.*

---

40. *colonel*] a trisyllable, as indicated by the spelling of *1592,* Corlonell,
which also shows the wavering of the word between 'coronel', from the
French, and 'colonel', from the Italian. *O.E.D.* remarks that up to 1590
'coronel' is far more frequent than 'colonel'.

41. *cornet*] squad of cavalry (from the banner at their head).

47. *handy*] hand-to-hand.

50. *rampiers*] ramparts.

52.] The first of several echoes of Garnier's description of the battle of
Thapsus in *Cornélie,* Act V: 'Bellonne ardant de rage, au plus fort de la
presse, / Couroit qui çà qui là.' In Kyd's later translation, *'Bellona,* fiered
with a quenchles rage, / Runnes vp and downe . . .' (*Cornelia,* v. 183–4).

53. *rain*] Collier's emendation brings out an appropriate image, to be
compared (from afar) with Milton's 'sharp sleet of arrowie showers' (*Paradise Regained,* III, 324).

54.] Cf. *Cornélie:* 'Ils rompent pique et lance, et les esclats pointus /
Bruyant sifflant par l'air, volent comme festus', and Kyd's rendering: 'The
shyuered Launces (ratling in the ayre) / Fly forth as thicke as moates about
the Sunne' (*Cornelia,* v. 170–1). See Appendix C.

dark] For *1594*'s 'improvement', *darkt,* see Introduction, p. xli. If *ran*
were retained in the preceding line, a case might be made for the preterite
here.

55–6.] 'Foot against foot, lance against lance; arms clash on arms and

On every side drop captains to the ground,
And soldiers, some ill-maim'd, some slain outright:
Here falls a body scinder'd from his head,
There legs and arms lie bleeding on the grass,   60
Mingled with weapons and unbowell'd steeds,
That scattering overspread the purple plain.
In all this turmoil, three long hours and more,
The victory to neither part inclin'd,
Till Don Andrea, with his brave lanciers,   65
In their main battle made so great a breach,
That, half dismay'd, the multitude retir'd:
But Balthazar, the Portingales' young prince,
Brought rescue and encourag'd them to stay:
Here-hence the fight was eagerly renew'd,   70
And in that conflict was Andrea slain—
Brave man at arms, but weak to Balthazar.
Yet while the prince, insulting over him,
Breath'd out proud vaunts, sounding to our reproach,
Friendship and hardy valour, join'd in one,   75
Prick'd forth Horatio, our Knight Marshal's son,
To challenge forth that prince in single fight:
Not long between these twain the fight endur'd,
But straight the prince was beaten from his horse

59. scinder'd] scindred *1592*; sundered *1602*.

---

man is assailed by man.' Boas and Schick note analogies and possible
sources in Statius, Virgil, and Curtius.
    59–60.] Cf. *Cornélie*: 'Aux uns vous eussiez veu la teste my-partie . . .
Aux uns la cuisse estoit ou l'espaule abbattue.' Once more, the echo here
influences Kyd's later version: 'Some should you see that had theyr heads
halfe clouen. . . Here lay an arme, and there a leg lay shiuer'd' (*Cornelia*,
v. 255–8).
    scinder'd] sundered; a rare form, probably from association/confusion
with Lat. *scindere* = to cleave (*O.E.D.*).
    61. *unbowell'd*] disembowelled. 'unboweld steeds' occurs in Heywood's
Rape of Lucrece, l. 2876.
    65. *lanciers*] lancers; this form is found into the 18th century.
    70. *Here-hence*] as a result of this (*O.E.D.*, 1). *O.E.D.* wrongly cites this
passage under *here-hence* 2 = from this point forward, from henceforth.
    73. *insulting*] exulting insolently.
    76. *Prick'd*] spurred.

F

And forc'd to yield him prisoner to his foe: 80
When he was taken, all the rest they fled,
And our carbines pursued them to the death,
Till Phoebus waning to the western deep,
Our trumpeters were charg'd to sound retreat.

King. Thanks good Lord General for these good news,   85
And for some argument of more to come,
Take this and wear it for thy sovereign's sake.

> *Give him his chain.*

But tell me now, hast thou confirm'd a peace?

Gen. No peace my liege, but peace conditional,
That if with homage tribute be well paid,   90
The fury of your forces will be stay'd:
And to this peace their viceroy hath subscrib'd,

> *Give the* KING *a paper.*

And made a solemn vow that during life
His tribute shall be truly paid to Spain.

King. These words, these deeds, become thy person well.   95
But now Knight Marshal, frolic with thy king,
For 'tis thy son that wins this battle's prize.

Hier. Long may he live to serve my sovereign liege,
And soon decay unless he serve my liege.   *A tucket afar off.*

King. Nor thou nor he shall die without reward: 100
What means the warning of this trumpet's sound?

Gen. This tells me that your grace's men of war,
Such as war's fortune hath reserv'd from death,
Come marching on towards your royal seat
To show themselves before your majesty,   105

---

83. waning] *1603;* wauing *1592.*   99. *A tucket afar off.*] *1592; following*
l. 100 in Dodsley.   101. the warning] *Schick;* this warning *1592.*   this
trumpet] *1592;* the trumpet *1615.*

---

83. *waning*] *1592*'s *waving* is generally retained, but it is probably a misprint. O.E.D., *wave, v.,* 5b, gives 'to decline' (of the sun) but cites only this
passage, wrongly dated 1615. The line in *Wily Beguiled* (l. 252), 'When
Phebus waues vnto the westerne deepe', is obviously derived from the
printed text of *The Spanish Tragedy.*

96. *frolic*] be gay. Hieronimo is not asked to skylark.

99. *tucket*] a flourish on a trumpet.

For so I gave in charge at my depart.
Whereby by demonstration shall appear
That all (except three hundred or few more)
Are safe return'd and by their foes enrich'd.

The Army enters, BALTHAZAR *between* LORENZO
and HORATIO, *captive.*

King. A gladsome sight, I long to see them here.   110

They enter and pass by.

Was that the warlike prince of Portingale,
That by our nephew was in triumph led?
Gen. It was, my liege, the prince of Portingale.
King. But what was he that on the other side
Held him by th' arm as partner of the prize?   115
Hier. That was my son, my gracious sovereign,
Of whom though from his tender infancy
My loving thoughts did never hope but well,
He never pleas'd his father's eyes till now,
Nor fill'd my heart with overcloying joys.   120
King. Go let them march once more about these walls,
That staying them we may confer and talk
With our brave prisoner and his double guard.
Hieronimo, it greatly pleaseth us,
That in our victory thou have a share,   125
By virtue of thy worthy son's exploit.

Enter [*the Army*] *again.*

Bring hither the young prince of Portingale,
The rest march on, but ere they be dismiss'd,
We will bestow on every soldier
Two ducats, and on every leader ten,   130

129–31. We ... soldier / Two ... ten, / That ... them.] *Manly;* We ...
ducats, / And ... know / Our ... them. *1592.*

117–19.] an awkward construction, but not an anacoluthon. 'And
though I never hoped but well of him, he never pleased (etc.).'

That they may know our largess welcomes them.

> *Exeunt all [the Army] but* BALTHAZAR,
> LORENZO, HORATIO.

Welcome Don Balthazar, welcome nephew,
And thou, Horatio, thou art welcome too:
Young prince, although thy father's hard misdeeds,
In keeping back the tribute that he owes,   135
Deserve but evil measure at our hands,
Yet shalt thou know that Spain is honourable.

Bal. The trespass that my father made in peace
Is now controll'd by fortune of the wars:
And cards once dealt, it boots not ask why so: 140
His men are slain, a weakening to his realm,
His colours seiz'd, a blot unto his name,
His son distress'd, a corsive to his heart:
These punishments may clear his late offence.

King. Ay Balthazar, if he observe this truce   145
Our peace will grow the stronger for these wars:
Meanwhile live thou, though not in liberty,
Yet free from bearing any servile yoke,
For in our hearing thy deserts were great,
And in our sight thyself art gracious.   150

Bal. And I shall study to deserve this grace.

King. But tell me, for their holding makes me doubt,
To which of these twain art thou prisoner?

Lor. To me, my liege.

Hor.   To me, my sovereign.

Lor. This hand first took his courser by the reins.   155

Hor. But first my lance did put him from his horse.

Lor. I seiz'd his weapon and enjoy'd it first.

---

142. unto] *1592;* upon *Dodsley.*

---

131. *largess*] liberality, bountifulness.
139. *controll'd*] held in check, hence, brought to an end, cancelled out.
143. *corsive*] corrosive. For the literal use, see Nashe, II, 147: 'Surgions lay Corsiues to any wounde, to eate out the dead-flesh.' For the figurative use, as here, cf. Chettle's *Hoffman,* l. 279: 'My ages corsiue, and my blacke sinnes curse'.

Hor. But first I forc'd him lay his weapons down.

King. Let go his arm, upon our privilege.   *Let him go.*

      Say worthy prince, to whether didst thou yield ?   160

Bal. To him in courtesy, to this perforce:

      He spake me fair, this other gave me strokes:

      He promis'd life, this other threaten'd death:

      He wan my love, this other conquer'd me:

      And truth to say I yield myself to both.   165

Hier. But that I know your grace for just and wise,

      And might seem partial in this difference,

      Enforc'd by nature and by law of arms

      My tongue should plead for young Horatio's right.

      He hunted well that was a lion's death,   170

      Not he that in a garment wore his skin:

      So hares may pull dead lions by the beard.

---

159. *upon our privilege*] sc. of absolute authority.

160. *whether*] which of the two.

164. *wan*] an alternative form of 'won'.

167. *And might seem partial*] Hieronimo is of course referring to himself and not to the king.

172.] a proverbial saying (Tilley H165) bringing together two proverbs from Erasmus' *Adagia*, which ultimately derive from P. Syrus' *Sententiae* (cf. Leishman's *Three Parnassus Plays*, p. 205) and Martial's *Epigrams* (cf. Nashe, *Works*, IV, 164), concerning (*a*) hares triumphing over dead lions and (*b*) the bravado of anyone's pulling a dead lion's beard. The conflation is found in one of Alciat's emblems (Green, pp. 304ff.) which pictures the hares tugging at a dead lion's mane and contains in the verses the phrase *sic cassi luce leonis | Conuellunt barbam vel timidi lepores.* (Whitney took over Alciat's emblem in 1586 but he is not Kyd's source.) In *Strange Newes* (1592), Nashe quotes directly from Kyd, '*So Hares may pull dead Lions by the beards. Memorandum:* I borrowed this sentence out of a Play' (*Works*, I, 271). The reference in ll. 170–1 is to the Fourth Fable of Avian (in Caxton) concerning the ass who sports himself in a lion's skin which he has found.

Lines 170–2 stand in perplexing relation to the lines in *King John* referring to Austria in Cœur-de-Lion's garment:

    —You are the hare of whom the proverb goes,
      Whose valour plucks dead lions by the beard:

        .   .   .   .   .

    —O, well did he become that lion's robe
      That did disrobe the lion of that robe!
    —It lies as sightly on the back of him

King. Content thee Marshal, thou shalt have no wrong,
    And for thy sake thy son shall want no right.
    Will both abide the censure of my doom?   175
Lor. I crave no better than your grace awards.
Hor. Nor I, although I sit beside my right.
King. Then by my judgment thus your strife shall end:
    You both deserve and both shall have reward.
    Nephew, thou took'st his weapon and his horse,   180
    His weapons and his horse are thy reward.
    Horatio, thou didst force him first to yield,
    His ransom therefore is thy valour's fee:
    Appoint the sum as you shall both agree.
    But nephew, thou shalt have the prince in guard,   185
    For thine estate best fitteth such a guest:
    Horatio's house were small for all his train.
    Yet in regard thy substance passeth his,

180. weapon] *1592;* weapons *1615.*

As great Alcides' shows upon an ass;   (II. i. 137–8, 141–4)
The date of *King John* is uncertain and so is that of *The Spanish Tragedy,* so
that dependence of one upon the other must be decided on internal evidence. Shakespeare is often given the precedence (see, e.g., Greg, *Shakespeare's First Folio,* pp. 254–5, following Dover Wilson), but the proverbial
background proves it not necessary. The images are appropriate to the situation in Kyd's play, would arise quite naturally to a writer, and would be
understood by the audience on their own merits and not by allusion. But if
in ll. 170–1 there is an allusion beyond the Avian fable, it might possibly be,
not to *King John,* but to *The Troublesome Reign of King John;* e.g. II. 131–2:
'Not you, Sir Doughty, with your lion's case.—Ah, joy betide his soul, to
whom that spoil belong'd!' If that play is the source of *King John,* Shakespeare may, in working over the passage, have recollected the proverbial
ornamentation which Kyd provides.

173.] Cf. *Jew of Malta,* I. 385, 'Content thee, *Barabas,* thou hast nought
but right.' See note to III. xii. 71.

175. *censure*] judgement.

177. *sit beside my right*] forgo my right. An odd phrase; presumably
Horatio thinks of placing himself outside the position his rights entitle him
to. It is possible that the reading should be *set beside* (set aside; see *O.E.D.,*
s.v. *beside,* 4b).

187.] Horatio's inferior social position is emphasized in the play and con-
tributes largely to Lorenzo's scorn and hatred towards him. Cf. II. iv. 60,
III. x. 57.

And that just guerdon may befall desert,
To him we yield the armour of the prince.   190
How likes Don Balthazar of this device?

Bal. Right well my liege, if this proviso were,
That Don Horatio bear us company,
Whom I admire and love for chivalry.

King. Horatio, leave him not that loves thee so.   195
Now let us hence to see our soldiers paid,
And feast our prisoner as our friendly guest.   *Exeunt.*

[I. iii]

   Enter VICEROY, ALEXANDRO, VILLUPPO[, Attendants].

Vice. Is our ambassador despatch'd for Spain?
Alex. Two days, my liege, are pass'd since his depart.
Vice. And tribute payment gone along with him?
Alex. Ay my good Lord.
Vice. Then rest we here awhile in our unrest,   5
And feed our sorrows with some inward sighs,
For deepest cares break never into tears.
But wherefore sit I in a regal throne?
This better fits a wretch's endless moan.   *Falls to the ground.*
Yet this is higher than my fortunes reach,   10
And therefore better than my state deserves.
Ay, ay, this earth, image of melancholy,
Seeks him whom fates adjudge to misery:
Here let me lie, now am I at the lowest.
   Qui jacet in terra non habet unde cadat.   15

I. iii. 9. *Falls to the ground.*] *1623; following l. 11 in 1592.*   14. am I] *1592;*
I am *1633.*

I. iii. 7.] Schick suggests an echo of Seneca, *Phaedra,* l. 607: *Curae leves
loquuntur, ingentes stupent.* But the notion is very common; e.g., Ralegh, 'To
the Queen': 'Our Passions are most like to Floods and streames; / The shal-
low Murmure; but the Deep are Dumb.' Cf. Tilley S664 and W130.

15–17.] 'If one lies on the ground, one can fall no further; in me, Fortune
has exhausted her power of hurting; there is nothing left that can harm me
more.' A typical pastiche: the sources were identified by W. P. Mustard,
P.Q., v (1926), 85–6; the first line is a tag from Alanus de Insulis, *Lib.*

In me consumpsit vires fortuna nocendo,
    Nil superest ut jam possit obesse magis.

Yes, Fortune may bereave me of my crown:
Here take it now: let Fortune do her worst,
She will not rob me of this sable weed: 20
O no, she envies none but pleasant things:
Such is the folly of despiteful chance!
Fortune is blind and sees not my deserts,
So is she deaf and hears not my laments:
And could she hear, yet is she wilful mad,   25
And therefore will not pity my distress.
Suppose that she could pity me, what then?
What help can be expected at her hands,
Whose foot is standing on a rolling stone
And mind more mutable than fickle winds?   30
Why wail I then, where's hope of no redress?
O yes, complaining makes my grief seem less.
My late ambition hath distain'd my faith,
My breach of faith occasion'd bloody wars,
Those bloody wars have spent my treasure,   35
And with my treasure my people's blood,
And with their blood, my joy and best belov'd,
My best belov'd, my sweet and only son.
O wherefore went I not to war myself?
The cause was mine, I might have died for both: 40
My years were mellow, his but young and green,

29. is] *Dodsley; not in 1592.*

Parab., cap. 2, l. 19, the second from Seneca's *Agamemnon*, l. 698 (*Fortuna vires ipsa consumpsit suas*), the third line is presumably Kyd's own composition.
    29. *rolling stone*] Fortune was commonly depicted standing on a sphere and so she appears in emblem-poetry (see Green, pp. 255, 261–3). Garnier's *Cornélie* has 'les piez . . . sur le haut d'une boule pliez', and in Kyd's translation the rolling stone turns up once more (I. 105). Pistol and Fluellen knew about the 'spherical stone, which rolls, and rolls, and rolls' (*Henry V*, III. vi. 37).
    33. *distain'd*] sullied.
    35, 36. *treasure*] trisyllabic in both places, 'treasu-er', although disyllabic elsewhere in the play.

My death were natural, but his was forc'd.

Alex. No doubt, my liege, but still the prince survives.

Vice. Survives! ay, where?

Alex. In Spain, a prisoner by mischance of war.   45

Vice. Then they have slain him for his father's fault.

Alex. That were a breach to common law of arms.

Vice. They reck no laws that meditate revenge.

Alex. His ransom's worth will stay from foul revenge.

Vice. No, if he liv'd the news would soon be here.   50

Alex. Nay, evil news fly faster still than good.

Vice. Tell me no more of news, for he is dead.

Vill. My sovereign, pardon the author of ill news,
And I'll bewray the fortune of thy son.

Vice. Speak on, I'll guerdon thee whate'er it be: 55
Mine ear is ready to receive ill news,
My heart grown hard 'gainst mischief's battery:
Stand up I say, and tell thy tale at large.

Vill. Then hear that truth which these mine eyes have seen.
When both the armies were in battle join'd,   60
Don Balthazar, amidst the thickest troops,
To win renown did wondrous feats of arms:
Amongst the rest I saw him hand to hand
In single fight with their lord-general:
Till Alexandro, that here counterfeits   65
Under the colour of a duteous friend,
Discharg'd his pistol at the prince's back,
As though he would have slain their general:
But therewithal Don Balthazar fell down,
And when he fell, then we began to fly: 70
But had he liv'd, the day had sure been ours.

Alex. O wicked forgery: O traitorous miscreant!

Vice. Hold thou thy peace! But now Villuppo, say,
Where then became the carcase of my son?

Vill. I saw them drag it to the Spanish tents.   75

---

54. *bewray*] reveal.
55. *guerdon*] reward.
72. *forgery*] malicious fabrication.

Vice. Ay, ay, my nightly dreams have told me this.
　　　Thou false, unkind, unthankful, traitorous beast,
　　　Wherein had Balthazar offended thee,
　　　That thou shouldst thus betray him to our foes ?
　　　Was't Spanish gold that bleared so thine eyes   80
　　　That thou couldst see no part of our deserts ?
　　　Perchance because thou art Terceira's lord
　　　Thou hadst some hope to wear this diadem,
　　　If first my son and then myself were slain :
　　　But thy ambitious thought shall break thy neck.   85
　　　Ay, this was it that made thee spill his blood,
　　　　　　　　　Take the crown and put it on again.
　　　But I'll now wear it till thy blood be spilt.
Alex. Vouchsafe, dread sovereign, to hear me speak.
Vice. Away with him, his sight is second hell,
　　　Keep him till we determine of his death.   90
　　　　　　　　[Exeunt Attendants with ALEXANDRO.]
　　　If Balthazar be dead, he shall not live.
　　　Villuppo, follow us for thy reward.   *Exit* VICEROY.
Vill. Thus have I with an envious forged tale
　　　Deceiv'd the king, betray'd mine enemy,
　　　And hope for guerdon of my villainy.   *Exit.* 95

[I. iv]

　　　　　　Enter HORATIO *and* BEL-IMPERIA.

Bel. Signior Horatio, this is the place and hour
　　　Wherein I must entreat thee to relate
　　　The circumstance of Don Andrea's death,
　　　Who, living, was my garland's sweetest flower,

---

83. diadem] Diadome *1592.*   90.1. [*Exeunt* . . .]] *no S.D. in 1592; They
take him out. Manly.*

---

　82. *Terceira's lord*] Boas remarks that the title of *Capitão Donatario* of
Terceira, or of any territory annexed to Portugal, would be inherited from
the original exploiter of the colony, and would carry with it almost despotic
sway.
　93. *envious*] malicious.

    And in his death hath buried my delights.   5
Hor. For love of him and service to yourself,
    I nill refuse this heavy doleful charge,
    Yet tears and sighs, I fear will hinder me.
    When both our armies were enjoin'd in fight,
    Your worthy chevalier amidst the thick'st,   10
    For glorious cause still aiming at the fairest,
    Was at the last by young Don Balthazar
    Encounter'd hand to hand: their fight was long,
    Their hearts were great, their clamours menacing,
    Their strength alike, their strokes both dangerous.   15
    But wrathful Nemesis, that wicked power,
    Envying at Andrea's praise and worth,
    Cut short his life to end his praise and worth.
    She, she herself, disguis'd in armour's mask
    (As Pallas was before proud Pergamus),   20
    Brought in a fresh supply of halberdiers,
    Which paunch'd his horse and ding'd him to the ground.
    Then young Don Balthazar with ruthless rage,
    Taking advantage of his foe's distress,
    Did finish what his halberdiers begun,   25
    And left not till Andrea's life was done.
    Then, though too late, incens'd with just remorse,
    I with my band set forth against the prince,
    And brought him prisoner from his halberdiers.
Bel. Would thou hadst slain him that so slew my love.   30
    But then was Don Andrea's carcase lost?
Hor. No, that was it for which I chiefly strove,

11.] 'striving always to perform the finest deeds for his glorious cause (of honour in Bel-imperia's eyes)'.

20.] Cf. *Aeneid*, II, 615–16 (Boas). But it was Juno who was 'girt with steel' (II, 613).

22. *paunch'd*] stabbed in the belly, disembowelled.

    ding'd] knocked, struck. Cf. Studley's trans. of Seneca's *Phaedra* (*Hippolytus*), Act IV, 'And dingd against the rugged Rocks his head doth oft rebound.'

27. *remorse*] sorrow, pity. The phrase 'incent with sole remorse' in a very similar context occurs in Watson's *Meliboeus*; see Appendix D.

Nor stepp'd I back till I recover'd him:
I took him up and wound him in mine arms,
And welding him unto my private tent,   35
There laid him down and dew'd him with my tears,
And sigh'd and sorrow'd as became a friend.
But neither friendly sorrow, sighs nor tears,
Could win pale death from his usurped right.
Yet this I did, and less I could not do,   40
I saw him honour'd with due funeral:
This scarf I pluck'd from off his liveless arm,
And wear it in remembrance of my friend.

Bel. I know the scarf, would he had kept it still,
For had he liv'd he would have kept it still,   45
And worn it for his Bel-imperia's sake:
For 'twas my favour at his last depart.
But now wear thou it both for him and me,
For after him thou hast deserv'd it best.
But for thy kindness in his life and death,   50
Be sure while Bel-imperia's life endures,
She will be Don Horatio's thankful friend.

Hor. And, madam, Don Horatio will not slack
Humbly to serve fair Bel-imperia.
But now if your good liking stand thereto,   55
I'll crave your pardon to go seek the prince,
For so the duke your father gave me charge.   *Exit.*

Bel. Ay, go Horatio, leave me here alone,
For solitude best fits my cheerless mood:
Yet what avails to wail Andrea's death,   60
From whence Horatio proves my second love?

35. welding] *1592;* wielding *Schick*[1].

---

35. *welding*] carrying. An alternative form of *wielding*, though for *wield* in
this sense, *O.E.D.* (4c) has only this example later than mid-15th century.
36. *dew'd him with my tears*] Examples of this figurative use of *dew* go
back to 1200 in *O.E.D.* The phrase was popular with the Elizabethans; cf.
2 Henry VI, III. ii. 340; *Tamburlaine*, Pt. 2, l. 3889; *Antonio's Revenge*,
ll. 998–9.
58–68.] Concerning Bel-imperia's motives, see Introduction, p. liv.

Had he not lov'd Andrea as he did,
He could not sit in Bel-imperia's thoughts.
But how can love find harbour in my breast,
Till I revenge the death of my beloved?   65
Yes, second love shall further my revenge.
I'll love Horatio, my Andrea's friend,
The more to spite the prince that wrought his end.
And where Don Balthazar, that slew my love,
Himself now pleads for favour at my hands,   70
He shall in rigour of my just disdain
Reap long repentance for his murd'rous deed:
For what was 't else but murd'rous cowardice,
So many to oppress one valiant knight,
Without respect of honour in the fight?   75
And here he comes that murder'd my delight.

Enter LORENZO *and* BALTHAZAR.

Lor. Sister, what means this melancholy walk?
Bel. That for a while I wish no company.
Lor. But here the prince is come to visit you.
Bel. That argues that he lives in liberty.   80
Bal. No madam, but in pleasing servitude.
Bel. Your prison then belike is your conceit.
Bal. Ay, by conceit my freedom is enthrall'd.
Bel. Then with conceit enlarge yourself again.
Bal. What if conceit have laid my heart to gage?   85
Bel. Pay that you borrow'd and recover it.
Bal. I die if it return from whence it lies.
Bel. A heartless man and live? A miracle!
Bal. Ay lady, love can work such miracles.
Lor. Tush, tush my lord, let go these ambages,   90

88. live] *1592;* lives *1602.*

---

82. *conceit*] fancy.
84. *enlarge*] set free.
85. *to gage*] as a pledge.
90. *ambages*] roundabout or indirect modes of speech. From 14th-century French, which took it from Latin, the word being the same in all

And in plain terms acquaint her with your love.

Bel. What boots complaint, when there's no remedy?

Bal. Yes, to your gracious self must I complain,
    In whose fair answer lies my remedy,
    On whose perfection all my thoughts attend,   95
    On whose aspect mine eyes find beauty's bower,
    In whose translucent breast my heart is lodg'd.

Bel. Alas my lord, these are but words of course,
    And but device to drive me from this place.

    She, in going in, lets fall her glove, which HORATIO,
        coming out, takes up.

Hor. Madam, your glove.   100

Bel. Thanks good Horatio, take it for thy pains.

Bal. Signior Horatio stoop'd in happy time.

Hor. I reap'd more grace than I deserv'd or hop'd.

Lor. My lord, be not dismay'd for what is past,
    You know that women oft are humorous: 105
    These clouds will overblow with little wind,
    Let me alone, I'll scatter them myself:
    Meanwhile let us devise to spend the time
    In some delightful sports and revelling.

Hor. The king, my lords, is coming hither straight,   110
    To feast the Portingal ambassador:
    Things were in readiness before I came.

Bal. Then here it fits us to attend the king,
    To welcome hither our ambassador
    And learn my father and my country's health.   115

    Enter the Banquet, Trumpets, the KING *and* AMBASSADOR.

99. device] deuise *1592;* deuisde *1599.*

---

three languages. Chaucer was apparently the first to use it in English. Reed
quotes *Wily Beguiled*, 'By Iesus, I cannot play the dissembler / And wooe
my loue with courting ambages' (M.S.R., ll. 948–9).

    98. *words of course*] conventional or routine phrases.

    99. *but device*] merely a device. The sense is not improved by reading
devis'd with *1599* and Brooke, and the reading has no authority.

    105. *humorous*] temperamental.

    115.1.] Many editors begin a new scene here. But the stage is not cleared

King. See Lord Ambassador, how Spain entreats
  Their prisoner Balthazar, thy viceroy's son:
  We pleasure more in kindness than in wars.
Amb. Sad is our king, and Portingale laments,
  Supposing that Don Balthazar is slain.   120
Bal. So am I slain, by beauty's tyranny.
  You see, my lord, how Balthazar is slain:
  I frolic with the Duke of Castile's son,
  Wrapp'd every hour in pleasures of the court,
  And grac'd with favours of his majesty.   125
King. Put off your greetings till our feast be done,
  Now come and sit with us and taste our cheer.

              Sit to the banquet.

  Sit down young prince, you are our second guest:
  Brother sit down, and nephew take your place:
  Signior Horatio, wait thou upon our cup,   130
  For well thou hast deserved to be honour'd.
  Now lordings fall to, Spain is Portugal,
  And Portugal is Spain, we both are friends,
  Tribute is paid, and we enjoy our right.
  But where is old Hieronimo, our marshal?   135
  He promis'd us, in honour of our guest,
  To grace our banquet with some pompous jest.

131. honour'd] honored *1592.*

---

and continuity is stressed by the King's first speech. Cf. the entry of the
King and State in *Hamlet*, v. ii.
 the Banquet] not necessarily the sumptuous meal the word now implies;
it could be something quite unpretentious (by Elizabethan standards), a
conveniently portable meal for theatrical purposes, and the King apolo-
gizes for the fare at l. 176. Nevertheless this feast is obviously elaborate.
 116. *entreats*] treats.
 121.] Schick punctuates thus: 'So am I!—slain by beauty's tyranny.'
1592 has no internal punctuation.
 125. *grac'd*] honoured. Kyd uses the word in several senses; see Index.
 131.] an awkward line to scan and *1592* gives no help. See Textual
Apparatus.
 137. *grace*] adorn, lend grace to (*O.E.D., v.,* 4).
 pompous] stately.
 jest] entertainment (*O.E.D.,* 8).

Enter HIERONIMO *with a* Drum, *three* Knights, *each his*
scutcheon: then he fetches three Kings, *they*
take their crowns and them captive.

Hieronimo, this masque contents mine eye,
Although I sound not well the mystery.

Hier. The first arm'd knight that hung his scutcheon up,   140
          He takes the scutcheon and gives it to the KING.

Was English Robert, Earl of Gloucester,
Who when King Stephen bore sway in Albion,
Arriv'd with five and twenty thousand men
In Portingale, and by success of war
Enforc'd the king, then but a Saracen,   145
To bear the yoke of the English monarchy.

King. My lord of Portingale, by this you see

137.1. with a *Drum*] 'It is more likely that . . . this indicates a character
. . . than that the Marshal himself carries a drum' (*MSR* (*1592*), p. xxvii).
Cf. *Halberts*, III. i. 30.1.

139. *mystery*] hidden meaning, allegorical significance. See note to I. i. 90.

140–57.] It is a problem to know where Kyd got his rosy account of
English triumphs in the Iberian lands. (*a*) Englishmen certainly helped in
the capture of Lisbon from the 'Saracen' in 1147 and Mayerne Turquet's
General History of Spain (published in France in 1586) mentions them; but
'there is no reason to suppose that Robert of Gloucester was ever in Portugal' (Boas). There is no hint in Holinshed or in chronicles like Grafton or
Hardyng or Fabyan to support Kyd. (*b*) Kyd is dealing with historical facts,
but has got them upside down. In 1381–2 Edmund Langley was on the side
of Portugal against Spain. Polydore Vergil deals fully with the campaign,
but there is nothing to suggest the razing of Lisbon's walls. Nor are the standard popular chronicles a possible source. (*c*) If Mariana's *History of Spain*
were not too late (Toledo, 1592), one might suggest that his account of the
battle of Najara (1367) in which John of Gaunt took part might have been
imperfectly remembered by Kyd. Whether it is Gaunt's expedition to
Spain of 1367 or, as Boas suggests, of 1386–7, I have found nothing in the
full accounts of Holinshed, Froissart, or Polydore Vergil to warrant Kyd's
account. But Holinshed (referring to 1386) talks of disagreement among
English writers about a battle in which the Duke of Castile was utterly
defeated; it is most unlikely that Kyd was alone in his views on Spain's history. Shakespeare may have been thinking of *The Spanish Tragedy* when he
wrote of 'great John of Gaunt, Which did subdue the greatest part of Spain'
(*3 Henry VI*, III. iii. 81–2), but P. A. Daniel noted the projected play in
Henslowe's *Diary*, I, 135, *The Conquest of Spayne by John a Gant*, as evidence of a popular belief not based on the chronicles.

That which may comfort both your king and you,
And make your late discomfort seem the less.
But say Hieronimo, what was the next ?   150
Hier. The second knight that hung his scutcheon up,

                    He doth as he did before.

Was Edmund, Earl of Kent in Albion,
When English Richard wore the diadem.
He came likewise and razed Lisbon walls,
And took the King of Portingale in fight: 155
For which, and other suchlike service done,
He after was created Duke of York.
King. This is another special argument,
That Portingale may deign to bear our yoke
When it by little England hath been yok'd.   160
But now Hieronimo, what were the last ?
Hier. The third and last, not least in our account, *Doing as before.*
Was as the rest a valiant Englishman,
Brave John of Gaunt, the Duke of Lancaster,
As by his scutcheon plainly may appear.   165
He with a puissant army came to Spain,
And took our King of Castile prisoner.
Amb. This is an argument for our viceroy,
That Spain may not insult for her success,
Since English warriors likewise conquer'd Spain,   170
And made them bow their knees to Albion.
King. Hieronimo, I drink to thee for this device,
Which hath pleas'd both the Ambassador and me:
Pledge me Hieronimo, if thou love the king.

                    Takes the cup of HORATIO.

My lord, I fear we sit but over-long,   175
Unless our dainties were more delicate:

152. Albion,] *1592;* Albion. *Manly.*   153. diadem.] *1592;* diadem,
Manly.   174. the] *1592;* thy *Schick.*

153.] Manly takes this line with the following and not with the preceding
line.
174.1. of] from.
176. *Unless*] See note at III. x. 36–8.

G

But welcome are you to the best we have.
Now let us in, that you may be despatch'd,
I think our council is already set.   *Exeunt omnes.*

[I. v]

Andrea. Come we for this from depth of underground,
          To see him feast that gave me my death's wound?
          These pleasant sights are sorrow to my soul,
          Nothing but league, and love, and banqueting!
Revenge. Be still Andrea, ere we go from hence,   5
          I'll turn their friendship into fell despite,
          Their love to mortal hate, their day to night,
          Their hope into despair, their peace to war,
          Their joys to pain, their bliss to misery.

I. v. 4. banqueting!] banqueting? *1592.*

Act II

Enter LORENZO *and* BALTHAZAR.

Lor. My lord, though Bel-imperia seem thus coy,
  Let reason hold you in your wonted joy:
  In time the savage bull sustains the yoke,
  In time all haggard hawks will stoop to lure,
  In time small wedges cleave the hardest oak,   5
  In time the flint is pierc'd with softest shower,
  And she in time will fall from her disdain,
  And rue the sufferance of your friendly pain.
Bal. No, she is wilder, and more hard withal,
  Than beast, or bird, or tree, or stony wall.   10
  But wherefore blot I Bel-imperia's name?
  It is my fault, not she, that merits blame.

Act II] Actus Secundus. *1592.*

---

1. *coy*] unresponsive.
3–10.] from Watson's *Hecatompathia* (Stationers' Register, 1582), Sonnet XLVII: 'In time the Bull is brought to weare the yoake; / In time all haggred Haukes will stoope the Lures; / In time small wedge will cleaue the sturdiest Oake; / In time the Marble weares with weakest shewres: / More fierce is my sweete loue, more hard withall, / Then Beast, or Birde, then Tree, or Stony wall.' Watson notes his debt to Serafino's 103rd Sonnet, but R. S. Forsythe (*P.Q.*, v (1926), 78–84) notes analogues and sources nearer home in Gascoigne, etc.; the images were extremely popular.
4. *stoop to lure*] the technical phrase for hawks, while they are being trained, coming down to their food (*haggard* = untamed).
8. *sufferance*] patient endurance, long-suffering.
9–28.] Balthazar's speech was famous: Boas quotes N. Field's take-off: 'Yet might she love me for my dimpled chin. / Ay, but she sees your beard is very thin' (*A Woman is a Weathercocke*, 1609, I. ii. 345–6).
12.] 'It is my shortcomings that are to blame, not Bel-imperia's nature.' *Fault* in a milder sense (*O.E.D.*, *sb.*, 3b) than at III. ii. 111.

My feature is not to content her sight,
My words are rude and work her no delight.
The lines I send her are but harsh and ill,   15
Such as do drop from Pan and Marsyas' quill.
My presents are not of sufficient cost,
And being worthless all my labour's lost.
Yet might she love me for my valiancy,
Ay, but that's slander'd by captivity.   20
Yet might she love me to content her sire,
Ay, but her reason masters his desire.
Yet might she love me as her brother's friend,
Ay, but her hopes aim at some other end.
Yet might she love me to uprear her state,   25
Ay, but perhaps she hopes some nobler mate.
Yet might she love me as her beauty's thrall,
Ay, but I fear she cannot love at all.

Lor. My lord, for my sake leave these ecstasies,
And doubt not but we'll find some remedy: 30
Some cause there is that lets you not be lov'd:
First that must needs be known and then remov'd.
What if my sister love some other knight?

Bal. My summer's day will turn to winter's night.

27. beauty's] *1615;* beauteous *1592;* duteous *conj. MSR (1592).*   29. these
ecstasies] *1592;* this ecstasy *Schick.*

---

13. *feature*] form, shape (*O.E.D., sb.,* 1), not the face in particular.
16. *Pan and Marsyas*] gods who had foolishly challenged Apollo to con-
tests in flute-playing.
quill is a reed and not a pen.
20. *slander'd*] brought into disrepute (*O.E.D., v.,* 2).
21–2.] Cf. the stychomyth in Garnier's *Bradamante,* II. i. 'Elle doit
approuver ce qui plaist à son père. / —L'amour ne se gouverne à l'appétit
d'autruy.'
27. *beauty's thrall*] The emendation accepted here is found first in Jonson's quotation—rather free quotation—of the lines, in *Poetaster* (1601),
III. iv. 221, fourteen years before it appeared in any edition of *The Spanish
Tragedy.* The phrase is found in *Soliman and Perseda,* IV. iii. 6.
29. *ecstasies*] unreasoning passions (lit. 'state of being outside oneself').
Schick and Boas read *this ecstasy* for the sake of the rhyme, but that is to
improve, not to emend.

Lor. I have already found a stratagem   35
    To sound the bottom of this doubtful theme.
    My lord, for once you shall be rul'd by me,
    Hinder me not whate'er you hear or see.
    By force or fair means will I cast about
    To find the truth of all this question out.   40
    Ho, Pedringano!
Ped.   Signior!
Lor.   *Vien qui presto.*

Enter PEDRINGANO.

Ped. Hath your lordship any service to command me ?
Lor. Ay Pedringano, service of import:
    And not to spend the time in trifling words,
    Thus stands the case; it is not long thou know'st,   45
    Since I did shield thee from my father's wrath
    For thy conveyance in Andrea's love,
    For which thou wert adjudg'd to punishment.
    I stood betwixt thee and thy punishment:
    And since, thou know'st how I have favour'd thee.   50
    Now to these favours will I add reward,
    Not with fair words, but store of golden coin,
    And lands and living join'd with dignities,
    If thou but satisfy my just demand.
    Tell truth and have me for thy lasting friend.   55
Ped. Whate'er it be your lordship shall demand,
    My bounden duty bids me tell the truth,
    If case it lie in me to tell the truth.
Lor. Then, Pedringano, this is my demand:
    Whom loves my sister Bel-imperia ?   60
    For she reposeth all her trust in thee:

41. *qui*] *Collier; que 1592.*   48. punishment] *1592;* banishment *Dodsley.*
53. living] *1592;* liuings *1602.*

---

37. *for once*] on this occasion (not implying a unique occasion).
41. Vien qui presto] Come here quickly (It.).
47. *conveyance*] clandestine or underhand service (*O.E.D.*, 11b).
58. *If case*] if it happens that ('if case be that . . .').

Speak man, and gain both friendship and reward:
I mean, whom loves she in Andrea's place?

Ped. Alas my lord, since Don Andrea's death,
    I have no credit with her as before,   65
    And therefore know not if she love or no.

Lor. Nay, if thou dally then I am thy foe,   [*Draw his sword.*]
    And fear shall force what friendship cannot win.
    Thy death shall bury what thy life conceals,
    Thou diest for more esteeming her than me.   70

Ped. O stay, my lord!

Lor. Yet speak the truth and I will guerdon thee,
    And shield thee from whatever can ensue,
    And will conceal whate'er proceeds from thee,
    But if thou dally once again, thou diest.   75

Ped. If Madam Bel-imperia be in love—

Lor. What, villain, ifs and ands?   [*Offer to kill him.*]

Ped. O stay my lord, she loves Horatio.   BALTHAZAR *starts back.*

Lor. What, Don Horatio our Knight Marshal's son?

Ped. Even him my lord.   80

Lor. Now say but how know'st thou he is her love,
    And thou shalt find me kind and liberal:
    Stand up I say, and fearless tell the truth.

Ped. She sent him letters which myself perus'd,
    Full fraught with lines and arguments of love,   85
    Preferring him before Prince Balthazar.

Lor. Swear on this cross, that what thou say'st is true,
    And that thou wilt conceal what thou hast told.

Ped. I swear to both by him that made us all.

Lor. In hope thine oath is true, here's thy reward,   90
    But if I prove thee perjur'd and unjust,
    This very sword whereon thou took'st thine oath,
    Shall be the worker of thy tragedy.

67. [*Draw his sword.*]] *1602; not in 1592.*   77. [*Offer to kill him.*]] *1602;*
not in 1592.   81. say] *Dodsley;* say, *1592.*   know'st thou] *1592;* thou
know'st *Dodsley.*

87. *this cross*] i.e., his sword-hilt.

Ped. What I have said is true, and shall for me
  Be still conceal'd from Bel-imperia.   95
  Besides, your honour's liberality
  Deserves my duteous service, even till death.
Lor. Let this be all that thou shalt do for me:
  Be watchful when, and where, these lovers meet,
  And give me notice in some secret sort.   100
Ped. I will my lord.
Lor. Then shalt thou find that I am liberal:
  Thou know'st that I can more advance thy state
  Than she, be therefore wise and fail me not.
  Go and attend her as thy custom is,   105
  Lest absence make her think thou dost amiss.

           Exit PEDRINGANO.

  Why so: *tam armis quam ingenio:*
  Where words prevail not, violence prevails:
  But gold doth more than either of them both.
  How likes Prince Balthazar this stratagem? 110
Bal. Both well, and ill: it makes me glad and sad:
  Glad, that I know the hinderer of my love,
  Sad, that I fear she hates me whom I love.
  Glad, that I know on whom to be reveng'd,
  Sad, that she'll fly me if I take revenge.   115
  Yet must I take revenge or die myself,
  For love resisted grows impatient.
  I think Horatio be my destin'd plague:
  First in his hand he brandished a sword,
  And with that sword he fiercely waged war, 120
  And in that war he gave me dangerous wounds,
  And by those wounds he forced me to yield,

---

107. tam armis quam ingenio] as much by force as by guile. Cf. the common *tam Marti quam Mercurio.*

117.] Cf. *Hero and Leander* (1593), 'But love resisted once, grows passionate' (II, 139); the sentence is frequently found in the figurative language of proverbs; cf. Tilley F265, S929.

119–29.] F. G. Hubbard may well be right in suggesting that these lines echo Watson's *Hecatompathia*, XLI (*P.M.L.A.*, XX (1905), 366–7).

And by my yielding I became his slave.
Now in his mouth he carries pleasing words,
Which pleasing words do harbour sweet conceits,   125
Which sweet conceits are lim'd with sly deceits,
Which sly deceits smooth Bel-imperia's ears,
And through her ears dive down into her heart,
And in her heart set him where I should stand.
Thus hath he ta'en my body by his force,   130
And now by sleight would captivate my soul:
But in his fall I'll tempt the destinies,
And either lose my life, or win my love. /

Lor. Let's go my lord, your staying stays revenge.
Do you but follow me and gain your love: 135
Her favour must be won by his remove.   *Exeunt.*

[II. ii]

Enter HORATIO *and* BEL-IMPERIA.

Hor. Now Madam, since by favour of your love
Our hidden smoke is turn'd to open flame,
And that with looks and words we feed our thoughts
(Two chief contents, where more cannot be had),
Thus in the midst of love's fair blandishments,   5
Why show you sign of inward languishments?

PEDRINGANO *showeth all to the* PRINCE *and* LORENZO,
placing them in secret [above].

II. ii. 3. thoughts] *1594;* though [ ] *1592.*   6.2. [*above*]] *This ed.; not in 1592.*

126. *lim'd*] i.e., made into snares.
127. *smooth*] flatter (*O.E.D., v.*, 5a).

II. ii. 6.1–2.] *1592* has two directions concerning the eavesdropping: the second, after l. 17, 'Balthazar aboue.', is omitted here, and *above* transferred to the end of the first direction. The double direction in *1592* may be explained in three ways: (i) the conspirators enter at l. 6 'and proceed unseen by the lovers to the gallery, where at l. 17 they remain "above" watching' (McIlwraith); (ii) the earlier direction is the author's and the later an addition by the book-keeper for stage-purposes; (iii) both directions are the

Bel. My heart, sweet friend, is like a ship at sea:
　　She wisheth port, where riding all at ease,
　　She may repair what stormy times have worn,
　　And leaning on the shore, may sing with joy　　　10
　　That pleasure follows pain, and bliss annoy.
　　Possession of thy love is th' only port
　　Wherein my heart, with fears and hopes long toss'd,
　　Each hour doth wish and long to make resort,
　　There to repair the joys that it hath lost,　　　15
　　And sitting safe, to sing in Cupid's quire
　　That sweetest bliss is crown of love's desire.

Bal. O sleep mine eyes, see not my love profan'd,
　　Be deaf my ears, hear not my discontent,
　　Die heart, another joys what thou deserv'st.　　　20

Lor. Watch still mine eyes, to see this love disjoin'd,
　　Hear still mine ears, to hear them both lament,
　　Live heart, to joy at fond Horatio's fall.

Bel. Why stands Horatio speechless all this while?

Hor. The less I speak, the more I meditate.　　　25

Bel. But whereon dost thou chiefly meditate?

---

9. may] *1602;* mad *1592;* made *1594.*   17.1. ^] *Balthazar aboue 1592;*
Balthazar *and* Lorenzo *alone 1610,* ∼ *aside Dodsley;* ∼ *above Schick.*
19. my ears] *1592;* mine ears *1615.*

---

author's, the second being made *currente calamo* to clarify what is not
obvious from the previous direction, namely, from what part of the stage
Balthazar speaks. The putative action in (i) is cumbersome and unnecessary; with (i) and with (ii), one would expect *Balthazar and Lorenzo above;*
many editors emend the text so. One would expect the book-keeper to
amend the original direction if clarity for the stage was his intention. (The
question of whether there is any evidence for the book-keeper's hand in
1592 is discussed in the Textual Introduction, pp. xxxi–xxxii.) In accepting (iii) I make an emendation which would serve the author's intention.

11.] Proverbial wisdom usually contradicts Bel-imperia, as perhaps we
are meant to recognize (cf. Tilley S908 and P408). Watson's *Teares of
Fancie* (published posthumously in 1593) appears to give the phrase the lie
direct: 'So haue I found and now too deerely trie, / That pleasure doubleth
paine and blisse annoy.' Yet it was a 'T.W.' who may be Watson who
wrote, 'Pleasure is the end of lingring smarts' (*Phoenix Nest*, 1593, ed.
Rollins, p. 98).

23. *fond*] foolish or infatuated.

Hor. On dangers past, and pleasures to ensue.
Bal. On pleasures past, and dangers to ensue.
Bel. What dangers and what pleasures dost thou mean?
Hor. Dangers of war, and pleasures of our love. 30
Lor. Dangers of death, but pleasures none at all.
Bel. Let dangers go, thy war shall be with me,
    But such a war, as breaks no bond of peace.
    Speak thou fair words, I'll cross them with fair words,
    Send thou sweet looks, I'll meet them with sweet looks, 35
    Write loving lines, I'll answer loving lines,
    Give me a kiss, I'll countercheck thy kiss:
    Be this our warring peace, or peaceful war.
Hor. But gracious madam, then appoint the field
    Where trial of this war shall first be made. 40
Bal. Ambitious villain, how his boldness grows!
Bel. Then be thy father's pleasant bower the field,
    Where first we vow'd a mutual amity:
    The court were dangerous, that place is safe.
    Our hour shall be when Vesper gins to rise, 45
    That summons home distressful travellers.
    There none shall hear us but the harmless birds:
    Happily the gentle nightingale
    Shall carol us asleep ere we be ware,
    And singing with the prickle at her breast, 50
    Tell our delight and mirthful dalliance.
    Till then each hour will seem a year and more.
Hor. But honey sweet, and honourable love,
    Return we now into your father's sight:

33. war] *Dodsley;* warring *1592.*

33. *war*] *1592*'s *warring* jars both metrically and rhetorically; the compositor's eye may have caught the word from l. 38.
  42. *bower*] See note on *arbour*, II. iv. 53.
  46. *travellers*] labourers ('travailers').
  48. *Happily*] haply (which would be a preferable reading, were the line not already short of a syllable).
  50. *prickle at her breast*] i.e., to keep her sharp woes waking, as Shakespeare and common legend have it.

    Dangerous suspicion waits on our delight.   55
Lor. Ay, danger mix'd with jealious despite
    Shall send thy soul into eternal night.   *Exeunt.*

[II. iii]
      Enter KING *of Spain, Portingale* AMBASSADOR,
            DON CYPRIAN, *&c.*

King. Brother of Castile, to the prince's love
    What says your daughter Bel-imperia ?
Cast. Although she coy it as becomes her kind,
    And yet dissemble that she loves the prince,
    I doubt not, I, but she will stoop in time.   5
    And were she froward, which she will not be,
    Yet herein shall she follow my advice,
    Which is to love him or forgo my love.
King. Then, Lord Ambassador of Portingale,
    Advise thy king to make this marriage up,   10
    For strengthening of our late-confirmed league :
    I know no better means to make us friends.
    Her dowry shall be large and liberal :
    Besides that she is daughter and half-heir
    Unto our brother here, Don Cyprian,   15
    And shall enjoy the moiety of his land,
    I'll grace her marriage with an uncle's gift,
    And this it is : in case the match go forward,
    The tribute which you pay shall be releas'd,

56. mix'd] *1592;* mixed *Hawkins.*   jealious] *conj. Kittredge;* ielalous *1592.*
II. iii. 11. league :] league. *1602;* league, *1592;* league *Collier.*

---

    56. *jealious*] a common enough form which saves the metre; Schick
accepted Kittredge's suggestion, once he knew about it.

    II. iii. 3. *coy it*] affect reserve.
    as becomes her kind] as it is her natural disposition as a woman to do.
    11.] The punctuation of *1592* leaves us free to take the line with either its
predecessor or its successor; Collier took the latter conjunction : the former
(following *1602*) is preferred here. There is but slight alteration in sense.
    16. *moiety*] half-share.

And if by Balthazar she have a son,   20
He shall enjoy the kingdom after us.
Amb. I'll make the motion to my sovereign liege,
    And work it if my counsel may prevail.
King. Do so my lord, and if he give consent,
    I hope his presence here will honour us   25
    In celebration of the nuptial day:
    And let himself determine of the time.
Amb. Will 't please your grace command me aught beside?
King. Commend me to the king, and so farewell.
    But where's Prince Balthazar to take his leave?   30
Amb. That is perform'd already, my good lord.
King. Amongst the rest of what you have in charge,
    The prince's ransom must not be forgot:
    That's none of mine, but his that took him prisoner,
    And well his forwardness deserves reward: 35
    It was Horatio, our Knight Marshal's son.
Amb. Between us there's a price already pitch'd,
    And shall be sent with all convenient speed.
King. Then once again farewell my lord.
Amb. Farewell my lord of Castile and the rest.   *Exit.*   40
King. Now brother, you must take some little pains
    To win fair Bel-imperia from her will:
    Young virgins must be ruled by their friends.
    The prince is amiable and loves her well,
    If she neglect him and forgo his love,   45
    She both will wrong her own estate and ours:
    Therefore, whiles I do entertain the prince
    With greatest pleasure that our court affords,
    Endeavour you to win your daughter's thought:
    If she give back, all this will come to naught.   *Exeunt.*   50

49. thought] *1615;* thoughts *1592.*

---

37. *pitch'd*] settled, determined.
38. *all convenient speed*] as quickly as possible.
42. *will*] wilfulness.
50. *give back*] i.e., 'turn her back on us'; cf. *O.E.D., back, sb.*[1], 24d. The
usual meaning, to retreat or yield, is clearly inappropriate.

[II. iv]

Enter HORATIO, BEL-IMPERIA, *and* PEDRINGANO.

Hor. Now that the night begins with sable wings
    To overcloud the brightness of the sun,
    And that in darkness pleasures may be done,
    Come Bel-imperia, let us to the bower,
    And there in safety pass a pleasant hour.   5
Bel. I follow thee my love, and will not back,
    Although my fainting heart controls my soul.
Hor. Why, make you doubt of Pedringano's faith?
Bel. No, he is as trusty as my second self.
    Go Pedringano, watch without the gate,   10
    And let us know if any make approach.
Ped. [*aside.*] Instead of watching, I'll deserve more gold
    By fetching Don Lorenzo to this match.   *Exit* PEDRINGANO.
Hor. What means my love?
Bel.   I know not what myself:
    And yet my heart foretells me some mischance.   15
Hor. Sweet say not so, fair fortune is our friend,
    And heavens have shut up day to pleasure us.
    The stars, thou seest, hold back their twinkling shine,
    And Luna hides herself to pleasure us.
Bel. Thou hast prevail'd, I'll conquer my misdoubt,   20
    And in thy love and counsel drown my fear:
    I fear no more, love now is all my thoughts.
    Why sit we not? for pleasure asketh ease.
Hor. The more thou sit'st within these leavy bowers,
    The more will Flora deck it with her flowers.   25
Bel. Ay, but if Flora spy Horatio here,
    Her jealous eye will think I sit too near.
Hor. Hark, madam, how the birds record by night,
    For joy that Bel-imperia sits in sight.

II. iv. 7. *controls*] overmasters (i.e., the heart denies the inclinations of the soul).

28. *record*] sing.

Bel. No, Cupid counterfeits the nightingale,   30
　　　　To frame sweet music to Horatio's tale.

Hor. If Cupid sing, then Venus is not far:
　　　　Ay, thou art Venus or some fairer star.

Bel. If I be Venus thou must needs be Mars,
　　　　And where Mars reigneth there must needs be wars.   35

Hor. Then thus begin our wars: put forth thy hand,
　　　　That it may combat with my ruder hand.

Bel. Set forth thy foot to try the push of mine.

Hor. But first my looks shall combat against thine.

Bel. Then ward thyself, I dart this kiss at thee.   40

Hor. Thus I retort the dart thou threw'st at me.

Bel. Nay then, to gain the glory of the field,
　　　　My twining arms shall yoke and make thee yield.

Hor. Nay then, my arms are large and strong withal:
　　　　Thus elms by vines are compass'd till they fall.   45

Bel. O let me go, for in my troubled eyes
　　　　Now may'st thou read that life in passion dies.

Hor. O stay awhile and I will die with thee,
　　　　So shalt thou yield and yet have conquer'd me.

Bel. Who's there? Pedringano! We are betray'd!   50

　　　Enter LORENZO, BALTHAZAR, SERBERINE, PEDRINGANO,
　　　　　　　　　　　disguised.

Lor. My lord, away with her, take her aside.

35. wars] *Dodsley;* warre *1592.*   44. withal] *1594;* with [ ] *1592.*
50. Who's there? Pedringano!] *Schick;* Whose there *Pedringano? 1592;*
Who's there? Pedringano? *Hazlitt.*

───

　　45.] a common image; cf. Virgil, *Georgics,* II, 221; see Green, pp. 307–9
and Tilley V61. But Horatio ingeniously twists the normal account for his
own ends; the point is usually that the vine held up the elm in its embraces
even after the elm was dead—an emblem of unswerving friendship. Only
Horatio (so far as I know) suggests that the vine pulls the elm down. Ll. 44–
5 are quoted (incorrectly) in *1 Return from Parnassus* (ed. Leishman),
ll. 1002–3.
　　48.] Harbage considers the sensuality of this passage unusual for the pre-
Shakespearian public theatre (*Shakespeare and the Rival Traditions,* pp.
201–2). For the double meaning in *die,* see Dryden's song, 'Whilst Alexis
lay prest', in *Marriage à la Mode,* IV. iii.

O sir, forbear, your valour is already tried.

Quickly despatch, my masters.   *They hang him in the arbour.*

Hor. What, will you murder me?

Lor. Ay, thus, and thus, these are the fruits of love.   *They stab him.*

Bel. O save his life and let me die for him!   56

O save him brother, save him Balthazar:

I lov'd Horatio but he lov'd not me.

Bal. But Balthazar loves Bel-imperia.

Lor. Although his life were still ambitious proud,   60

Yet is he at the highest now he is dead.

Bel. Murder! murder! Help, Hieronimo, help!

Lor. Come stop her mouth, away with her.

Exeunt[, *leaving Horatio's body*].

[II. v]

Enter HIERONIMO *in his shirt, &c.*

Hier. What outcries pluck me from my naked bed,

63.1. *Exeunt*[, *leaving Horatio's body*].] *This ed.; Exeunt. 1592.*

53.] There seems every reason for believing that the stage-property serving as the *arbour* (hitherto called *bower* in the text) was much like that illustrated in the famous woodcut on the t.p. of *1615*, sc. a trellis-work arch, not wide, but quite deep, adorned with 'leaves' (?) (so that Isabella may call it a 'fatal pine' in IV. ii). There would be a bench for the lovers to sit on. Such a property would be an ideal hanging-machine; perhaps it served also for Pedringano's gallows. Probably the arbour stood at the back of the stage between the doors. Hosley (privately) compares the arbour in *Looking Glass for London and England*, a 'brave arbour' and, though small enough to rise from a trap, large enough 'for fair Remilia to desport her in'. It would be possible to argue that the arbour was only a conventional tree; Isabella's later actions would be more realistic; Hieronimo refers to 'a tree' on which his son was hanged at IV. iv. 111; the author of the 'Painter scene' clearly thought of a tree (see 4th Addition, ll. 6off.). A stage tree was used for hangings, cf. *Massacre at Paris*, ll. 496–7: 'Lets hang him heere vpon this tree . . . *They hang him.*' Arch or tree, hangings were not a difficulty on the Elizabethan stage, to judge from their frequency.

II. v.] It is strictly incorrect to begin a new scene, since the stage is not clear, and many recent edd. continue the previous scene. But since it is only a corpse that occupies the stage, it has seemed better to follow the traditional division.

1. *naked bed*] a common phrase, not created by Kyd as an unwary reader of Boas' note might suppose; e.g., R. Edwardes in *Paradise of Dainty*

And chill my throbbing heart with trembling fear,
Which never danger yet could daunt before?
Who calls Hieronimo? Speak, here I am.
I did not slumber, therefore 'twas no dream,   5
No, no, it was some woman cried for help,
And here within this garden did she cry,
And in this garden must I rescue her:
But stay, what murd'rous spectacle is this?
A man hang'd up and all the murderers gone,   10
And in my bower, to lay the guilt on me:
This place was made for pleasure not for death.

                                        He cuts him down.

Those garments that he wears I oft have seen—
Alas, it is Horatio my sweet son!
O no, but he that whilom was my son.   15
O was it thou that call'dst me from my bed?
O speak, if any spark of life remain:
I am thy father. Who hath slain my son?
What savage monster, not of human kind,
Hath here been glutted with thy harmless blood,   20
And left thy bloody corpse dishonour'd here,
For me amidst this dark and deathful shades
To drown thee with an ocean of my tears?
O heavens, why made you night to cover sin?
By day this deed of darkness had not been.   25
O earth, why didst thou not in time devour

22. this] *1592;* these *1633.*

Devices (1576): 'In going to my naked bed as one that would have slept'.
    15. *whilom*] formerly, in the past.
    17.] Cf. Shakespeare's 'If any spark of life be yet remaining', *3 Henry VI,*
v. vi. 66.
    20.] For a parallel in Marlowe, see the end of Appendix C.
    22. *this*] *1633*'s *these* is followed by most edd. (not Schick²) and may be
less awkward to modern ears, but *this* is a form of the plural found up to
1622 (*apud O.E.D.*, s.v. *these, Illustration of Forms,* γ). It is used again
before a double epithet at III. ix. 4. Cf. Shakespeare, 'this two days', 'this
twenty years' (Schmidt, s.v. *this*). Even later examples may be found in
Massinger, *Bondman,* I. i. 21, 'this wars'; *Picture,* V. iii. 216, 'upon this
terms'.

The vild profaner of this sacred bower ?
O poor Horatio, what hadst thou misdone,
To leese thy life ere life was new begun ?
O wicked butcher, whatsoe'er thou wert,   30
How could thou strangle virtue and desert ?
Ay me most wretched, that have lost my joy,
In leesing my Horatio, my sweet boy!

Enter ISABELLA.

Isab. My husband's absence makes my heart to throb—
        Hieronimo!   35
Hier. Here Isabella, help me to lament,
        For sighs are stopp'd, and all my tears are spent.
Isab. What world of grief—My son Horatio!
      ' O where's the author of this endless woe ?
Hier. To know the author were some ease of grief,   40
        For in revenge my heart would find relief.
Isab. Then is he gone ? and is my son gone too ?
        O gush out, tears, fountains and floods of tears,
        Blow, sighs, and raise an everlasting storm:
        For outrage fits our cursed wretchedness.   45
Hier. Sweet lovely rose, ill-pluck'd before thy time, [*First Addition;*
        Fair worthy son, not conquer'd but betray'd: *see p.* 122]
        I'll kiss thee now, for words with tears are stay'd.
Isab. And I'll close up the glasses of his sight,
        For once these eyes were only my delight.   50

31. could] *1592;* could'st *1602.*   48. stay'd] staide *1603;* stainde *1592.*

---

29. *leese*] lose; not uncommon, but conquered by the modern form during the following century.
  new begun] i.e., after the wars ?
38. *What world of grief*—] not an exclamation, as previous edd. imply,
but the start of a remark which is broken off as Isabella recognizes the body.
45. *outrage*] passionate behaviour.
46. *Sweet lovely rose*] So Hotspur refers to the dead Richard, *1 Henry IV*,
I. iii. 175. Cf. also *Soliman and Perseda*, v. iv. 81: 'Faire springing Rose, ill
pluckt before thy time' (Sarrazin).
49. *glasses of his sight*] Boas compares *Coriolanus*, III. ii. 117: '—and
schoolboys' tears take up / The glasses of my sight.'

H

Hier. Seest thou this handkercher besmear'd with blood?
    It shall not from me till I take revenge:
    Seest thou those wounds that yet are bleeding fresh?
    I'll not entomb them till I have reveng'd:
    Then will I joy amidst my discontent,   55
    Till then my sorrow never shall be spent.
Isab. The heavens are just, murder cannot be hid,
    Time is the author both of truth and right,
    And time will bring this treachery to light.
Hier. Meanwhile, good Isabella, cease thy plaints,   60
    Or at the least dissemble them awhile:
    So shall we sooner find the practice out,
    And learn by whom all this was brought about.
    Come Isabel, now let us take him up,   *They take him up.*
    And bear him in from out this cursed place.   65
    I'll say his dirge, singing fits not this case.
    O aliquis mihi quas pulchrum ver educat herbas
            HIERONIMO *sets his breast unto his sword.*

54. reveng'd] *1592;* reuenge *1623.*   67. ver] *1594; var* 1592.   *educat*]
1615; educet 1592.

51–2.] Compare the use of the napkin dipped in Rutland's blood in
3 Henry VI, I. iv. 79–80 and 157–9. Since the incident is not in Shakespeare's source, he may have borrowed the idea from Kyd.
    54. *reveng'd] 1623*'s reading is preferred by Hazlitt and Schick. The only
argument can be one of balancing l. 52, for this absolute or intransitive use
of the verb is common.
    57. *murder cannot be hid*] a well-worn axiom; for some 16th-century
examples, see Tilley M1315.
    58–9.] proverbial; Tilley T324.
    62. *practice*] contrivance, evil-scheming.
    67–80.] 'A pastiche, in Kyd's singular fashion, of tags from classical
poetry, and lines of his own composition' (Boas). There are reminiscences
of Lucretius, Virgil, and Ovid. The emendation *herbarum* for *irraui* (l. 73) is
indefensible, except on the ground of sense and the source in Tibullus which
was suggested by Traube (see Schick's note). 'Let someone mix for me
herbs which the beautiful spring brings forth, and let a medicine be given
for our pain: or let him offer juices, if there are any which will bring oblivion
to our minds. I shall myself gather whatever herbs the sun brings forth,
throughout the mighty world, into the fair realms of light. I shall myself
drink whatever poison the sorceress contrives, whatever herbs, too, the

Misceat, et nostor detur medicina dolori;
Aut, si qui faciunt animis oblivia, succos
Praebeat; ipse metam magnum quaecunque per orbem   70
Gramina Sol pulchras effert in luminis oras;
Ipse bibam quicquid meditatur saga veneni,
Quicquid et herbarum vi caeca nenia nectit:
Omnia perpetiar, lethum quoque, dum semel omnis
Noster in extincto moriatur pectore sensus.   75
Ergo tuos oculos nunquam, mea vita, videbo,
Et tua perpetuus sepelivit lumina somnus?
Emoriar tecum, sic, sic juvat ire sub umbras.
At tamen absistam properato cedere letho,
Ne mortem vindicta tuam tum nulla sequatur.   80

    Here he throws it from him and bears the body away.

---

69. *animis*] conj. D. R. Dudley; *annum 1592*; *annorum* Hawkins.   *oblivia*]
Hawkins; *oblimia 1592*.   70. *metam*] Hawkins; *metum 1592*.   *magnum*]
1594; *magnam 1592*.   *quaecunque*] Hawkins; *quicunque 1592*.   71. *effert
in luminis oras*] conj. Traube; *effecit in luminis oras 1592*; *ejecit lucis in oras*
Hawkins.   72. *veneni*] *1594*; *veneri 1592*.   73. *herbarum*] Schick; *irraui
1592*; *irarum* Hawkins.   *vi caeca*] Hawkins; *euecæca 1592*.   *nenia*]
Hawkins; *menia 1592*.   75. *pectore*] *1594*; *pectora 1592*.   80. *tum*]
Hawkins; *tam 1592*.

---

goddess of spells weaves together by her secret power. All things I shall
essay, death even, until all feeling dies at once in my dead heart. Shall I
never again, my life, see your face, and has eternal sleep buried your
light? I shall die with you—so, so would I rejoice to go to the shades
below. But none the less, I shall keep myself from a hasty death, in case
then no revenge should follow your death.'

80.1. and bears the body away] perhaps *and they bear*? The action is not
very clear, and the directions may indicate revision, second thoughts, or the
book-keeper's hand. They *take him up* at l. 64, but Hieronimo cannot be
holding him while he *sets his breast unto his sword* (l. 67) or *throws it* [his
sword?] *from him.* It is arguable (see Introduction, p. xxxii) that the text is
a conflation of a literary version and an abridged version for the stage in
which the dirge is omitted; if so, the first *They take him up* would be the
sole direction before *Exeunt.* But in spite of clear inconsistency, the directions in the text may be found actable: Hieronimo and Isabella tend and
half-raise the body, which Isabella supports while Hieronimo recites the
dirge. Hieronimo then lifts the body and carries it offstage in his arms.

[II. vi]

Andrea. Brought'st thou me hither to increase my pain ?
          I look'd that Balthazar should have been slain:
          But 'tis my friend Horatio that is slain,
          And they abuse fair Bel-imperia,
          On whom I doted more than all the world,   5
          Because she lov'd me more than all the world.
Revenge. Thou talk'st of harvest when the corn is green:
          The end is crown of every work well done:
          The sickle comes not till the corn be ripe.
          Be still, and ere I lead thee from this place,   10
          I'll show thee Balthazar in heavy case.

II. vi. 5. On] *1599;* Or *1592.*

II. vi. 8.] a version of one of the commonest sayings, *Finis coronat opus.*
Cf. 'T.W.', 'The end of eu'ry worke doth crowne the same' (*Phoenix Nest,*
ed. Rollins, p. 98).

Act III

[III. i]

       Enter VICEROY of Portingale, Nobles, VILLUPPO.

Vice. Infortunate condition of kings,
   Seated amidst so many helpless doubts!
   First we are plac'd upon extremest height,
   And oft supplanted with exceeding heat,
   But ever subject to the wheel of chance: 5
   And at our highest never joy we so,
   As we both doubt and dread our overthrow.
   So striveth not the waves with sundry winds
   As fortune toileth in the affairs of kings,
   That would be fear'd, yet fear to be belov'd,   10
   Sith fear or love to kings is flattery:
   For instance lordings, look upon your king,
   By hate deprived of his dearest son,
   The only hope of our successive line.
1 Nob. I had not thought that Alexandro's heart   15
   Had been envenom'd with such extreme hate:
   But now I see that words have several works,

Act III] Actus Tertius *1592*.   0.1. Nobles, VILLUPPO] *Brooke; Nobles,*
Alexandro, Villuppo 1592.   4. heat] *1592;* hate *1599*.   15. *1 Nob.*]
Nob. 1592.

1–11.] an adaptation of Seneca's *Agamemnon,* 57–73 (Boas).
   4. *heat*] All edd. read *hate* with *1599,* but the reading has no authority and
there is not the slightest reason for suspecting that *heat* is wrong: the meaning of passion, anger, or fury is regular and common.
   8. *striveth*] The inversion makes permissible what is for us a false concord; it is unlikely that we have here the rare plural in *-th* (cf. Franz, §156).
   11. *Sith*] since.
   17. *words have several works*] i.e., words are not always related to deeds.

And there's no credit in the countenance.

Vill. No; for, my lord, had you beheld the train
    That feigned love had colour'd in his looks,   20
    When he in camp consorted Balthazar,
    Far more inconstant had you thought the sun,
    That hourly coasts the centre of the earth,
    Than Alexandro's purpose to the prince.

Vice. No more Villuppo, thou hast said enough,   25
    And with thy words thou slay'st our wounded thoughts.
    Nor shall I longer dally with the world,
    Procrastinating Alexandro's death:
    Go some of you and fetch the traitor forth,
    That as he is condemned he may die.   30

Enter ALEXANDRO *with a* Nobleman *and* Halberts.

2 Nob. In such extremes will naught but patience serve.
Alex. But in extremes what patience shall I use?
    Nor discontents it me to leave the world,
    With whom there nothing can prevail but wrong.
2 Nob. Yet hope the best.
Alex.   'Tis Heaven is my hope.   35
    As for the earth, it is too much infect
    To yield me hope of any of her mould.
Vice. Why linger ye? Bring forth that daring fiend

---

26. slay'st] slaiest *1592;* staiest *Boas.*   31. *2 Nob.*] *Nob. 1592.*

18.] Cf. *Duchess of Malfi*, I. i. 250; *Macbeth*, I. iv. 11–12.

19–20.] Villuppo is a little confused: what he says is: 'had you beheld the treachery [*train*] which feigned love had disguised [*colour'd*] in his looks ...' But the point is that the treachery could *not* be seen. He means, 'Had you beheld the feigned love in his looks, disguising the treachery of his heart ...'

22–3.] from Garnier's *Cornélie*, Act II, but whereas Garnier uses the perpetual movement of the heavens and the seasons as an image of mutability, Kyd stresses the constancy of the regular cycles of the sun. Once again Kyd recalled the lines here when making his translation of *Cornélie*.

23. *the centre of the earth*] 'this centre of the universe, the earth'.

26. *slay'st*] Boas' *staiest* appears to derive from a misreading of the ligature fl.

30.1. Halberts] i.e., Halberdiers.

And let him die for his accursed deed.

Alex. Not that I fear the extremity of death,   40
    For nobles cannot stoop to servile fear,
    Do I, O king, thus discontented live.
    But this, O this, torments my labouring soul,
    That thus I die suspected of a sin,
    Whereof, as heavens have known my secret thoughts,   45
    So am I free from this suggestion.

Vice. No more, I say! to the tortures! when!
    Bind him, and burn his body in those flames

                         They bind him to the stake.

    That shall prefigure those unquenched fires
    Of Phlegethon prepared for his soul.   50

Alex. My guiltless death will be aveng'd on thee,
    On thee, Villuppo, that hath malic'd thus,
    Or for thy meed hast falsely me accus'd.

Vill. Nay Alexandro, if thou menace me,
    I'll lend a hand to send thee to the lake   55
    Where those thy words shall perish with thy works,
    Injurious traitor, monstrous homicide!

             Enter AMBASSADOR.

Amb. Stay, hold a while,
    And here, with pardon of his majesty,
    Lay hands upon Villuppo.

Vice.   Ambassador,   60
    What news hath urg'd this sudden entrance?

Amb. Know, sovereign lord, that Balthazar doth live.

58–61. Stay ... while, / And ... majesty, / Lay ... Ambassador, / What ...
entrance?] *Schick;* Stay ... Maiestie, / Lay ... *Villuppo.* / Embassadour
... entrance? *1592.*

---

46. *suggestion*] false accusation (*O.E.D.*, 3).
    47. *when!*] a common exclamation denoting impatience; the successive
editors of Dodsley (including Hazlitt) emended to *to the tortures with him!*
    52. *malic'd*] entertained malice. A rare intransitive usage (*O.E.D.*, *v.*, 2).
    53. *meed*] reward.
    55. *lake*] infernal, of course.
    61. *entrance*] trisyllabic. Cf. *Romeo & Juliet,* I. iv. 8.

Vice. What say'st thou ? liveth Balthazar our son ?

Amb. Your highness' son, Lord Balthazar, doth live;

And, well entreated in the court of Spain,   65

Humbly commends him to your majesty.

These eyes beheld, and these my followers,

With these, the letters of the king's commends,

Gives him letters.

Are happy witnesses of his highness' health.

The KING *looks on the letters, and proceeds.*

Vice. 'Thy son doth live, your tribute is receiv'd,   70

Thy peace is made, and we are satisfied :

The rest resolve upon as things propos'd

For both our honours and thy benefit.'

Amb. These are his highness' farther articles.

He gives him more letters.

Vice. Accursed wretch, to intimate these ills   75

Against the life and reputation

Of noble Alexandro !—Come, my lord,

Let him unbind thee that is bound to death,

To make a quital for thy discontent.   *They unbind him.*

Alex. Dread lord, in kindness you could do no less,   80

Upon report of such a damned fact:

---

77. Come, my lord,] *This ed.; come my Lord vnbinde him. 1592.*

---

68. *commends*] greetings, compliments (*O.E.D., sb.*, 3).

77.] See textual notes: the final *unbind him* of *1592* gives the line thirteen syllables; Le Gay Brereton (quoted by Schick²) thought *unbind him* to be the original S.D. Kittredge (quoted by Manly) thought *my lord* hypermetrical. It is far better that the King's gentler tone, with *Come, my lord,* should mark a turn from Villuppo to Alexandro than to accept with *1592* a continuation to the first, i.e., *Come, my lord, unbind him!,* with a very awkward transition to a new hearer in the next line. Either the compositor's eye has anticipated the direction two lines below or the author has failed to strike out a direction placed too early. It is possible the passage as a whole contains erasure and rewriting, for Alexandro's first remark after release is a reply to an apology which the King has not made.

79. *quital*] requital.

They unbind him] a passive sense only: *He is unbound,* by Villuppo, as the King orders.

80. *in kindness*] naturally.

But thus we see our innocence hath sav'd
The hopeless life which thou, Villuppo, sought
By thy suggestions to have massacred.

Vice. Say, false Villuppo! wherefore didst thou thus   85
Falsely betray Lord Alexandro's life?
Him whom thou know'st that no unkindness else,
But even the slaughter of our dearest son,
Could once have mov'd us to have misconceiv'd?

Alex. Say, treacherous Villuppo, tell the king,   90
Or wherein hath Alexandro us'd thee ill?

Vill. Rent with remembrance of so foul a deed,
My guilty soul submits me to thy doom:
For, not for Alexandro's injuries,
But for reward, and hope to be preferr'd,   95
Thus have I shamelessly hazarded his life.

Vice. Which, villain, shall be ransom'd with thy death,
And not so mean a torment as we here
Devis'd for him, who thou said'st slew our son,
But with the bitterest torments and extremes   100
That may be yet invented for thine end.

                              ALEXANDRO *seems to entreat.*
Entreat me not, go take the traitor hence.

                              Exit VILLUPPO [*guarded*].
And, Alexandro, let us honour thee
With public notice of thy loyalty.
To end those things articulated here   105
By our great lord, the mighty King of Spain,
We with our council will deliberate.
Come, Alexandro, keep us company.   *Exeunt.*

---

91. Or] *1592; not in Hazlitt.*

---

98. *mean*] temperate, moderate.

[III. ii]

Enter HIERONIMO.

Hier. O eyes, no eyes, but fountains fraught with tears;
    O life, no life, but lively form of death;
    O world, no world, but mass of public wrongs,
    Confus'd and fill'd with murder and misdeeds;
    O sacred heavens! if this unhallow'd deed,   5
    If this inhuman and barbarous attempt,
    If this incomparable murder thus
    Of mine, but now no more my son,
    Shall unreveal'd and unrevenged pass,
    How should we term your dealings to be just,   10
    If you unjustly deal with those that in your justice trust?
    The night, sad secretary to my moans,
    With direful visions wake my vexed soul,
    And with the wounds of my distressful son
    Solicit me for notice of his death.   15
    The ugly fiends do sally forth of hell,
    And frame my steps to unfrequented paths,
    And fear my heart with fierce inflamed thoughts.
    The cloudy day my discontents records,
    Early begins to register my dreams   20
    And drive me forth to seek the murderer.
    Eyes, life, world, heavens, hell, night, and day,

III. ii. 13. wake] *1592;* wakes *Dodsley.*   15. Solicit] *1592;* Solicits *Dodsley.*

III. ii. 1.] Rollins, in pointing out the similarity of this line to 'T.W.' 's 'Mine eies, now eies no more, but seas of teares', notes many Italian and French versions of a figure which is commonplace; e.g., Petrarch, *Rime,* 161, 'oi occhi miei, occhi non già, ma fonti', or De Baif, 'O mes yeux, non plus yeux, mais de pleurs deux fontaines' (*Phoenix Nest,* p. 201). Hieronimo's speech became a kind of rallying-point for all who would pour scorn on the absurdities of the Kydean rhetoric; see, e.g., *Everyman in his Humour,* I. v. 57–8 and Introduction, pp. l and lxvii.

12. *secretary to my moans*] 'the confidant to whom my moans are uttered' (Boas). This phrase is cited in *O.E.D., secretary, sb.*[1], 1b.

13. *wake*] plural for singular, probably by attraction to *visions;* cf. false concords in *solicit* (l. 15) and *drive* (l. 21).

18. *fear*] frighten (*O.E.D., v.,* 1).

See, search, shew, send, some man, some mean, that may—

A letter falleth.

What's here ? a letter ? tush, it is not so!

A letter written to Hieronimo!   *Red ink.*   25

'For want of ink, receive this bloody writ.

Me hath my hapless brother hid from thee:

Revenge thyself on Balthazar and him,

For these were they that murdered thy son.

Hieronimo, revenge Horatio's death,   30

And better fare than Bel-imperia doth.'

What means this unexpected miracle ?

My son slain by Lorenzo and the prince!

What cause had they Horatio to malign ?

Or what might move thee, Bel-imperia,   35

To accuse thy brother, had he been the mean ?

Hieronimo beware, thou art betray'd,

And to entrap thy life this train is laid.

Advise thee therefore, be not credulous:

This is devised to endanger thee,   40

That thou by this Lorenzo shouldst accuse,

And he, for thy dishonour done, should draw

Thy life in question, and thy name in hate.

Dear was the life of my beloved son,

And of his death behoves me be reveng'd: 45

Then hazard not thine own, Hieronimo,

But live t' effect thy resolution.

I therefore will by circumstances try

---

23. See . . . may] *Manly;* See . . . some man, / Some . . . may *1592.*   26.
For] *1602; Bel.* For *1592.*   29. murdered] murdred *1592.*   32. What]
1602; Hiero What *1592.*

---

25. *Red ink*] perhaps an author's instruction; the phrase is otherwise
inexplicable; see Introduction, p. xxxi.

34. *malign*] hate (*O.E.D., v.,* 4).

38. *train*] snare, trap (*O.E.D., sb.*², 1b); cf. III. i. 19.

48. *circumstances*] 'circumstantial evidence'. I believe Boas is wrong in
glossing 'roundabout, indirect methods' and citing in support *Merchant of
Venice,* I. i. 154. *O.E.D.,* 6, would confine this usage to speech, 'beating
about the bush'; Hieronimo is after further information, and we should

What I can gather to confirm this writ,
And, heark'ning near the Duke of Castile's house,   50
Close if I can with Bel-imperia,
To listen more, but nothing to bewray.

Enter PEDRINGANO.

Now, Pedringano!
Ped.   Now, Hieronimo!
Hier. Where's thy lady?
Ped.   I know not; here's my lord.

Enter LORENZO.

Lor. How now, who's this? Hieronimo?
Hier.   My lord.   55
Ped. He asketh for my lady Bel-imperia.
Lor. What to do, Hieronimo? The duke my father hath
    Upon some disgrace awhile remov'd her hence,
    But if it be aught I may inform her of,
    Tell me, Hieronimo, and I'll let her know it.   60
Hier. Nay, nay, my lord, I thank you, it shall not need,
    I had a suit unto her, but too late,
    And her disgrace makes me unfortunate.
Lor. Why so, Hieronimo? use me.
Hier. O no, my lord, I dare not, it must not be.   *[Second Addition; see p. 124]*
    I humbly thank your lordship.
Lor.   Why then, farewell.   66
Hier. My grief no heart, my thoughts no tongue can tell.   *Exit.*
Lor. Come hither Pedringano, seest thou this?
Ped. My lord, I see it, and suspect it too.
Lor. This is that damned villain Serberine,   70
    That hath, I fear, reveal'd Horatio's death.

53. Now, Pedringano!] *Schick; Hiero.* Now ~ *1592.*

---

paraphrase: 'I will try to find out other facts which may give credence to this accusation.' *by circumstances* will be better understood if it is taken with *confirm* and not with *try.*

Ped. My lord, he could not, 'twas so lately done,
    And since, he hath not left my company.
Lor. Admit he have not, his condition's such,
    As fear or flattering words may make him false.   75
    I know his humour, and therewith repent
    That e'er I us'd him in this enterprise.
    But Pedringano, to prevent the worst,
    And 'cause I know thee secret as my soul,
    Here for thy further satisfaction take thou this,   80
                          Gives him more gold.
    And hearken to me—thus it is devis'd:
    This night thou must, and prithee so resolve,
    Meet Serberine at Saint Luigi's Park—
    Thou know'st 'tis here hard by behind the house;
    There take thy stand, and see thou strike him sure,   85
    For die he must, if we do mean to live.
Ped. But how shall Serberine be there, my lord?
Lor. Let me alone, I'll send to him to meet
    The prince and me, where thou must do this deed.
Ped. It shall be done, my lord, it shall be done,   90
    And I'll go arm myself to meet him there.
Lor. When things shall alter, as I hope they will,
    Then shalt thou mount for this: thou know'st my mind.
                        Exit PEDRINGANO.

    Che le Ieron!

                Enter Page.

Page.   My lord?

83. Saint Luigi's] *Manly, Schick; S. Liugis 1592.*

---

74. *condition*] nature, disposition.
83. *Saint Luigi's Park*] If the emendation is correct, Kyd is incorrect, for Luigi is not a Spanish name.
88. *Let me alone*] 'trust me'.
93. *mount*] Lorenzo enjoys his own jokes; that the same terms can apply to promotion or to hanging has already inspired his wit; cf. II. iv. 61.
94. Che le Ieron] 'An unintelligible expression, possibly a corruption of the page's name' (Boas).

Lor.   Go, sirrah, to Serberine,
      And bid him forthwith meet the prince and me   95
      At Saint Luigi's Park, behind the house—
      This evening, boy!
Page.   I go, my lord.
Lor. But sirrah, let the hour be eight o' clock:
      Bid him not fail.
Page.   I fly, my lord.   *Exit.*
Lor. Now to confirm the complot thou hast cast   100
      Of all these practices, I'll spread the watch,
      Upon precise commandment from the king,
      Strongly to guard the place where Pedringano
      This night shall murder hapless Serberine.
      Thus must we work that will avoid distrust,   105
      Thus must we practise to prevent mishap,
      And thus one ill another must expulse.
      This sly enquiry of Hieronimo
      For Bel-imperia breeds suspicion,
      And this suspicion bodes a further ill.   110
      As for myself, I know my secret fault,
      And so do they, but I have dealt for them.
      They that for coin their souls endangered,
      To save my life, for coin shall venture theirs:
      And better it's that base companions die,   115
      Than by their life to hazard our good haps.

94–7. Go . . . Serberine, / And . . . me / At . . . house— / This . . . boy! . . .]
Boas; Goe . . . forthwith, / Meet . . . Parke, / Behinde . . . boy. / *1592;*
Go sirrah, / To . . . meet / The Prince . . . Park, / Behind . . . boy. . . .
Manly, Schick.   96. Luigi's] *Manly, Schick; Liugis 1592.*   98. *Lor.*]
1602; not in 1592.   108–9. This . . . Hieronimo / For . . . suspicion,]
Hawkins; This . . . suspition, *1592.*   115. it's] its *1592;* tis *1599.*

---

   100. *complot*] plot.
   cast] contrived, schemed (*O.E.D.*, v., 43b).
   107.] The saying is frequently found in one form or another. Tilley
(D174) quotes Taverner's translation of Erasmus, 'One disceyt dryueth
out an other.'
   111. *fault*] misdeed, offence (*O.E.D.*, 5a). For *secret fault*, see Psalm 19:
12 (Coverdale).
   115. *companions*] fellows (used contemptuously).

Nor shall they live, for me to fear their faith:
I'll trust myself, myself shall be my friend,
For die they shall, slaves are ordain'd to no other end.   *Exit.*

[III. iii]

Enter PEDRINGANO *with a pistol.*

Ped. Now, Pedringano, bid thy pistol hold,
    And hold on, Fortune! once more favour me,
    Give but success to mine attempting spirit,
    And let me shift for taking of mine aim!
    Here is the gold, this is the gold propos'd: 5
    It is no dream that I adventure for,
    But Pedringano is possess'd thereof.
    And he that would not strain his conscience
    For him that thus his liberal purse hath stretch'd,
    Unworthy such a favour may he fail,   10
    And, wishing, want, when such as I prevail.
    As for the fear of apprehension,
    I know, if need should be, my noble lord
    Will stand between me and ensuing harms:
    Besides, this place is free from all suspect.   15
    Here therefore will I stay and take my stand.

Enter the Watch.

1. I wonder much to what intent it is
    That we are thus expressly charg'd to watch.
2. 'Tis by commandment in the king's own name.
3. But we were never wont to watch and ward   20
    So near the duke his brother's house before.
2. Content yourself, stand close, there's somewhat in't.

III. iii. 1. Ped.] *1602; not in 1592.*

III. iii. 4.] 'And I'll look after pointing the pistol.'
    15. *suspect*] suspicion.
    20. *watch and ward*] patrol, keep a guard. Originally part of the legal definition of the duties of a sentinel.

Enter SERBERINE.

Ser. Here, Serberine, attend and stay thy pace,
    For here did Don Lorenzo's page appoint
    That thou by his command shouldst meet with him.   25
    How fit a place, if one were so dispos'd,
    Methinks this corner is to close with one.

Ped. Here comes the bird that I must seize upon:
    Now, Pedringano, or never play the man!

Ser. I wonder that his lordship stays so long,   30
    Or wherefore should he send for me so late?

Ped. For this, Serberine, and thou shalt ha't.   *Shoots the dag.*
    So, there he lies, my promise is perform'd.

The Watch.

1.   Hark gentlemen, this is a pistol shot.

2.   And here's one slain; stay the murderer.   35

Ped. Now by the sorrows of the souls in hell,
                            He strives with the Watch.

    Who first lays hand on me, I'll be his priest.

3.   Sirrah, confess, and therein play the priest,
    Why hast thou thus unkindly kill'd the man?

Ped. Why? because he walk'd abroad so late.   40

3.   Come sir, you had been better kept your bed,
    Than have committed this misdeed so late.

2.   Come, to the Marshal's with the murderer!

1.   On to Hieronimo's! help me here
    To bring the murder'd body with us too.   45

Ped. Hieronimo! Carry me before whom you will:
    Whate'er he be, I'll answer him and you,
    And do your worst, for I defy you all.   *Exeunt.*

---

43. Come,] *1602;* Come *1592.*

---

    32. dag] 'a kind of heavy pistol or hand-gun' (*O.E.D.*).
    37. *I'll be his priest*] i.e., smooth his passage to the next world, make an end
of him. See Tilley P587 for other examples of the saying.
    39. *unkindly*] unnaturally.

[III. iv]

Enter LORENZO *and* BALTHAZAR.

Bal. How now my lord, what makes you rise so soon?
Lor. Fear of preventing our mishaps too late.
Bal. What mischief is it that we not mistrust?
Lor. Our greatest ills we least mistrust, my lord,
    And inexpected harms do hurt us most.   5
Bal. Why, tell me Don Lorenzo, tell me, man,
    If aught concerns our honour and your own.
Lor. Nor you nor me, my lord, but both in one,
    For I suspect, and the presumption's great,
    That by those base confederates in our fault   10
    Touching the death of Don Horatio,
    We are betray'd to old Hieronimo.
Bal. Betray'd, Lorenzo? tush, it cannot be.
Lor. A guilty conscience, urged with the thought
    Of former evils, easily cannot err: 15
    I am persuaded, and dissuade me not,
    That all's revealed to Hieronimo.
    And therefore know that I have cast it thus—

[*Enter* Page.]

    But here's the page. How now, what news with thee?
Page. My lord, Serberine is slain.   20
Bal. Who? Serberine, my man?
Page. Your highness' man, my lord.
Lor. Speak page, who murdered him?
Page. He that is apprehended for the fact.
Lor. Who?   25

III. iv. 5. inexpected] *1599;* in expected *1592;* unexpected *1623.*   18.1.
[*Enter* Page.]] *1615; not in 1592.*

III. iv. 2. *preventing*] in the usual sense of anticipating, being beforehand,
hence 'Fear of being too late to avert our mishaps'.
   3. *mistrust*] 'suspect the existence of or anticipate the occurrence of
[something evil]' (*O.E.D., v.,* 3).
   24. *fact*] crime, evil deed. Cf. mod. 'accessary before the fact'.

I

Page. Pedringano.

Bal. Is Serberine slain, that lov'd his lord so well?
       Injurious villain, murderer of his friend!

Lor. Hath Pedringano murder'd Serberine?
       My lord, let me entreat you to take the pains   30
       To exasperate and hasten his revenge
       With your complaints unto my lord the king.
       This their dissension breeds a greater doubt.

Bal. Assure thee, Don Lorenzo, he shall die,
       Or else his highness hardly shall deny.   35
       Meanwhile, I'll haste the marshal-sessions:
       For die he shall for this his damned deed.   *Exit* BALTHAZAR.

Lor. Why so, this fits our former policy,
       And thus experience bids the wise to deal.
       I lay the plot, he prosecutes the point,   40
       I set the trap, he breaks the worthless twigs
       And sees not that wherewith the bird was lim'd.
       Thus hopeful men, that mean to hold their own,
       Must look like fowlers to their dearest friends.
       He runs to kill whom I have holp to catch,   45
       And no man knows it was my reaching fatch.
       'Tis hard to trust unto a multitude,
       Or anyone, in mine opinion,
       When men themselves their secrets will reveal.

                Enter a Messenger *with a letter.*

                Boy!   50
Page. My lord.
Lor. What's he?

---

31. *exasperate*] make harsh.

35. *hardly shall deny*] shall show harshness in denying me. The sentiment
is in keeping with Balthazar's ineffectual character and makes more sense
of *Or else* than the usual gloss, e.g., McIlwraith, 'shall find it hard to refuse'.

36. *marshal-sessions*] The Knight Marshal's 'sessions' were called the
court of Marshalsea; but the correct term was no doubt too English.

45. *holp*] helped. Boas compares *Tempest*, I. ii. 62–3.

46. *reaching*] reaching forward, designing, far-seeing.
   fatch] = fetch: stratagem, contrivance (*O.E.D., fetch, sb.*[1], 2).

Mes.   I have a letter to your lordship.

Lor. From whence?

Mes.   From Pedringano that's imprison'd.

Lor. So, he is in prison then?

Mes.   Ay, my good lord.

Lor. What would he with us? He writes us here   55
  To stand good lord and help him in distress.
  Tell him I have his letters, know his mind,
  And what we may, let him assure him of.
  Fellow, begone: my boy shall follow thee.   *Exit* Messenger.
  This works like wax, yet once more try thy wits.   60
  Boy, go convey this purse to Pedringano:
  Thou know'st the prison, closely give it him,
  And be advis'd that none be there about.
  Bid him be merry still, but secret:
  And though the marshal-sessions be today,   65
  Bid him not doubt of his delivery.
  Tell him his pardon is already sign'd,
  And thereon bid him boldly be resolv'd:
  For were he ready to be turned off
  (As 'tis my will the uttermost be tried),   70
  Thou with his pardon shalt attend him still:
  Show him this box, tell him his pardon's in't,
  But open't not, and if thou lov'st thy life,
  But let him wisely keep his hopes unknown;
  He shall not want while Don Lorenzo lives.   75
  Away!

55–6. What . . . here / To . . . distress.] *Manly;* What . . . vs? / He writes
. . . distres. *1592.*   75–6. He . . . lives. / Away!] *Hazlitt;* He . . . away.
1592.

---

56. *stand good lord*] act the part of good lord, or patron; a stock phrase
(*O.E.D.*, s.v. *stand, v.,* 15c).

62. *closely*] secretly.

64. *secret*] The scansion here, and at III. x. 10, suggests that the word is
trisyllabic.

69. *turned off*] hanged.

73. *and if*] if.

Page.   I go my lord, I run.
Lor. But sirrah, see that this be cleanly done.   *Exit* Page.
            Now stands our fortune on a tickle point,
            And now or never ends Lorenzo's doubts.
            One only thing is uneffected yet,   80
            And that's to see the executioner.
            But to what end? I list not trust the air
            With utterance of our pretence therein,
            For fear the privy whisp'ring of the wind
            Convey our words amongst unfriendly ears,   85
            That lie too open to advantages.
            E quel che voglio io, nessun lo sa,
            Intendo io: quel mi basterà.   *Exit.*

[III. v]

Enter Boy *with the box.*

Page. My master hath forbidden me to look in this box, and
by my troth 'tis likely, if he had not warned me, I should
not have had so much idle time: for we men's-kind in our
minority are like women in their uncertainty: that they
are most forbidden, they will soonest attempt: so I now.   5
By my bare honesty, here's nothing but the bare empty
box: were it not sin against secrecy, I would say it were a
piece of gentlemanlike knavery. I must go to Pedringano,

---

81. see] *1592;* fee *conj. Edwards.*   87–8. E quel . . . basterà.] *Hawkins,
Schick; Et quel que voglio Ii nessun le sa, | Intendo io quel mi bassara.
1592.*

III. v. 1. Page] *not in 1592;* Boy. *1615.*

---

78. *tickle*] delicately balanced, ticklish.
79. *ends*] singular for plural in inversion; cf. III. i. 8.
81. *see*] I have a strong suspicion that 'fee' is a misprint for 'fee'; the
remark would be more in character and more powerful. But one cannot
tamper with a reading which makes good sense.
82. *list not*] have no wish to.
83. *pretence*] intention (*O.E.D.,* 3).
87–8.] 'And what I want, no-one knows; I understand, and that's enough
for me,'

and tell him his pardon is in this box, nay, I would have
sworn it, had I not seen the contrary. I cannot choose but   10
smile to think how the villain will flout the gallows, scorn
the audience, and descant on the hangman, and all pre-
suming of his pardon from hence. Will 't not be an odd
jest, for me to stand and grace every jest he makes, pointing my finger at this box, as who would say, 'Mock on,   15
here's thy warrant.' Is't not a scurvy jest, that a man
should jest himself to death? Alas, poor Pedringano, I
am in a sort sorry for thee, but if I should be hanged with
thee, I cannot weep.   *Exit.*

[III. vi]

Enter HIERONIMO *and the* Deputy.

Hier. Thus must we toil in other men's extremes,
      That know not how to remedy our own,
      And do them justice, when unjustly we,
      For all our wrongs, can compass no redress.
      But shall I never live to see the day   5
      That I may come, by justice of the heavens,
      To know the cause that may my cares allay?
      This toils my body, this consumeth age,
      That only I to all men just must be,
      And neither gods nor men be just to me.   10
Dep. Worthy Hieronimo, your office asks
      A care to punish such as do transgress.
Hier. So is't my duty to regard his death
      Who, when he liv'd, deserv'd my dearest blood:
      But come, for that we came for, let's begin,   15
      For here lies that which bids me to be gone.

III. vi. 15. But ... begin,] *1602;* But come, for that we came for lets begin,
1592; But come, for that we came for: let's begin, *1615.*

III. vi. 0.1. *Deputy*] the official title of the assistant to the Knight Marshal.
13. *regard*] care for, show concern for.
16. *For here*] i.e., in his heart or his head, which he touches. Boas suggests
he refers to the bloody kercher.

Enter Officers, Boy *and* PEDRINGANO,
with a letter in his hand, bound.

Dep. Bring forth the prisoner, for the court is set.
Ped. Gramercy boy, but it was time to come,
    For I had written to my lord anew
    A nearer matter that concerneth him,   20
    For fear his lordship had forgotten me;
    But sith he hath remember'd me so well—
    Come, come, come on, when shall we to this gear?
Hier. Stand forth, thou monster, murderer of men,
    And here, for satisfaction of the world,   25
    Confess thy folly and repent thy fault,
    For there's thy place of execution.
Ped. This is short work: well, to your marshalship
    First I confess, nor fear I death therefore,
    I am the man, 'twas I slew Serberine.   30
    But sir, then you think this shall be the place
    Where we shall satisfy you for this gear?
Dep. Ay, Pedringano.
Ped.   Now I think not so.
Hier. Peace impudent, for thou shalt find it so:
    For blood with blood shall, while I sit as judge,   35
    Be satisfied, and the law discharg'd;
    And though myself cannot receive the like,
    Yet will I see that others have their right.
    Despatch! the fault's approved and confess'd,
    And by our law he is condemn'd to die.   40
Hangman. Come on sir, are you ready?
Ped. To do what, my fine officious knave?
Hangm. To go to this gear.

40.1. ʌ] *1592; Enter Hangman 1615.*

---

    23. *gear*] affair, business; cf. following note.
    32. *for this gear*] for this behaviour, deed, or action. Cf. Nashe, ii, 181, 'Ile hamper him like a iade as he is for this geare.'
    39. *approved*] proved.
    40.] It is unnecessary to provide an entry for the Hangman here since he is one of the officers who enter at the start of the scene.

Ped. O sir, you are too forward; thou wouldst fain furnish
me with a halter, to disfurnish me of my habit, so I should   45
go out of this gear, my raiment, into that gear, the rope;
but hangman, now I spy your knavery, I'll not change
without boot, that's flat.

Hangm. Come sir.

Ped. So then, I must up?   50

Hangm. No remedy.

Ped. Yes, but there shall be for my coming down.

Hangm. Indeed, here's a remedy for that.

Ped. How? be turned off?

Hangm. Ay truly; come, are you ready? I pray sir, despatch: 55
the day goes away.

Ped. What, do you hang by the hour? If you do, I may chance
to break your old custom.

Hangm. Faith, you have reason, for I am like to break your
young neck.   60

Ped. Dost thou mock me, hangman? Pray God I be not preserved to break your knave's pate for this!

Hangm. Alas sir, you are a foot too low to reach it, and I hope
you will never grow so high while I am in the office.

Ped. Sirrah, dost see yonder boy with the box in his hand?   65

Hangm. What, he that points to it with his finger?

Ped. Ay, that companion.

Hangm. I know him not, but what of him?

Ped. Dost thou think to live till his old doublet will make thee
a new truss?   70

44–8. O sir . . . that's flat.] *Prose as Schick;* O sir . . . habit. / So I . . . rope. /
But Hangman . . . flat. *1592.*   55–6. Ay truly . . . away.] *Schick;* I truely
. . . ready. / I pray . . . away. *1592.*

44.] The compositor of *1592* has occasionally given Pedringano's and the
Hangman's speeches the appearance of a kind of Whitmanesque verse by
beginning a new sentence or main clause on a fresh line. But there is no
doubt at all that they speak prose. Cf. note on 4th Addition, l. 107.

45. *disfurnish me of my habit*] alluding to the custom which grants the
hangman his victim's clothes.

70. *truss*] close-fitting breeches or trousers; in the succeeding speech the
hangman puns on another meaning of the word—to hang.

Hangm. Ay, and many a fair year after, to truss up many an
    honester man than either thou or he.

Ped. What hath he in his box, as thou think'st?

Hangm. Faith, I cannot tell, nor I care not greatly. Methinks
    you should rather hearken to your soul's health.   75

Ped. Why, sirrah hangman? I take it, that that is good for the
    body is likewise good for the soul: and it may be, in that
    box is balm for both.

Hangm. Well, thou art even the merriest piece of man's flesh
    that e'er groaned at my office door.   80

Ped. Is your roguery become an office, with a knave's name?

Hangm. Ay, and that shall all they witness that see you seal it
    with a thief's name.

Ped. I prithee request this good company to pray with me.

Hangm. Ay marry sir, this is a good motion: my masters, you   85
    see here's a good fellow.

Ped. Nay, nay, now I remember me, let them alone till some
    other time, for now I have no great need.

Hier. I have not seen a wretch so impudent!
    O monstrous times, where murder's set so light,   90
    And where the soul, that should be shrin'd in heaven,
    Solely delights in interdicted things,
    Still wand'ring in the thorny passages
    That intercepts itself of happiness.
    Murder, O bloody monster—God forbid   95
    A fault so foul should scape unpunished.
    Despatch, and see this execution done:
    This makes me to remember thee, my son. *Exit* HIERONIMO.

Ped. Nay, soft, no haste.

Dep. Why, wherefore stay you? have you hope of life?   100

Ped. Why, ay.

Hangm. As how?

74–5. Faith . . . health.] *Prose as Schick;* Faith . . . greatly. / Me thinks . . .
health. *1592.*   84. pray with me] *1592;* pray for me *1602.*

94.] presumably 'which prevent it (the soul) from attaining happiness'.
Since the construction is so clumsy it is impossible to know whether *intercepts* is a correct or incorrect singular, or a rare plural-form. Cf. III. xiv. 50.

Ped. Why, rascal, by my pardon from the king.

Hangm. Stand you on that? then you shall off with this.

He turns him off.

Dep. So, executioner; convey him hence,   105
    But let his body be unburied.
    Let not the earth be choked or infect
    With that which heaven contemns and men neglect.   *Exeunt.*

[III. vii]

Enter HIERONIMO.

Hier. Where shall I run to breathe abroad my woes,
    My woes, whose weight hath wearied the earth?
    Or mine exclaims, that have surcharg'd the air
    With ceaseless plaints for my deceased son?
    The blust'ring winds, conspiring with my words,   5
    At my lament have mov'd the leaveless trees,
    Disrob'd the meadows of their flower'd green,
    Made mountains marsh with spring-tides of my tears,
    And broken through the brazen gates of hell.
    Yet still tormented is my tortur'd soul   10
    With broken sighs and restless passions,
    That winged mount, and, hovering in the air,
    Beat at the windows of the brightest heavens,
    Soliciting for justice and revenge:
    But they are plac'd in those empyreal heights   15
    Where, countermur'd with walls of diamond,

108. heaven] *1594;* heauens *1592.*

III. vii. 1. *Hier.*] *1603; not in 1592.*   15. empyreal] *Schick*[1]*; imperiall 1592.*

III. vii. 8.] a violent image, but Kyd liked the latter part well enough to re-use it in *Cornelia,* v. 420, 'And dewe your selues with springtides of your teares'. The first part is transmuted in the same translation (I. 40) and again there is no parallel in Garnier: 'with their blood made marsh the parched plaines'.

15. *empyreal*] *1592*'s *imperiall* is only a spelling variant.

16. *countermur'd*] doubly-walled. Cf. Studley's translation of Seneca's *Phaedra (Hippolytus),* Act II: 'countermured castle strong'.

I find the place impregnable, and they
Resist my woes, and give my words no way.

Enter Hangman *with a letter.*

Hangm. O lord sir, God bless you sir, the man sir, Petergade
   sir, he that was so full of merry conceits—   20
Hier. Well, what of him?
Hangm. O lord sir, he went the wrong way, the fellow had a
   fair commission to the contrary. Sir, here is his passport;
   I pray you sir, we have done him wrong.
Hier. I warrant thee, give it me.   25
Hangm. You will stand between the gallows and me?
Hier. Ay, ay.
Hangm. I thank your lord-worship.   *Exit* Hangman.
Hier. And yet, though somewhat nearer me concerns,
   I will, to ease the grief that I sustain,   30
   Take truce with sorrow while I read on this.
   'My lord, I writ as mine extremes requir'd,
   That you would labour my delivery:
   If you neglect, my life is desperate,
   And in my death I shall reveal the troth.   35
   You know, my lord, I slew him for your sake,
   And as confederate with the prince and you,
   Won by rewards and hopeful promises,
   I holp to murder Don Horatio, too.'
   Holp he to murder mine Horatio?   40
   And actors in th' accursed tragedy
   Wast thou, Lorenzo, Balthazar and thou,

---

28. lord-worship] L. worship *1592*.   32. writ] *Manly;* write *1592*.
requir'd] *1592;* require *1623*.   37. as] *This ed.;* was *1592*.

---

32. *writ*] Manly's simple emendation, though it has not been popular,
must be correct.

37. *as confederate*] To read *as* instead of *was* relieves us of having to
choose between intolerable syntax and a sheer mis-statement. It is clear,
from what we know and from what Hieronimo immediately says, that the
last three lines of the letter go together; Pedringano was not a confederate
of the prince in the murder of Serberine. But the last three lines cannot be
read together as they stand in *1592*.

Of whom my son, my son, deserv'd so well ?
What have I heard, what have mine eyes beheld ?
O sacred heavens, may it come to pass   45
That such a monstrous and detested deed,
So closely smother'd, and so long conceal'd,
Shall thus by this be venged or reveal'd ?
Now see I what I durst not then suspect,
That Bel-imperia's letter was not feign'd,   50
Nor feigned she, though falsely they have wrong'd
Both her, myself, Horatio and themselves.
Now may I make compare, 'twixt hers and this,
Of every accident; I ne'er could find
Till now, and now I feelingly perceive,   55
They did what heaven unpunish'd would not leave.
O false Lorenzo, are these thy flattering looks ?
Is this the honour that thou didst my son ?
And Balthazar, bane to thy soul and me,
Was this the ransom he reserv'd thee for ?   60
Woe to the cause of these constrained wars,
Woe to thy baseness and captivity,
Woe to thy birth, thy body and thy soul,
Thy cursed father, and thy conquer'd self!
And bann'd with bitter execrations be   65
The day and place where he did pity thee!
But wherefore waste I mine unfruitful words,
When naught but blood will satisfy my woes ?

54. accident; I] accident, I *1592;* accident. I *Manly;* accident I *Dodsley.*

50–1. *was not feign'd, Nor feigned she*] 'He is relieved of two doubts, whether or not Bel-imperia really wrote the letter, and if so whether or not she was telling the truth' (McIlwraith).

53–6.] 'Now, from the two letters, I can piece together the whole occurrence. I could never satisfy myself before, though now it is brought right home to me, that these men committed the murder—which heaven was bound to bring to light and punish.' Edd. have made nonsense of an admittedly difficult passage by ignoring *1592*'s stop after *accident*; Manly preserves it.

65. *bann'd*] cursed.

I will go plain me to my lord the king,
And cry aloud for justice through the court,   70
Wearing the flints with these my wither'd feet,
And either purchase justice by entreats
Or tire them all with my revenging threats.   *Exit.*

[III. viii]

Enter ISABELLA *and her* Maid.

Isab. So that you say this herb will purge the eye,
And this the head?
Ah, but none of them will purge the heart:
No, there's no medicine left for my disease,
Nor any physic to recure the dead.   *She runs lunatic.*   5
Horatio! O where's Horatio?

Maid. Good madam, affright not thus yourself
With outrage for your son Horatio:
He sleeps in quiet in the Elysian fields.

Isab. Why, did I not give you gowns and goodly things,   10
Bought you a whistle and a whipstalk too,
To be revenged on their villainies?

Maid. Madam, these humours do torment my soul.

Isab. My soul? poor soul, thou talks of things

[III. viii]] Act IV *Hawkins.*   2–3. And ... head? / Ah, ... heart:] *Manly;*
And ... hart: *1592.*   14. talks] *1592;* talk'st *1623.*

---

69. *plain me*] complain (*O.E.D., v.,* 4a).

III. viii.] Hawkins and others begin here a new Act. Although Biesterfeldt
(p. 85) has argued that there is a break in the action at this point, we have no
authority for making the change, or for postulating the loss of one of the
scenes between Andrea and Revenge which conclude the Acts, as *MSR*
(*1602*), p. xxii, and Oliphant suggest (*Shakespeare and his Fellow-Drama-
tists,* 1929). Act III is extremely long, but Schick noted that the 'Senecan'
Thebais and *Octavia* had been divided into four acts, and there is some information about four-act Latin Renaissance plays in L. Bradner, *Studies in
the Renaissance,* IV (1957), 35ff.
      5. *recure*] restore to health.
      8. *outrage*] Cf. II. v. 45.
      11. *whipstalk*] whipstock (dialectal form).
      13. *humours*] extravagant emotions.

Thou know'st not what—my soul hath silver wings,　15
That mounts me up unto the highest heavens,
To heaven, ay, there sits my Horatio,
Back'd with a troop of fiery cherubins,
Dancing about his newly-healed wounds,
Singing sweet hymns and chanting heavenly notes,　20
Rare harmony to greet his innocence,
That died, ay, died, a mirror in our days.
But say, where shall I find the men, the murderers,
That slew Horatio? Whither shall I run
To find them out that murdered my son?　　　*Exeunt.*　25

[III. ix]

BEL-IMPERIA *at a window.*

Bel. What means this outrage that is offer'd me?
　Why am I thus sequester'd from the court?
　No notice? Shall I not know the cause
　Of this my secret and suspicious ills?
　Accursed brother, unkind murderer,　　　　　　5
　Why bends thou thus thy mind to martyr me?
　Hieronimo, why writ I of thy wrongs,
　Or why art thou so slack in thy revenge?
　Andrea, O Andrea, that thou sawest

16. mounts] *1592;* mount *Dodsley.*

III. ix. 4. this] *1592;* these *1633.*　　6. bends] *1592;* bend'st *1623.*

15–22.] There seems to be a connexion between these lines and T. Watson's elegy on Walsingham, *Melibœus* (1590), written in Latin with an English translation. See Appendix D.

16. *mounts*] either a plural in -s, or a confusion, as to the subject, between *soul* and *wings.* Cf. *intercepts* at III. vi. 94.

21. *greet*] acclaim, honour, salute (*not* welcome). An unusual usage. *O.E.D., v.*¹, 3d, 'to honour with a gift', has no example after 1362, but cf. *O.E.D.,* 3e, the Spenserian 'to offer congratulations'.

22. *mirror*] paragon, model of excellence (*O.E.D., sb.*, 5b).

III. ix. 2. *sequester'd*] kept apart in seclusion.

3. *notice*] information.

6. *bends*] applies, directs.

Me for thy friend Horatio handled thus,   10
And him for me thus causeless murdered.
Well, force perforce, I must constrain myself
To patience, and apply me to the time,
Till heaven, as I have hop'd, shall set me free.

Enter CHRISTOPHIL.

Chris. Come, Madam Bel-imperia, this may not be.   *Exeunt.*   15

[III. x]

Enter LORENZO, BALTHAZAR, *and the* Page.

Lor. Boy, talk no further, thus far things go well.
        Thou art assur'd that thou sawest him dead?
Page. Or else, my lord, I live not.
Lor.   That's enough.
        As for his resolution in his end,
        Leave that to him with whom he sojourns now.   5
        Here, take my ring, and give it Christophil,
        And bid him let my sister be enlarg'd,
        And bring her hither straight.   *Exit* Page.
        This that I did was for a policy
        To smooth and keep the murder secret,   10
        Which as a nine-days' wonder being o'er-blown,
        My gentle sister will I now enlarge.
Bal. And time, Lorenzo, for my lord the duke,
        You heard, enquired for her yester-night.
Lor. Why, and, my lord, I hope you heard me say   15
        Sufficient reason why she kept away:

III. x. 2. assur'd] *1592;* assurèd *Schick*[1].   sawest] *1592;* saw'st *Schick*[1].

---

13. *apply me to the time*] conform to the times, submit to things as they
are. The phrase 'obey the time', with the same sense, is frequently found.
14.1. Enter CHRISTOPHIL] presumably 'above', appearing at Bel-
imperia's side. It is unusual to have action on the 'upper-stage' alone, but it
would be rather absurd for Christophil to enter below and retire after saying
his one line; the line is clearly to accompany a leading-off.

III. x. 10. *secret*] Cf. III. iv. 64.

But that's all one. My lord, you love her?
Bal.   Ay.
Lor. Then in your love beware, deal cunningly,
Salve all suspicions, only soothe me up;
And if she hap to stand on terms with us,   20
As for her sweetheart, and concealment so,
Jest with her gently: under feigned jest
Are things conceal'd that else would breed unrest.
But here she comes.

Enter BEL-IMPERIA.

Now, sister—
Bel.   Sister? No,
Thou art no brother, but an enemy;   25
Else wouldst thou not have us'd thy sister so:
First, to affright me with thy weapons drawn,
And with extremes abuse my company:
And then to hurry me, like whirlwind's rage,
Amidst a crew of thy confederates,   30
And clap me up where none might come at me,
Nor I at any to reveal my wrongs.
What madding fury did possess thy wits?
Or wherein is't that I offended thee?
Lor. Advise you better, Bel-imperia,   35
For I have done you no disparagement,
Unless, by more discretion than deserv'd,
I sought to save your honour and mine own.

24–5. But ... No, / Thou ... enemy;] *Manly;* But ... comes. / Now Sister. / Sister ... enemy. *1592.*   24. Now] *Lor.* Now *1592.*

19.] 'Smooth over all suspicions and above all back me up in what I say'. *salve* suggests a healing ointment. *soothe,* see *O.E.D.,* 3.
20. *stand on terms*] insist on conditions, make difficulties.
21.] 'Lorenzo's jaunty and laconic allusion to Horatio's murder and Bel-imperia's secret detention is highly characteristic' (Boas).
36–8.] 'If I have humiliated you, it was only in the course of my attempt (which showed more consideration than you deserved) to save your honour and my own.' For *unless* = unless it were that, cf. I. iv. 176.
disparagement] a lowering of dignity, humiliation (*O.E.D., disparage,* 2).

Bel. Mine honour! why Lorenzo, wherein is't
    That I neglect my reputation so,   40
    As you, or any, need to rescue it?
Lor. His highness and my father were resolv'd
    To come confer with old Hieronimo,
    Concerning certain matters of estate
    That by the viceroy was determined.   45
Bel. And wherein was mine honour touch'd in that?
Bal. Have patience, Bel-imperia; hear the rest.
Lor. Me next in sight as messenger they sent,
    To give him notice that they were so nigh:
    Now when I came, consorted with the prince,   50
    And unexpected in an arbour there
    Found Bel-imperia with Horatio—
Bel. How then?
Lor. Why then, remembering that old disgrace
    Which you for Don Andrea had endur'd,   55
    And now were likely longer to sustain,
    By being found so meanly accompanied,
    Thought rather, for I knew no readier mean,
    To thrust Horatio forth my father's way.
Bal. And carry you obscurely somewhere else,   60
    Lest that his highness should have found you there.
Bel. Even so, my lord? And you are witness
    That this is true which he entreateth of?
    You, gentle brother, forged this for my sake,
    And you, my lord, were made his instrument: 65

44–5.] 'Concerning certain matters about possessions which the viceroy
had given up'. Lorenzo would make the King come to discuss law with
Hieronimo; *estate* may therefore be taken as the antecedent of *that*, explaining the singular *was*. For *determine*, see *O.E.D.*, I, 'to conclude, terminate',
and *determination*, Ib, 'the cessation of an estate or interest of any kind',
quoting an act of Henry VII, 'After the dettermynacions of the states ... by
deth ... or any other wise'.

57. *meanly accompanied*] Horatio's social inferiority again.

59. *forth*] out of.

64.] The uncontracted *forged* is kept, although the line is thus given a
hypermetrical syllable, because Bel-imperia's sardonic tone demands that
the final stress fall on *my*, not *sake*.

A work of worth, worthy the noting too!
But what's the cause that you conceal'd me since?

Lor. Your melancholy, sister, since the news
    Of your first favourite Don Andrea's death,
    My father's old wrath hath exasperate.   70

Bal. And better was't for you, being in disgrace,
    To absent yourself and give his fury place.

Bel. But why had I no notice of his ire?

Lor. That were to add more fuel to your fire,
    Who burnt like Aetna for Andrea's loss.   75

Bel. Hath not my father then enquir'd for me?

Lor. Sister, he hath, and thus excus'd I thee.

                      He whispereth in her ear.
    But Bel-imperia, see the gentle prince,
    Look on thy love, behold young Balthazar,
    Whose passions by thy presence are increas'd,   80
    And in whose melancholy thou mayst see
    Thy hate, his love; thy flight, his following thee.

Bel. Brother, you are become an orator,
    I know not, I, by what experience,
    Too politic for me, past all compare,   85
    Since last I saw you; but content yourself,
    The prince is meditating higher things.

Bal. 'Tis of thy beauty then, that conquers kings:
    Of those thy tresses, Ariadne's twines,

75. for] *1592;* and *MSR (1592).*

70.] See III. iv. 31; cf. *Cornelia,* III. iii. 128: 'His wrath against you 'twill exasperate,' and *Edward II*, l. 478, 'But that will more exasperate his wrath.' The phrase is also found in the old *King Leir.*

72. *give his fury place*] Though the meaning is not obscure, this is an unusual figurative use of *give place,* and there is no parallel in *O.E.D.* (cf. *place, sb.,* 23).

75. *for*] *M.S.R.*'s *and* appears to be an error.

89–90.] He means that her hairs are the bonds which have made him a prisoner (*twines* = cords or threads, *surpris'd* = captured). The source of the couplet is Sonnet x of Du Bellay's *L'Olive:* 'Ces cheveux d'or sont les liens, Madame, / Dont fut premier ma liberté surprise.' Daniel, in translating the same sonnet (*Delia,* XIV), uses almost the same words as Kyd in the second line: 'Those amber locks, are those same nets my deere, / Where-

       Wherewith my liberty thou hast surpris'd: 90
       Of that thine ivory front, my sorrow's map,
       Wherein I see no haven to rest my hope.
Bel. To love, and fear, and both at once, my lord,
       In my conceit, are things of more import
       Than women's wits are to be busied with.   95
Bal. 'Tis I that love.
Bel.   Whom?
Bal.   Bel-imperia.
Bel. But I that fear.
Bal.   Whom?
Bel.   Bel-imperia.
Lor. Fear yourself?
Bel.   Ay, brother.
Lor.   How?
Bel.   As those
       That what they love are loath and fear to lose.
Bal. Then, fair, let Balthazar your keeper be.   100
Bel. No, Balthazar doth fear as well as we:
       Et tremulo metui pavidum junxere timorem,
           Et vanum stolidae proditionis opus.   *Exit.*
Lor. Nay, and you argue things so cunningly,
       We'll go continue this discourse at court.   105
Bal. Led by the loadstar of her heavenly looks,

98–9. . . . As those / That . . . lose.] *Manly;* As those, . . . loose. *1592.*
101. doth fear] *doth feare 1592.*   102. Et] *Hawkins; Est 1592.*   103. Et]
1592; Est Manly, Schick.

---

with my libertie thou didst surprize.' This was published in 1591, but it is
unlikely that Kyd borrowed from Daniel, since his *twines* is much nearer to
liens than Daniel's *nets.* Why Kyd inserted Ariadne is a puzzle; Ariadne
used a thread to guide Theseus through the Labyrinth, but she did not tie
him up with it. Possibly Kyd confused Ariadne with Arachne the weaver
who turned into a spider, and who therefore has more to do with enmeshing
people; compare Shakespeare's uncertainty over 'Ariachne' in *Troilus and
Cressida*, v. ii. 152.
    91. *front*] forehead.
    102–3.] 'Another piece of classical patchwork, of which the meaning is
obscure' (Boas). 'They joined dismayed dread to quaking fear, a futile deed
of sottish betrayal.'

Wends poor oppressed Balthazar,
As o'er the mountains walks the wanderer,
Incertain to effect his pilgrimage.   *Exeunt.*

[III. xi]

    Enter two Portingales, *and* HIERONIMO *meets them.*

1.   By your leave, sir.
Hier. Good leave have you, nay, I pray you go,   [*Third Addition;*
    For I'll leave you, if you can leave me, so.   *see p.* 125]
2.   Pray you, which is the next way to my lord the duke's ?
Hier. The next way from me.
1.   To his house, we mean.   5
Hier. Oh, hard by, 'tis yon house that you see.
2.   You could not tell us if his son were there ?
Hier. Who, my lord Lorenzo ?
1.   Ay, sir.
      He goeth in at one door and comes out at another.
Hier.   Oh, forbear,
    For other talk for us far fitter were.
    But if you be importunate to know   10
    The way to him, and where to find him out,
    Then list to me, and I'll resolve your doubt.
    There is a path upon your left-hand side,
    That leadeth from a guilty conscience
    Unto a forest of distrust and fear,   15
    A darksome place and dangerous to pass:
    There shall you meet with melancholy thoughts,

III. xi. 3. me, so] *Schick²;* me so *1592.*   8–9. . . . . Oh, forbear, / For . . .
were.] *Hazlitt;* Oh forbeare . . . were. *1592.*

---

109. *Incertain to effect*] doubtful that he will achieve.

   III. xi. 4. *next*] nearest.
   13.] Cf. I. i. 63: the left-hand path led to the deepest hell. The resemblance noted by Sarrazin between the passage which follows and Spenser's
Cave of Despair (*F.Q.*, I, ix, 33 and 34) is, as Boas says, probably only
accidental.

Whose baleful humours if you but uphold,
It will conduct you to despair and death:
Whose rocky cliffs when you have once beheld,   20
Within a hugy dale of lasting night,
That, kindled with the world's iniquities,
Doth cast up filthy and detested fumes—
Not far from thence, where murderers have built
A habitation for their cursed souls,   25
There, in a brazen cauldron fix'd by Jove
In his fell wrath upon a sulphur flame,
Yourselves shall find Lorenzo bathing him
In boiling lead and blood of innocents.

1.   Ha, ha, ha!

Hier.   Ha, ha, ha!   30
          Why, ha, ha, ha! Farewell, good, ha, ha, ha!   *Exit.*

2.   Doubtless this man is passing lunatic,
          Or imperfection of his age doth make him dote.
          Come, let's away to seek my lord the duke.   *[Exeunt.]*

[III. xii]

Enter HIERONIMO *with a poniard in one hand, and
a rope in the other.*

Hier. Now sir, perhaps I come and see the king,

18. uphold] *1592;* behold *1618.*   22. kindled] *1594;* kind'ed [*broken* l ?]
1592.   30–1. *Hier.* . . . good, ha, ha, ha!] Boas; *one line 1592.*   34.
[*Exeunt.*]] *1602; not in 1592.*

---

18. *uphold*] sustain, continue in. This sense (*O.E.D.*, 2) is more likely
than anything connected with *O.E.D.*, 3c, to nourish.
     21. *hugy*] huge.

     III. xii. 0.1.] Cf. *Looking Glass for London and England,* 'Enter the Usurer,
with a halter in one hand, a dagger in the other.' Boas remarks, 'Hieronimo
appears with the stock "properties" of a would-be suicide', and compares
Spenser, *F.Q.*, I, ix, 29 and Skelton's *Magnyfycence,* ll. 2312ff.
     poniard] dagger.
     1–5.] Hieronimo has acuteness enough to expect obstacles, though he
does not seem to confine the enmity to Lorenzo and Balthazar.
     1–24.] Hieronimo's speech begins in quatrains and continues in a loose
rhyme-scheme to the end.

The king sees me, and fain would hear my suit:
Why, is not this a strange and seld-seen thing,
That standers-by with toys should strike me mute?
Go to, I see their shifts, and say no more.   5
Hieronimo, 'tis time for thee to trudge:
Down by the dale that flows with purple gore,
Standeth a fiery tower: there sits a judge
Upon a seat of steel and molten brass,
And 'twixt his teeth he holds a firebrand,   10
That leads unto the lake where hell doth stand.
Away, Hieronimo, to him be gone:
He'll do thee justice for Horatio's death.
Turn down this path, thou shalt be with him straight,
Or this, and then thou need'st not take thy breath: 15
This way, or that way? Soft and fair, not so:
For if I hang or kill myself, let's know
Who will revenge Horatio's murder then?
No, no! fie, no! pardon me, I'll none of that:
                    He flings away the dagger and halter.
This way I'll take, and this way comes the king,   20
                    He takes them up again.
And here I'll have a fling at him, that's flat:
And, Balthazar, I'll be with thee to bring,
And thee, Lorenzo! Here's the king, nay, stay,

---

3. *seld*] seldom.

4. *toys*] The word usually denotes the frivolous and petty; here, perhaps, vain triflings, nonsense, or possibly idle minds.

6. *trudge*] make off, get moving (O.E.D., *v*.¹, 1c); cf. *Comedy of Errors*, III. ii. 158: ' 'Tis time, I think, to trudge, pack and be gone.' That the word does not imply slowness is seen from *Alphonsus of Aragon*, Act II, 'I saw you trudging in such posting haste.'

14–15. *this path . . . Or this*] Hieronimo brandishes the poniard and then the rope; the same indecision is in Skelton's *Magnyfycence* (see note to 0.1); Massinger echoes this passage in *Believe as You List*, ll. 1959–64.

17–18.] the same ideas as in the Latin dirge, II. v. 78–80 (Schick).

22. *I'll be with thee to bring*] a common enough phrase, capable of various meanings, some bawdy. Here, 'I'll get the upper hand of you' or 'I'll be even with you' or any phrase which will convey forcible retaliation and conquest. Schmidt (s.v. *bring*) has a useful note; see also Deighton's note to *Troilus and Cressida*, I. ii. 304 (Arden ed.) for parallels.

And here, ay here, there goes the hare away.

Enter KING, AMBASSADOR, CASTILE *and* LORENZO.

King. Now show, Ambassador, what our viceroy saith: 25
    Hath he receiv'd the articles we sent?
Hier. Justice, O justice to Hieronimo!
Lor. Back! seest thou not the king is busy?
Hier. Oh, is he so?
King. Who is he that interrupts our business?   30
Hier. Not I. Hieronimo, beware: go by, go by.
Amb. Renowned king, he hath receiv'd and read
    Thy kingly proffers, and thy promis'd league,
    And, as a man extremely overjoy'd
    To hear his son so princely entertain'd,   35
    Whose death he had so solemnly bewail'd,
    This, for thy further satisfaction
    And kingly love, he kindly lets thee know:
    First, for the marriage of his princely son
    With Bel-imperia, thy beloved niece,   40
    The news are more delightful to his soul,
    Than myrrh or incense to the offended heavens.
    In person therefore will he come himself,
    To see the marriage rites solemnized,
    And, in the presence of the court of Spain,   45
    To knit a sure, inexplicable band
    Of kingly love, and everlasting league,
    Betwixt the crowns of Spain and Portingale.

46. inexplicable] *1594;* inexecrable *1592;* inextricable *Hawkins.*

---

24. *there goes the hare away*] Tilley H157. A saying with several uses, often (as here) with reference to losing something one has tried to achieve or hold. Not, I think, as Boas: 'Here the matter ends' or as Schick: 'There is the game I want to hunt.' Hieronimo is afraid of losing the King.

31. *go by, go by*] literally, go aside; 'be careful, don't run your head into trouble.' 'Go by, Jeronimo' became a stock Elizabethan phrase. See Boas' note for references to this passage in Shakespeare, Dekker, Middleton, Fletcher, etc.

46. *inexplicable*] that cannot be untied, indissoluble. See Textual Introduction, pp. xli–xlii, for the textual problems involved in this reading.

There will he give his crown to Balthazar,

And make a queen of Bel-imperia.   50

King. Brother, how like you this our viceroy's love ?

Cast. No doubt, my lord, it is an argument

Of honourable care to keep his friend,

And wondrous zeal to Balthazar his son:

Nor am I least indebted to his grace,   55

That bends his liking to my daughter thus.

Amb. Now last, dread lord, here hath his highness sent

(Although he send not that his son return)

His ransom due to Don Horatio.

Hier. Horatio ? who calls Horatio ?   60

King. And well remember'd, thank his majesty.

Here, see it given to Horatio.

Hier. Justice, O justice, justice, gentle king!

King. Who is that ? Hieronimo ?

Hier. Justice, O justice! O my son, my son,   65

My son, whom naught can ransom or redeem!

Lor. Hieronimo, you are not well-advis'd.

Hier. Away Lorenzo, hinder me no more,

For thou hast made me bankrupt of my bliss.

Give me my son! You shall not ransom him.   70

Away! I'll rip the bowels of the earth,

                                        He diggeth with his dagger.

And ferry over to th'Elysian plains,

And bring my son to show his deadly wounds.

Stand from about me!

I'll make a pickaxe of my poniard,   75

And here surrender up my marshalship:

74–5. Stand . . . me! / I'll . . . poniard,] *Schick;* Stand . . . poniard, *1592.*

61–2.] The King's ignorance is extraordinary. See Introduction, p. lviii.

71.] Boas compares *Jew of Malta* (?1590), l. 147, 'Ripping the bowels of the earth for them [precious stones]'. The parallel is striking but I do not think the evidence suggests that Marlowe 'probably imitated Kyd'. Marlowe's sequence of ideas is more poetically appropriate and suggests that he was the originator of the phrase. But since it could be argued that the crudity in Kyd is appropriate to Hieronimo, the question of precedence must remain open.

      For I'll go marshal up the fiends in hell,
      To be avenged on you all for this.
King. What means this outrage?
      Will none of you restrain his fury?   80
Hier. Nay, soft and fair: you shall not need to strive,
      Needs must he go that the devils drive.   *Exit.*
King. What accident hath happ'd Hieronimo?
      I have not seen him to demean him so.
Lor. My gracious lord, he is with extreme pride,   85
      Conceiv'd of young Horatio his son,
      And covetous of having to himself
      The ransom of the young prince Balthazar,
      Distract, and in a manner lunatic.
King. Believe me, nephew, we are sorry for't: 90
      This is the love that fathers bear their sons:
      But gentle brother, go give to him this gold,
      The prince's ransom: let him have his due,
      For what he hath Horatio shall not want:
      Haply Hieronimo hath need thereof.   95
Lor. But if he be thus helplessly distract,
      'Tis requisite his office be resign'd,
      And given to one of more discretion.
King. We shall increase his melancholy so.
      'Tis best that we see further in it first: 100
      Till when, ourself will not exempt the place.

79–80. What ... outrage? / Will ... fury?] *Hawkins;* What ... fury? *1592*.
82. Needs] *1592;* For needs *Schick.*   the] *1592;* all the *Hazlitt.*   101.
not exempt] *This ed.;* exempt *1592;* execute *conj. Collier;* hold exempt
Hazlitt; exempt him *Boas.*

---

    79. *outrage*] extravagant outburst.
    82.] Tilley D278.
    83. *happ'd Hieronimo*] happened to Hieronimo. See *O.E.D., hap, v.*[1], 1b
for this use of indirect object.
    84. *demean him*] conduct himself, behave.
    101.] It is very hard to make any sense out of *1592* ('ourself will exempt
the place'), and the line is a syllable short. In trying to produce the correct
reformation, we must be led by the sense of the passage, which is that the
King is anxious not to make a change in the Marshalship until he has made
further enquiries, for fear of upsetting Hieronimo. *hold exempt* (keep

And brother, now bring in the ambassador,
That he may be a witness of the match
'Twixt Balthazar and Bel-imperia,
And that we may prefix a certain time,   105
Wherein the marriage shall be solemniz'd,
That we may have thy lord the viceroy here.

Amb. Therein your highness highly shall content
His majesty, that longs to hear from hence.

King. On then, and hear you, lord ambassador.   *Exeunt.* 110

[*Fourth Addition; see p.* 127]

[III. xiii]

Enter HIERONIMO *with a book in his hand.*

Hier. Vindicta mihi !

Ay, heaven will be reveng'd of every ill,
Nor will they suffer murder unrepaid:
Then stay, Hieronimo, attend their will,
For mortal men may not appoint their time.   5
Per scelus semper tutum est sceleribus iter.

III. xiii. 1. *Hier.*] *not in 1592.*

---

vacant) and *exempt him* (excuse him) are therefore dubious alternatives, apart from the strain on the word *exempt*, because they imply some kind of suspension of the Knight Marshal. Collier's *execute* is an inspired emendation, and gives some justification to the emphatic *ourself*, but it still implies suspension, and it is scarcely credible that the King would so demean himself. In suggesting that a *not* has fallen out before *exempt*, we are still left with an intransigent *exempt*. O.E.D., 3 gives 'to debar, exclude *from* the enjoyment or participation in something'; an elliptical construction must be supposed here, 'I will not debar him from the position'.

III. xiii. 1. *Vindicta mihi !*] The book in Hieronimo's hand is obviously a Seneca, from the excerpts read later in the speech, but Boas is surely wrong in suggesting that here Hieronimo is reading from *Octavia, Et hoc sat est ? . . . haec vindicta debetur mihi ?* ('And is this enough ? . . . Is this the vengeance due to me ?'). This sense would be fitting for Hieronimo's mood at this point, but the succeeding words make it obvious that Schick and Bowers are right (cf. *M.L.N.*, liii (1938), 590) in saying that Hieronimo quotes first the biblical 'Vengeance is mine, I will repay, saith the Lord.'

6.] Cf. Seneca, *Agamemnon*, l. 115: *per scelera semper sceleribus tutum est iter* ('The safe way for crime is always through crime').

Strike, and strike home, where wrong is offer'd thee,
For evils unto ills conductors be,
And death's the worst of resolution:
For he that thinks with patience to contend   10
To quiet life, his life shall easily end.
Fata si miseros juvant, habes salutem;
Fata si vitam negant, habes sepulchrum.
If destiny thy miseries do ease,
Then hast thou health, and happy shalt thou be: 15
If destiny deny thee life, Hieronimo,
Yet shalt thou be assured of a tomb:
If neither, yet let this thy comfort be,
Heaven covereth him that hath no burial.
And to conclude, I will revenge his death!   20
But how? not as the vulgar wits of men,
With open, but inevitable ills,
As by a secret, yet a certain mean,
Which under kindship will be cloaked best.
Wise men will take their opportunity,   25
Closely and safely fitting things to time:
But in extremes advantage hath no time,
And therefore all times fit not for revenge.
Thus therefore will I rest me in unrest,
Dissembling quiet in unquietness,   30

12–13.] From Seneca's *Troades*, ll. 510–12; Hieronimo interprets in the
succeeding lines.

19.] 'This is Lucan's *Caelo tegitur qui non habet urnam* (*Pharsalia*, vii,
818)' (Schick).

22.] 'The sense is not satisfactory. We should expect a contrast between
the open and therefore by no means "inevitable ills" employed by vulgar
wits, and the secret yet certain method which Hieronimo contemplates'
(Boas). Would it strain the construction too much to take *inevitable* as in
fact a contrast to *open*? Cf. Bowers, pp. 78–9, for a discussion of the passage.

23. *mean*] measure, course of action.

24. *kindship*] kindness.

27–8.] Hieronimo appears to argue that it is only in desperate situations
(*extremes*) that one does not wait for a favourable opportunity (*advantage*);
revenge is a serious and deliberate retaliation and can only be exacted at the
right moment.

Not seeming that I know their villainies,
That my simplicity may make them think
That ignorantly I will let all slip:
For ignorance, I wot, and well they know,
Remedium malorum iners est.   35
Nor aught avails it me to menace them,
Who, as a wintry storm upon a plain,
Will bear me down with their nobility.
No, no, Hieronimo, thou must enjoin
Thine eyes to observation, and thy tongue   40
To milder speeches than thy spirit affords,
Thy heart to patience, and thy hands to rest,
Thy cap to courtesy, and thy knee to bow,
Till to revenge thou know, when, where, and how.

A noise within.

How now, what noise? what coil is that you keep?   45

Enter a Servant.

Ser. Here are a sort of poor petitioners,
    That are importunate, and it shall please you sir,
    That you should plead their cases to the king.
Hier. That I should plead their several actions?
    Why, let them enter, and let me see them.   50

Enter three Citizens *and an* Old Man.

1. So I tell you this, for learning and for law,
    There's not any advocate in Spain
    That can prevail, or will take half the pain
    That he will, in pursuit of equity.
Hier. Come near, you men that thus importune me.   55
    [*Aside.*] Now must I bear a face of gravity,

44.1. *A noise within*] *1602; follows l. 45 in 1592.*   52. There's] Theres
1592; There is *Hawkins.*

35.] 'Is an idle remedy for ills'; from Seneca, *Oedipus,* l. 515: *Iners
malorum remedium ignorantia est* (Sarrazin, *Anglia,* xiii, 127).
    45. *what . . . keep*] 'what is all this fuss about?'
    46. *sort*] group, gathering.

  For thus I us'd, before my marshalship,
  To plead in causes as corregidor.—
  Come on sirs, what's the matter ?

2.   Sir, an action.

Hier. Of battery ?

1.   Mine of debt.

Hier.   Give place.   60

2. No sir, mine is an action of the case.

3. Mine an *ejectione firmae* by a lease.

Hier. Content you sirs, are you determined
  That I should plead your several actions ?

1. Ay sir, and here's my declaration.   65

2. And here is my band.

3.   And here is my lease.

           They give him papers.

Hier. But wherefore stands yon silly man so mute,
  With mournful eyes and hands to heaven uprear'd ?
  Come hither father, let me know thy cause.

Senex. O worthy sir, my cause but slightly known 70
  May move the hearts of warlike Myrmidons
  And melt the Corsic rocks with ruthful tears.

Hier. Say father, tell me what's thy suit ?

---

62. *firmae*] *Fleischer;* firma *1592.* 66. here is my band] *1592;* here's ~
Hazlitt. 66.1. *papers.*] *1594;* papers: *1592* [*broken* s].

---

 58. *corregidor*] properly, the chief magistrate of a Spanish town, but the
title was used with some latitude by Elizabethan writers and here obviously
means 'advocate'. Cf. Webster, *Devil's Law Case,* II. i. 13.

 61. *action of the case*] An action not within the limited jurisdiction of the
Common Pleas needed a special writ to cover it. These special writs were
known as 'actions of trespass on the case' or 'actions on the case'. See
Shakespeare's England, I, 390–1, but the best account is in Jacob's *Law Dict.*
Cf. Webster, *Cure for a Cuckold,* IV. i. 62–70.

 62. ejectione firmae] a writ to eject a tenant from his holding before the
expiration of his lease; see Jacob's *Law Dict.* The phrase was common
enough to be used figuratively and facetiously by Nashe (III, 156).

 66. *band*] bond.

 67. *silly*] poor, to be pitied.

 71.] Cf. *Aeneid,* II, 6–8 (W. P. Mustard).

 72. *Corsic rocks*] rocks of Corsica. Seneca's *Corsici rupes*; *Octavia,* 382
(Schick).

Senex. No sir, could my woes
    Give way unto my most distressful words,   75
    Then should I not in paper, as you see,
    With ink bewray what blood began in me.
Hier. What's here? 'The humble supplication
    Of Don Bazulto for his murder'd son.'
Senex. Ay sir.
Hier.   No sir, it was my murder'd son,   80
    O my son, my son, O my son Horatio!
    But mine, or thine, Bazulto, be content.
    Here, take my handkercher and wipe thine eyes,
    Whiles wretched I in thy mishaps may see
    The lively portrait of my dying self.   85
                He draweth out a bloody napkin.
    O no, not this: Horatio, this was thine,
    And when I dy'd it in thy dearest blood,
    This was a token 'twixt thy soul and me
    That of thy death revenged I should be.
    But here, take this, and this—what, my purse?—   90
    Ay this and that, and all of them are thine,
    For all as one are our extremities.
1. O see the kindness of Hieronimo!
2. This gentleness shows him a gentleman.
Hier. See, see, O see thy shame, Hieronimo,   95
    See here a loving father to his son!
    Behold the sorrows and the sad laments
    That he delivereth for his son's decease!
    If love's effects so strives in lesser things,
    If love enforce such moods in meaner wits,   100
    If love express such power in poor estates:
    Hieronimo, whenas a raging sea,

80–1. . . . my murder'd son, / O my son . . . Horatio!] *Manly;* . . . my murdred sonne, oh my sonne. / My sonne . . . *Horatio. 1592.*   90. what, my purse?] *Dodsley;* what my purse? *1592; Senex.* What, thy purse? *Hazlitt.*   102. whenas] conj. *Boas;* when as *1592;* as when conj. *Kittredge.*

102–7.] A very clumsy passage, however reformed; Hawkins' reading (*o'erturneth*) gives the best sense. *whenas* = when. I suppose we are to

Toss'd with the wind and tide, o'erturneth then
The upper billows, course of waves to keep,
Whilst lesser waters labour in the deep: 105
Then sham'st thou not, Hieronimo, to neglect
The sweet revenge of thy Horatio?
Though on this earth justice will not be found,
I'll down to hell, and in this passion
Knock at the dismal gates of Pluto's court,   110
Getting by force, as once Alcides did,
A troop of Furies and tormenting hags
To torture Don Lorenzo and the rest.
Yet lest the triple-headed porter should
Deny my passage to the slimy strond,   115
The Thracian poet thou shalt counterfeit:
Come on, old father, be my Orpheus,
And if thou canst no notes upon the harp,
Then sound the burden of thy sore heart's grief,
Till we do gain that Proserpine may grant   120
Revenge on them that murdered my son:
Then will I rent and tear them thus and thus,
Shivering their limbs in pieces with my teeth.

                                        Tear the papers.

1.   O sir, my declaration!   *Exit* HIERONIMO *and they after.*
2.   Save my bond!   125

                Enter HIERONIMO.

Save my bond!

---

103. o'erturneth then] *Hawkins;* ore turnest then *1592;* ore-turned then
1618; o'erturneth thee *conj. Gollancz.*   121. murdered] murdred *1592.*

---

understand that in a storm it is the surface waters which are under real
stress and which keep the necessary *course of waves,* and that Hieronimo
considers himself like the labouring lesser waters compared with the much-
moved Bazulto. Since the old man is a *meaner wit,* Hieronimo is ashamed of
his lethargy. In spite of the tortuousness of the language, there is a strong
resemblance to Hamlet's feelings of guilt after the First Player's exhibition
of grief.

   111. *Alcides*] Hercules: the reference is to the last of the Labours.
   118. *canst*] knowest.
   122. *rent*] rend.

3.   Alas, my lease! it cost me ten pound,
       And you, my lord, have torn the same.
Hier. That cannot be, I gave it never a wound,
       Shew me one drop of blood fall from the same: 130
       How is it possible I should slay it then?
       Tush, no; run after, catch me if you can.

                              Exeunt all but the Old Man.
                    BAZULTO *remains till* HIERONIMO *enters again,*
                              who, staring him in the face, speaks.
Hier. And art thou come, Horatio, from the depth,
       To ask for justice in this upper earth?
       To tell thy father thou art unreveng'd,   135
       To wring more tears from Isabella's eyes,
       Whose lights are dimm'd with over-long laments?
       Go back my son, complain to Aeacus,
       For here's no justice: gentle boy be gone,
       For justice is exiled from the earth: 140
       Hieronimo will bear thee company.
       Thy mother cries on righteous Rhadamanth
       For just revenge against the murderers.
Senex. Alas my lord, whence springs this troubled speech?
Hier. But let me look on my Horatio: 145
       Sweet boy, how art thou chang'd in death's black shade!
       Had Proserpine no pity on thy youth?
       But suffer'd thy fair crimson-colour'd spring
       With wither'd winter to be blasted thus?
       Horatio, thou art older than thy father: 150
       Ah ruthless fate, that favour thus transforms!
Senex. Ah my good lord, I am not your young son.
Hier. What, not my son? thou, then, a fury art,
       Sent from the empty kingdom of black night
       To summon me to make appearance   155

151. fate] *Dodsley;* Father *1592.*

---

   151. *favour*] countenance, looks. *1592*'s *Father*, which Dodsley emended
to *fate*, is an obvious piece of dittography; Manly and Schick[2] retain
father, but Schick's explanation of *that favour thus transforms!* as an absolute construction is far-fetched.

        Before grim Minos and just Rhadamanth,
        To plague Hieronimo that is remiss
        And seeks not vengeance for Horatio's death.
Senex. I am a grieved man, and not a ghost,
        That came for justice for my murder'd son.   160
Hier. Ay, now I know thee, now thou nam'st thy son,
        Thou art the lively image of my grief:
        Within thy face, my sorrows I may see.
        Thy eyes are gumm'd with tears, thy cheeks are wan,
        Thy forehead troubled, and thy mutt'ring lips   165
        Murmur sad words abruptly broken off,
        By force of windy sighs thy spirit breathes,
        And all this sorrow riseth for thy son:
        And selfsame sorrow feel I for my son.
        Come in old man, thou shalt to Isabel,   170
        Lean on my arm: I thee, thou me shalt stay,
        And thou, and I, and she, will sing a song,
        Three parts in one, but all of discords fram'd—
        Talk not of cords, but let us now be gone,
        For with a cord Horatio was slain.   *Exeunt.* 175

[III. xiv]

     Enter KING of Spain, *the* DUKE, VICEROY, *and*
    LORENZO, BALTHAZAR, DON PEDRO, *and* BEL-IMPERIA.

King. Go brother, it is the Duke of Castile's cause,
        Salute the viceroy in our name.
Cast.   I go.
Vice. Go forth, Don Pedro, for thy nephew's sake,
        And greet the Duke of Castile.

161. thy] *1623;* my *1592.*   166. off,] *1592;* off *Manly.*

III. xiv. 1–2. Go . . . cause, / Salute . . . I go.] *1610; as prose in 1592.*   1. it
is] *1592;* tis *1610.*

  166–7.] Most edd. follow Boas and Manly in carrying the sense on
through the two lines, *thy spirit breathes* becoming a relative clause. But the
original punctuation, followed here, gives as good sense.

Pedro.　　　　　　　　　　It shall be so.

King. And now to meet these Portuguese,　　　　　　5
　　　　For as we now are, so sometimes were these,
　　　　Kings and commanders of the western Indies.
　　　　Welcome, brave viceroy, to the court of Spain,
　　　　And welcome, all his honourable train:
　　　　'Tis not unknown to us, for why you come,　　　10
　　　　Or have so kingly cross'd the seas:
　　　　Sufficeth it, in this we note the troth
　　　　And more than common love you lend to us.
　　　　So is it that mine honourable niece
　　　　(For it beseems us now that it be known)　　　15
　　　　Already is betroth'd to Balthazar:
　　　　And by appointment and our condescent
　　　　To-morrow are they to be married.
　　　　To this intent we entertain thyself,
　　　　Thy followers, their pleasure and our peace:　　20
　　　　Speak, men of Portingale, shall it be so?
　　　　If ay, say so: if not, say flatly no.

Vice. Renowned king, I come not as thou think'st,
　　　　With doubtful followers, unresolved men,
　　　　But such as have upon thine articles　　　25
　　　　Confirm'd thy motion and contented me.
　　　　Know sovereign, I come to solemnize
　　　　The marriage of thy beloved niece,
　　　　Fair Bel-imperia, with my Balthazar—
　　　　With thee, my son, whom sith I live to see,　　30
　　　　Here take my crown, I give it her and thee,
　　　　And let me live a solitary life,
　　　　In ceaseless prayers,

11. seas] *1592;* raging seas *Hazlitt.*

6–7.] Kyd is far from accurate; Portuguese imperialism had been directed towards India, Africa, and the East. Either Kyd was thinking of colonies in Brazil, or he simply confused the East and West Indies.

11.] an amusing howler in the light of the General's better knowledge at I. ii. 22–3.

17. *condescent*] assent.

L

To think how strangely heaven hath thee preserv'd.

King. See brother, see, how nature strives in him!   35
　　Come worthy viceroy, and accompany
　　Thy friend with thine extremities:
　　A place more private fits this princely mood.

Vice. Or here or where your highness thinks it good.

Exeunt all but CASTILE *and* LORENZO.

Cast. Nay stay, Lorenzo, let me talk with you.   40
　　Seest thou this entertainment of these kings?

Lor. I do my lord, and joy to see the same.

Cast. And knowest thou why this meeting is?

Lor. For her, my lord, whom Balthazar doth love,
　　And to confirm their promis'd marriage.   45

Cast. She is thy sister?

Lor.   Who, Bel-imperia?
　　Ay, my gracious lord, and this is the day
　　That I have long'd so happily to see.

Cast. Thou wouldst be loath that any fault of thine
　　Should intercept her in her happiness.   50

Lor. Heavens will not let Lorenzo err so much.

Cast. Why then Lorenzo, listen to my words:
　　It is suspected and reported too,
　　That thou, Lorenzo, wrong'st Hieronimo,
　　And in his suits towards his majesty   55
　　Still keep'st him back, and seeks to cross his suit.

Lor. That I, my lord—?

Cast. I tell thee son, myself have heard it said,
　　When to my sorrow I have been asham'd
　　To answer for thee, though thou art my son: 60
　　Lorenzo, know'st thou not the common love
　　And kindness that Hieronimo hath won
　　By his deserts within the court of Spain?

37. with thine] *1592;* to strive with thine *Manly.* 46–8. She . . . Bel-
imperia? / Ay . . . day / That . . . see.] She . . . Sister? / Who . . . Lord, /
And . . . see. *1592.*

37. *extremities*] intense emotions (*O.E.D.,* 4).
50. *intercept*] interrupt, break in upon.

Or seest thou not the king my brother's care
In his behalf, and to procure his health?   65
Lorenzo, shouldst thou thwart his passions,
And he exclaim against thee to the king,
What honour were't in this assembly,
Or what a scandal were't among the kings
To hear Hieronimo exclaim on thee?   70
Tell me, and look thou tell me truly too,
Whence grows the ground of this report in court?
Lor. My lord, it lies not in Lorenzo's power
To stop the vulgar, liberal of their tongues:
A small advantage makes a water-breach,   75
And no man lives that long contenteth all.
Cast. Myself have seen thee busy to keep back
Him and his supplications from the king.
Lor. Yourself, my lord, hath seen his passions,
That ill-beseem'd the presence of a king,   80
And for I pitied him in his distress,
I held him thence with kind and courteous words,
As free from malice to Hieronimo
As to my soul, my lord.
Cast. Hieronimo, my son, mistakes thee then.   85
Lor. My gracious father, believe me so he doth.
But what's a silly man, distract in mind,
To think upon the murder of his son?
Alas, how easy is it for him to err!

74. vulgar, liberal] *Dodsley;* vulgar liberall *1592.*   79. hath] *1592;* have *1602.*

---

74. *liberal*] licentious.
75. *advantage*] There is no exact parallel in *O.E.D.*, but cf. *advantage,* 4, 'a favourable occasion, an opportunity'. The image of waters flooding through a small break is not uncommon; cf. Ralegh, *Ocean To Cynthia,* ll. 221ff., and Spenser, *F.Q.*, VI, i, 21.
81. *And for*] Most modern edd. follow Boas in putting a comma between *and* and *for*, making a parenthesis of *for I pitied him in his distress*, and losing the force of the (now obsolete) meaning of *for* = 'because'; cf. *Tempest,* I. ii. 272: 'and for thou wast a spirit too delicate, . . . she did confine thee'; see Schmidt, s.v. *for, conj.,* 2.

But for his satisfaction and the world's,   90
'Twere good, my lord, that Hieronimo and I
Were reconcil'd, if he misconster me.
Cast. Lorenzo thou hast said, it shall be so,
Go one of you and call Hieronimo.

Enter BALTHAZAR *and* BEL-IMPERIA.

Bal. Come Bel-imperia, Balthazar's content,   95
My sorrow's ease and sovereign of my bliss,
Sith heaven hath ordain'd thee to be mine:
Disperse those clouds and melancholy looks,
And clear them up with those thy sun-bright eyes
Wherein my hope and heaven's fair beauty lies.   100
Bel. My looks, my lord, are fitting for my love,
Which, new begun, can show no brighter yet.
Bal. New-kindled flames should burn as morning sun.
Bel. But not too fast, lest heat and all be done.
I see my lord my father.
Bal.   Truce, my love,   105
I will go salute him.
Cast.   Welcome Balthazar,
Welcome brave prince, the pledge of Castile's peace:
And welcome Bel-imperia. How now, girl?
Why com'st thou sadly to salute us thus?
Content thyself, for I am satisfied,   110
It is not now as when Andrea liv'd,
We have forgotten and forgiven that,
And thou art graced with a happier love.
But Balthazar, here comes Hieronimo,
I'll have a word with him.   115

Enter HIERONIMO *and a* Servant.

102. no brighter] *1594;* brighter *1592.*   105-7. I see ... my love, / I will
... Balthazar, / Welcome ... peace:] *Manly, Schick;* I see ... Father. /
Truce ... him. / Welcome ... Prince, / The ... peace: *1592.*

92. *misconster*] interpret wrongly, misconstrue.
100. *lies*] singular verb after double subject, as frequently in Elizabethan
English.

Hier. And where's the duke ?
Ser.   Yonder.
Hier.   Even so:
  What new device have they devised, trow ?
  Pocas palabras, mild as the lamb,
  Is't I will be reveng'd ? no, I am not the man.
Cast. Welcome Hieronimo.   120
Lor. Welcome Hieronimo.
Bal. Welcome Hieronimo.
Hier. My lords, I thank you for Horatio.
Cast. Hieronimo, the reason that I sent
  To speak with you, is this.
Hier.   What, so short ?   125
  Then I'll be gone, I thank you for't.
Cast. Nay, stay, Hieronimo! Go call him, son.
Lor. Hieronimo, my father craves a word with you.
Hier. With me, sir ? why my lord, I thought you had done.
Lor. [*aside.*] No, would he had.
Cast.   Hieronimo, I hear   130
  You find yourself aggrieved at my son
  Because you have not access unto the king,
  And say 'tis he that intercepts your suits.
Hier. Why, is not this a miserable thing, my lord ?
Cast. Hieronimo, I hope you have no cause,   135
  And would be loath that one of your deserts
  Should once have reason to suspect my son,
  Considering how I think of you myself.
Hier. Your son Lorenzo ? whom, my noble lord ?
  The hope of Spain, mine honourable friend ?   140
  Grant me the combat of them, if they dare.
                         Draws out his sword.

116–17. . . . Even so: / What . . . trow ?] *Manly, Schick;* Euen so . . . tro ?
1592.   128. Lor.] *1602; not in 1592.*   130. Hieronimo, I hear] *begins*
l. 131 in 1592.

118. Pocas palabras] 'few words' (Spanish). Another phrase which became part of the furniture of Elizabethan drama.
  133. *intercepts*] stands in the way of.

I'll meet him face to face to tell me so.

These be the scandalous reports of such

As love not me, and hate my lord too much.

Should I suspect Lorenzo would prevent   145

Or cross my suit, that lov'd my son so well ?

My lord, I am asham'd it should be said.

Lor. Hieronimo, I never gave you cause.

Hier. My good lord, I know you did not.

Cast.   There then pause,

And for the satisfaction of the world,   150

Hieronimo, frequent my homely house,

The Duke of Castile, Cyprian's ancient seat,

And when thou wilt, use me, my son, and it:

But here, before Prince Balthazar and me,

Embrace each other, and be perfect friends.   155

Hier. Ay marry my lord, and shall:

Friends, quoth he ? see, I'll be friends with you all:

Specially with you, my lovely lord;

For divers causes it is fit for us

That we be friends, the world is suspicious,   160

And men may think what we imagine not.

Bal. Why, this is friendly done, Hieronimo.

Lor. And thus, I hope, old grudges are forgot.

Hier. What else ? it were a shame it should not be so.

Cast. Come on, Hieronimo, at my request;   165

144. love] *1610;* loues *1592.*   149–50. . . . There then pause, / And . . .
world,] *Hawkins;* There then pause . . . world, *1592.*   158. Specially]
1592; Especially *Dodsley.*   163. And thus, I hope,] *Dodsley;* And that
I hope *1592.*

144. *love*] There is a case for retaining *1592*'s *loves* in spite of the inconsistency with *hate*, on the ground that Hieronimo's speech is no longer
always logical; Manly, Boas, Schick[2] preserve the original, but I feel it more
likely that there has been a compositor's slip.

145. *prevent*] forestall.

151. *homely*] hospitable, 'home-like' (*O.E.D.*, 3); the more usual meaning
is 'plain', 'simple', even 'crude'.

163. *And thus*] See Textual Notes; recent edd. have not made good sense
by returning to the original and punctuating *And that I hope: old grudges are
forgot ?*

Let us entreat your company today.

> *Exeunt [all but* HIERONIMO].

Hier. Your lordship's to command.—Pha! keep your way.

Chi mi fa più carezze che non suole,

Tradito mi ha, o tradir mi vuole.   *Exit.*

[III. xv]

> Ghost [*of* ANDREA] *and* REVENGE.

Andrea. Awake, Erichtho! Cerberus, awake!

Solicit Pluto, gentle Proserpine,

To combat, Acheron and Erebus!

For ne'er by Styx and Phlegethon in hell

.   .   .   .

167. Pha!] *Pha: 1592;* Pah! *Schick;* Pho! *conj. MSR (1592).*   Pha! . . .
way.] *separate line 1592.*   168. Chi] *Manly, Schick; Mi.* Chi *1592; Mi!*
Chi *Hawkins.*   fa più carezze] *Hawkins; fa? Pui Correzza 1592.*   suole]
Hawkins; sule 1592. 169. mi ha] *Hawkins; viha 1592. o tradir mi]*
Hawkins; otrade 1592.   vuole] Hawkins; vule 1592.

III. xv. 0.1. Ghost] *This ed.;* Enter Ghoast *1592.*   1. Andrea.] *Ghost. 1592*
(*and throughout*).   Erichtho] *Fleischer;* Erictha *1592;* Alecto *Hazlitt.*
3. Acheron] *Hawkins;* Achinon *1592.*   Erebus] *Hawkins;* Ericus *1592.*
4. ne'er] *Dodsley;* neere *1592.   in hell] Schick; ends l. 3 in 1592.*

---

167. *Pha!*] It seems unnecessary to modernize the exclamation with
Schick. *O.E.D.* has examples of *Phah* and *Pho* as exclamations of disgust in
1592 and 1601.

168–9.] 'He who shows unaccustomed fondness for me has betrayed me
or wants to betray me.' Keller (*Archiv*, ciii, 387) points out that a slightly
different form of this proverb is to be found in Sandford's *Garden of
Pleasure* (1573), a translation of Guicciardini's *Proverbs of Piovano*, and in
Florio's *First Fruits* (1578), f. 26r. J. C. Maxwell (*P.Q.*, xxx (1951), 86)
would omit *mi* before *vuole* on the grounds of scansion and greater fidelity
to *1592*.

III. xv. 0.1.] *Enter* is omitted since Andrea and Revenge are clearly on
stage the whole time. Concerning the extent of the corruption in the scene
which follows, see Introduction, pp. xxxiii–xxxiv.

1. *Erichtho*] 'This means, of course, the Thessalian sorceress Erichtho,
well known from Lucan, Ovid, Dante, and Goethe's *Faust.* She is often
introduced in the Elizabethan drama (*cp.* especially Marston's *Sophonisba*)'
(Schick).

4–7.] Although this passage is extremely corrupt, something faintly

Nor ferried Charon to the fiery lakes   6
Such fearful sights as poor Andrea sees!
Revenge, awake!
Revenge. Awake? for why?
Andrea. Awake, Revenge, for thou art ill-advis'd   10
To sleep; awake! what, thou art warn'd to watch!
Revenge. Content thyself, and do not trouble me.
Andrea. Awake, Revenge, if love, as love hath had,
Have yet the power or prevalence in hell!
Hieronimo with Lorenzo is join'd in league   15
And intercepts our passage to revenge:
Awake, Revenge, or we are woe-begone!
Revenge. Thus worldlings ground, what they have dream'd, upon.
Content thyself, Andrea; though I sleep,
Yet is my mood soliciting their souls: 20
Sufficeth thee that poor Hieronimo
Cannot forget his son Horatio.
Nor dies Revenge although he sleep awhile,
For in unquiet, quietness is feign'd,
And slumb'ring is a common worldly wile.   25
Behold, Andrea, for an instance how

---

6. Nor ferried] *1592;* O'er-ferried *Schick.*   7. sees!] sees *1602;* see ? *1592.*
11. To sleep] *1594;* Thsleep *1592.*   awake!] awake: *1633;* away, *1592.*
14. prevalence] preuailance *1592.*   17. begone] *1594;* degone *1592.*

---

approaching meaning can be perceived, and emendations are saved, if we
suppose that a line to balance l. 7 has dropped out after l. 4, something of
the order of *Was I distress'd with outrage sore as this.*

11. *awake!*] Manly, Boas, and Brooke retain *away* but repunctuate 'To
sleep away what thou art warn'd to watch.' Hawkins' emendation preserves the principle of *1592*'s punctuation and no-one can cavil at an extra
awake! in this scene.

14. *prevalence*] *1592*'s spelling indicates the meaning (*O.E.D.*, 1).

18. *ground ... upon*] found their beliefs on what is a mere dream or fancy.
Cf. *O.E.D., ground, v.,* 4b, intransitive for reflexive.

20. *mood*] The meaning 'mind' or 'thought' which suggests itself was
obsolescent or obsolete in Kyd's day (*O.E.D., sb.*[1], 1); it is just possible that
the meaning 'anger' would fit this context (*O.E.D., sb.*[1], 2b).

24.] If the text of this scene represents a 'reported' version, this line
could be explained as an inapposite recollection of Hieronimo's *dissembling
quiet in unquietness* (III. xiii. 30).

Revenge hath slept, and then imagine thou
What 'tis to be subject to destiny.

Enter a Dumb Show.

Andrea. Awake, Revenge, reveal this mystery.
Revenge. The two first, the nuptial torches bore,   30
 As brightly burning as the mid-day's sun:
 But after them doth Hymen hie as fast,
 Clothed in sable, and a saffron robe,
 And blows them out and quencheth them with blood,
 As discontent that things continue so.   35
Andrea. Sufficeth me, thy meaning's understood,
 And thanks to thee and those infernal powers
 That will not tolerate a lover's woe.
 Rest thee, for I will sit to see the rest.
Revenge. Then argue not, for thou hast thy request.   40

---

30. bore] boare *1592;* bear *Fleischer, Manly.*   40.1. ʌ] *Exeunt. 1592.*

29. *mystery*] See note to I. i. 90.

Act IV

Enter BEL-IMPERIA *and* HIERONIMO.

Bel. Is this the love thou bear'st Horatio?
    Is this the kindness that thou counterfeits?
    Are these the fruits of thine incessant tears?
    Hieronimo, are these thy passions,
    Thy protestations and thy deep laments,   5
    That thou wert wont to weary men withal?
    O unkind father, O deceitful world!
    With what excuses canst thou show thyself,
    With what . . . . . .
    From this dishonour and the hate of men?—   10
    Thus to neglect the loss and life of him
    Whom both my letters and thine own belief
    Assures thee to be causeless slaughtered.
    Hieronimo, for shame, Hieronimo,
    Be not a history to after-times   15
    Of such ingratitude unto thy son.
    Unhappy mothers of such children then,

Act IV] Actus Quartus *1592*.   9. With what . . .] With what dishonour, and the hate of men, *1592; not in Schick.*

9.] The line in *1592* contains the first two words of the preceding line and then the last six words of the succeeding line. The best explanation is that the line ran, perhaps as Boas suggests, *With what devices seek thyself to save*, or something of that order. It may be the compositor, after *With what*, almost went on with the line above, which begins in the same way; made too violent a correction and jumped to the line below, and never saw what he had done.

13. *Assures*] singular verb after double subject once more. Cf. Franz, §673.
17–20.] anacoluthon.

But monstrous fathers, to forget so soon
The death of those whom they with care and cost
Have tender'd so, thus careless should be lost.   20
Myself, a stranger in respect of thee,
So lov'd his life, as still I wish their deaths,
Nor shall his death be unreveng'd by me,
Although I bear it out for fashion's sake:
For here I swear in sight of heaven and earth,   25
Shouldst thou neglect the love thou shouldst retain
And give it over and devise no more,
Myself should send their hateful souls to hell,
That wrought his downfall with extremest death.
Hier. But may it be that Bel-imperia   30
Vows such revenge as she hath deign'd to say?
Why then, I see that heaven applies our drift,
And all the saints do sit soliciting
For vengeance on those cursed murderers.
Madam, 'tis true, and now I find it so,   35
I found a letter, written in your name,
And in that letter, how Horatio died.

---

32. applies] *1592;* applauds *conj. Collier.*

---

20. *tender'd*] cherished, looked after.
21. *stranger . . . thee*] a stranger to him compared with you, his father.
24. *bear it out for fashion's sake*] make a pretence of accepting the situation for the sake of appearances. *Bear it out* is a difficult phrase, and parallels to suit this context are hard to come by, in *O.E.D.* or elsewhere, though the phrase occurs frequently.
fashion's sake] Cf. *O.E.D., fashion, sb.,* 7.
32. *applies our drift*] *either* supports what we are working towards *or* directs our course. A most difficult phrase, though Collier's emendation is a last resort. *drift* = 'that at which one drives' as used in modern English with reference to an argument, etc., hence 'direction', 'intention', or, possibly, 'plan', 'scheme', as frequently in Shakespeare. *applies* may be as III. ix. 13 = 'assent', 'conform', or, by association, 'comply'; but, if so, the construction needs a preposition (cf. *O.E.D.,* 19). Or it may be (*O.E.D.,* 22) echoing *applicare navem* = guide, direct. Schick[1] supported the latter sense, but his paraphrase as a whole is wrong, viz.: 'Heaven furthers our drifting plans, brings them to a definite goal'; Hieronimo is conscious of receiving, not direction, but encouragement from above, and the paraphrase should be, 'Heaven is assisting us towards our goal'.

Pardon, O pardon, Bel-imperia,
My fear and care in not believing it,
Nor think I thoughtless think upon a mean   40
To let his death be unreveng'd at full,
And here I vow (so you but give consent,
And will conceal my resolution)
I will ere long determine of their deaths,
That causeless thus have murdered my son.   45

Bel. Hieronimo, I will consent, conceal,
And aught that may effect for thine avail,
Join with thee to revenge Horatio's death.

Hier. On then, whatsoever I devise,
Let me entreat you grace my practices;   50
For why, the plot's already in mine head.
Here they are.

Enter BALTHAZAR *and* LORENZO.

Bal.   How now, Hieronimo?
What, courting Bel-imperia?

Hier.   Ay my lord,
Such courting as, I promise you,
She hath my heart, but you, my lord, have hers.   55

Lor. But now, Hieronimo, or never,
We are to entreat your help.

Hier.   My help?
Why my good lords, assure yourselves of me,
For you have given me cause,
Ay, by my faith have you.

---

45. murdered] *1602;* murderd *1592.*   52-61.] *Lineation as Schick; 1592*
reads: Heere they are. / How now ... *Bel-imperia.* / I my lord ... promise
you / She hath ... hers. / But now ... your helpe. / My help ... of me. /
For you ... haue you. / It pleasde ... Embassadour.

---

39. *care*] caution.
47. *avail*] assistance (*O.E.D., sb.,* 2) rather than profit (*O.E.D.,* 1).
50. *grace*] give favour to, support, 'be gracious to' (*O.E.D., v.,* 2).
52.] The metre of the remainder of this scene is frequently defective: see
Textual Introduction, p. xxxiv. Attempts to supply its deficiencies are only
made if there seems some possibility of restoring the original rhythms.

Bal.   It pleas'd you   60
    ⌈At the entertainment of the ambassador⌉
    To grace the king so much as with a show:
    Now were your study so well furnished,
    As for the passing of the first night's sport
    To entertain my father with the like,   65
    Or any such-like pleasing motion,
    Assure yourself it would content them well.
Hier. Is this all?
Bal. Ay, this is all.
Hier. Why then I'll fit you, say no more.   70
    When I was young, I gave my mind
    And plied myself to fruitless poetry:
    Which though it profit the professor naught,
    Yet is it passing pleasing to the world.
Lor. And how for that?
Hier.   Marry, my good lord, thus—   75
    And yet methinks you are too quick with us—
    When in Toledo there I studied,
    It was my chance to write a tragedy,
    See here my lords,   *He shows them a book.*
    Which long forgot, I found this other day.   80
    Now would your lordships favour me so much
    As but to grace me with your acting it—
    I mean each one of you to play a part—
    Assure you it will prove most passing strange
    And wondrous plausible to that assembly.   85

---

62. *grace*] honour. Balthazar shows a typical obsequiousness in talking of
an official's being pleased to grace the King.

66. *motion*] entertainment, 'show'. The word is first recorded in the sense
of a puppet-show in 1589 (*O.E.D.*, *sb.*, 13a); the more general sense here is
possibly unique, but the only possible alternative sense—idea, or suggestion—seems most unlikely.

70. *I'll fit you*] The phrase has a double sense: (a) 'I'll provide what you
need' (*O.E.D.*, *fit*, *v.*¹, 11), and (b) 'I'll pay you out' or 'I'll punish you as
you deserve'. Usage (b) was well-established before 1625, the date of
O.E.D.'s first quotation (s.v. *fit*, *v.*¹, 12). Cf. Massinger and Field, *The
Fatal Dowry* (?1619; before 1620), III. i. 253.

85. *plausible*] acceptable, agreeable (*O.E.D.*, 2).

Bal. What, would you have us play a tragedy?

Hier. Why, Nero thought it no disparagement,
   And kings and emperors have ta'en delight
   To make experience of their wits in plays!

Lor. Nay, be not angry, good Hieronimo,   90
   The prince but asked a question.

Bal. In faith, Hieronimo, and you be in earnest,
   I'll make one.

Lor. And I another.

Hier. Now my good lord, could you entreat   95
   Your sister Bel-imperia to make one—
   For what's a play without a woman in it?

Bel. Little entreaty shall serve me, Hieronimo,
   For I must needs be employed in your play.

Hier. Why, this is well; I tell you, lordings,   100
   It was determined to have been acted
   By gentlemen and scholars too,
   Such as could tell what to speak.

Bal. And now it shall be play'd by princes and courtiers,
   Such as can tell how to speak,   105
   If, as it is our country manner,
   You will but let us know the argument.

Hier. That shall I roundly. The chronicles of Spain
   Record this written of a knight of Rhodes:
   He was betroth'd and wedded at the length 110

105. speak,] speak: *1592.*

---

87. *disparagement*] Cf. note on III. x. 36–8.

89. *experience*] trial.

105.] Although these unmetrical exchanges may be corrupt, some edd. do not help the sense by preserving *1592*'s colon after *speak.* I see no value in the opposition of *what to speak* (l. 103) and *how to speak,* and doubt that the variation is authoritative. Balthazar says (a little disdainfully) that princes and courtiers can tell what to speak as well as gentlemen and scholars—if only Hieronimo will be good enough to explain the plot to them.

108. *roundly*] directly, without ado. The story of Soliman and Perseda is found in J. Yver's *Printemps d'Iver* (1572) translated by H. Wotton in 1578 as *Courtlie Controversie of Cupids Cautels.* The relevant parts of the latter are reprinted in Sarrazin, pp. 12–39.

  To one Perseda, an Italian dame,
  Whose beauty ravish'd all that her beheld,
  Especially the soul of Soliman,
  Who at the marriage was the chiefest guest.
  By sundry means sought Soliman to win   115
  Perseda's love, and could not gain the same.
  Then gan he break his passions to a friend,
  One of his bashaws whom he held full dear;
  Her had this bashaw long solicited,
  And saw she was not otherwise to be won   120
  But by her husband's death, this knight of Rhodes,
  Whom presently by treachery he slew.
  She, stirr'd with an exceeding hate therefore,
  As cause of this slew Soliman,
  And to escape the bashaw's tyranny   125
  Did stab herself: and this the tragedy.
Lor. O excellent!
Bel.   But say, Hieronimo,
  What then became of him that was the bashaw?
Hier. Marry thus, moved with remorse of his misdeeds,
  Ran to a mountain top and hung himself.   130
Bal. But which of us is to perform that part?
Hier. Oh, that will I, my lords, make no doubt of it:
  I'll play the murderer, I warrant you,
  For I already have conceited that.
Bal. And what shall I?   135
Hier. Great Soliman, the Turkish emperor.
Lor. And I?
Hier. Erastus, the knight of Rhodes.
Bel. And I?
Hier. Perseda, chaste and resolute.   140
  And here, my lords, are several abstracts drawn,

127–8. O excellent . . . Hieronimo, / What . . . bashaw?] *Boas;* O excellent. / But say . . . him / That . . . Bashaw? *1592.*

134. *conceited*] formed a conception of; Hieronimo says that the idea of playing a murderer has been in his mind some time.

For each of you to note your parts,
And act it as occasion's offer'd you.
You must provide a Turkish cap,
A black mustachio and a fauchion; 145

Gives a paper to BALTHAZAR.

You with a cross like to a knight of Rhodes;

Gives another to LORENZO.

And madam, you must attire yourself

He giveth BEL-IMPERIA *another.*

Like Phoebe, Flora, or the Huntress,
Which to your discretion shall seem best.
And as for me, my lords, I'll look to one, 150
And with the ransom that the viceroy sent
So furnish and perform this tragedy,
As all the world shall say Hieronimo
Was liberal in gracing of it so.

Bal. Hieronimo, methinks a comedy were better. 155

Hier. A comedy?

Fie, comedies are fit for common wits:
But to present a kingly troop withal,
Give me a stately-written tragedy,
Tragedia cothurnata, fitting kings, 160
Containing matter, and not common things.
My lords, all this must be performed
As fitting for the first night's revelling.
The Italian tragedians were so sharp of wit,
That in one hour's meditation 165
They would perform anything in action.

---

148. Huntress] huntresse *1592;* Hunteress *Schick;* huntresse Dian *conj.*
Kittredge. 156–7. A comedy ? / Fie . . . wits:] A Comedie, . . . wits *1592.*
160. *cothurnata*] *Dodsley; cother nato 1592.*

---

145. *fauchion*] falchion, a broad curved sword; the spelling is a variant
which shows the proper pronunciation.
154. *gracing*] See I. iv. 137.
160. Tragedia cothurnata] buskin'd tragedy, i.e., the most serious and
stately.
164–6.] a reference to the improvisations of the *commedia dell' arte.*

Lor. And well it may, for I have seen the like
 In Paris, 'mongst the French tragedians.
Hier. In Paris ? mass, and well remembered!
 There's one thing more that rests for us to do.   170
Bal. What's that, Hieronimo ? forget not anything.
Hier. Each one of us must act his part
 In unknown languages,
 That it may breed the more variety.
 As you, my lord, in Latin, I in Greek,   175
 You in Italian, and for because I know
 That Bel-imperia hath practised the French,
 In courtly French shall all her phrases be.
Bel. You mean to try my cunning then, Hieronimo.
Bal. But this will be a mere confusion,   180
 And hardly shall we all be understood.
Hier. It must be so, for the conclusion
 Shall prove the invention and all was good:
 And I myself in an oration,
 And with a strange and wondrous show besides,   185
 That I will have there behind a curtain,
 Assure yourself shall make the matter known.
 And all shall be concluded in one scene,
 For there's no pleasure ta'en in tediousness.
Bal. [*aside to* LORENZO.] How like you this ?   190
Lor. Why thus, my lord,
 We must resolve to soothe his humours up.
Bal. On then, Hieronimo, farewell till soon.
Hier. You'll ply this gear ?

169. remembered] remembred *1592.* 185–6.] *As 1602; lines transposed in 1592.* 192. We must resolve] *ends l. 191 in 1592.* 194. gear ?] geere. *1592.*

---

173. *In unknown languages*] For the problems raised by this unfulfilled promise, see Introduction, pp. xxxiv–xxxvii.
 181. *hardly*] with difficulty.
 192. *soothe . . . up*] indulge him in his whims, humour him (*O.E.D., soothe,* 4b). Cf. *Alphonsus of Aragon,* Act IV: 'Are they wax'd so frolic now of late / As that they think that mighty Amurack / Dares do no other than to soothe them up ?'

M

Lor.   I warrant you.
                          Exeunt all but HIERONIMO.
Hier.   Why, so:
    Now shall I see the fall of Babylon,   195
    Wrought by the heavens in this confusion.
    And if the world like not this tragedy,
    Hard is the hap of old Hieronimo.   *Exit.*

[IV. ii]
                Enter ISABELLA *with a weapon.*

Isab. Tell me no more! O monstrous homicides!
    Since neither piety nor pity moves
    The king to justice or compassion,
    I will revenge myself upon this place
    Where thus they murder'd my beloved son.   5
                          She cuts down the arbour.
    Down with these branches and these loathsome boughs
    Of this unfortunate and fatal pine:
    Down with them Isabella, rent them up
    And burn the roots from whence the rest is sprung:
    I will not leave a root, a stalk, a tree,   10
    A bough, a branch, a blossom, nor a leaf,
    No, not an herb within this garden plot—
    Accursed complot of my misery.
    Fruitless for ever may this garden be,
    Barren the earth, and blissless whosoever   15

194–5. . . . Why so: / Now . . . Babylon,] Why so . . . Babilon, *1592.*

IV. ii. 1. *Isab.*] *not in 1592.*

---

195. *the fall of Babylon*] See Revelation, chap. 18. But in view of the plan
for a confusion of tongues it may be that the tower of Babylon, i.e., Babel,
is in Hieronimo's mind. (I owe this suggestion to Mrs E. E. Duncan-Jones.)

IV. ii. 5.1.] Presumably Isabella goes through the motions or strips the
arbour of its leaves. See note to II. iv. 53.
    8. *rent*] See III. xiii. 122.

Imagines not to keep it unmanur'd!
An eastern wind commix'd with noisome airs
Shall blast the plants and the young saplings,
The earth with serpents shall be pestered,
And passengers, for fear to be infect,   20
Shall stand aloof, and looking at it, tell,
'There, murder'd, died the son of Isabel.'
Ay, here he died, and here I him embrace:
See where his ghost solicits with his wounds
Revenge on her that should revenge his death.   25
Hieronimo, make haste to see thy son,
For sorrow and despair hath cited me
To hear Horatio plead with Rhadamanth:
Make haste, Hieronimo, to hold excus'd
Thy negligence in pursuit of their deaths,   30
Whose hateful wrath bereav'd him of his breath.
Ah nay, thou dost delay their deaths,
Forgives the murderers of thy noble son,
And none but I bestir me—to no end.
And as I curse this tree from further fruit,   35
So shall my womb be cursed for his sake,
And with this weapon will I wound the breast,

She stabs herself.

The hapless breast, that gave Horatio suck.   [*Exit.*]

27. cited] scited *1592*.   29. to hold excus'd] *1592;* or hold accus'd *Hazlitt*.
34. me—to no end] me to no end *1592*.   37.1. *She stabs herself.*] *1592;*
after l. *38* in *1602*.

---

16. *unmanur'd*] uncultivated.
20. *passengers*] passers-by.
27. *hath*] singular after double subject.
cited] summoned.
38. [*Exit.*]] The compositor was very cramped at the foot of the page
(K2) and a direction for removing Isabella's body may be missing. Isabella
has no curtains to fall behind; there could be no better proof that an inner-
stage did not exist than the very next direction, which shows Hieronimo
having to arrange a curtain to conceal Horatio's body. Isabella must some-
how be got off stage; in spite of all modern edd., the place for the direction
to stab herself is, as in *1592*, before the last line; by inserting a simple *Exit*
we establish no theory about what is missing from *1592*, but, if she is to drag

[IV. iii]

Enter HIERONIMO; *he knocks up the curtain.*
Enter the DUKE *of* CASTILE.

Cast. How now Hieronimo, where's your fellows,
    That you take all this pain?
Hier. O sir, it is for the author's credit
    To look that all things may go well:
    But good my lord, let me entreat your grace   5
    To give the king the copy of the play:
    This is the argument of what we show.
Cast. I will, Hieronimo.
Hier. One thing more, my good lord.
Cast. What's that?   10
Hier. Let me entreat your grace,
    That when the train are pass'd into the gallery
    You would vouchsafe to throw me down the key.
Cast. I will, Hieronimo.   *Exit* CASTILE.
Hier. What, are you ready, Balthazar?   15
    Bring a chair and a cushion for the king.

Enter BALTHAZAR *with a chair.*

---

herself, wounded, off-stage, she has one line to speak as she does so. Hosley notes (privately) that in Davenant's *The Just Italian* (1629) the wounded Altamont leaves the stage, alone, with the direction, 'Reeles off, Exit.' (H1ᵛ).

IV. iii. 0.1. knocks up the curtain] It is difficult to judge what precisely Hieronimo does. (i) What is involved in 'knocking up' a curtain? Probably a hasty hanging of a curtain in a prepared place, but *O.E.D.* gives only late examples (s.v. *knock, v.,* 14c (*knock together*), and 16d (*knock up*), referring to hasty constructions for a temporary purpose). (ii) Where was the curtain? The best suggestion is that it hung over one of the doors, so that Horatio's body could conveniently be brought behind it.

12–13.] The gallery is not a balcony but the hall; it is clear from the action later, and (as Hosley points out) from Balthazar's bringing on a chair for the King (l. 16), that the audience of the play-within-the-play is on the main stage with the actors. *throw me down the key* must therefore mean 'throw the key down [on the floor] for me'.

Well done Balthazar, hang up the title,
Our scene is Rhodes; what, is your beard on?
Bal. Half on, the other is in my hand.
Hier. Despatch for shame, are you so long? *Exit* BALTHAZAR.   20
Bethink thyself, Hieronimo,
Recall thy wits, recompt thy former wrongs
Thou hast receiv'd by murder of thy son,
And lastly, not least, how Isabel,
Once his mother and thy dearest wife,   25
All woe-begone for him hath slain herself.
Behoves thee then, Hieronimo, to be reveng'd:
The plot is laid of dire revenge:
On then, Hieronimo, pursue revenge,
For nothing wants but acting of revenge.   *Exit* HIERONIMO.

[IV. iv]

    Enter Spanish KING, VICEROY, *the* DUKE OF CASTILE,
                and their train.

King. Now, Viceroy, shall we see the tragedy
Of Soliman the Turkish emperor,
Perform'd of pleasure by your son the prince,
My nephew, Don Lorenzo, and my niece.
Vice. Who, Bel-imperia?   5
King. Ay, and Hieronimo our marshal,
At whose request they deign to do't themselves:
These be our pastimes in the court of Spain.
Here brother, you shall be the book-keeper: 9
This is the argument of that they show.   *He giveth him a book.*

---

22. recompt] *1592;* recount *1602.*

---

17. *title*] For the use of title-boards and locality-labels in public and private theatres, see *Eliz. Stage,* III, 126–7, 154.
19.] Marston, in *Antonio's Revenge* (1599), attempts some sophisticated humour by making Balurdo enter 'with a beard half-off, half on', saying 'the tyring man hath not glewd on my beard halfe fast enough. Gods bores, it wil not stick to fal off.'

Gentlemen, this play of HIERONIMO *in sundry languages, was*
thought good to be set down in English more largely,
for the easier understanding to every
public reader.

Enter BALTHAZAR, BEL-IMPERIA, *and* HIERONIMO.

Bal. *Bashaw, that Rhodes is ours, yield heavens the honour,*
    And holy Mahomet, our sacred prophet:
    And be thou grac'd with every excellence
    That Soliman can give, or thou desire.
    But thy desert in conquering Rhodes is less   15
    Than in reserving this fair Christian nymph,
    Perseda, blissful lamp of excellence,
    Whose eyes compel, like powerful adamant,
    The warlike heart of Soliman to wait.
King. See, Viceroy, that is Balthazar your son   20
    That represents the emperor Soliman:
    How well he acts his amorous passion.
Vice. Ay, Bel-imperia hath taught him that.
Cast. That's because his mind runs all on Bel-imperia.
Hier. *Whatever joy earth yields betide your majesty.*   25
Bal. *Earth yields no joy without Perseda's love.*
Hier. *Let then Perseda on your grace attend.*
Bal. *She shall not wait on me, but I on her:*
    Drawn by the influence of her lights, I yield.
    But let my friend, the Rhodian knight, come forth,   30
    Erasto, dearer than my life to me,
    That he may see Perseda, my beloved.

Enter Erasto.

King. Here comes Lorenzo; look upon the plot,
    And tell me, brother, what part plays he?
Bel. *Ah my Erasto, welcome to Perseda.*   35

10.1.] For the problem posed by this note, see Introduction, pp. xxxiv,
xxxvi-xxxix.
35.] The use of the third person and frequent vocatives indicates the

Lor. *Thrice happy is Erasto that thou liv'st,*
    Rhodes' loss is nothing to Erasto's joy:
    Sith his Perseda lives, his life survives.
Bal. *Ah Bashaw, here is love between Erasto*
    And fair Perseda, sovereign of my soul.   40
Hier. *Remove Erasto, mighty Soliman,*
    And then Perseda will be quickly won.
Bal. *Erasto is my friend, and while he lives*
    Perseda never will remove her love.
Hier. *Let not Erasto live to grieve great Soliman.*   45
Bal. *Dear is Erasto in our princely eye.*
Hier. *But if he be your rival, let him die.*
Bal. *Why, let him die, so love commandeth me.*
    Yet grieve I that Erasto should so die.
Hier. *Erasto, Soliman saluteth thee,*   50
    And lets thee wit by me his highness' will,
    Which is, thou shouldst be thus employ'd.   *Stab him.*
Bel.   *Ay me,*
    Erasto ! see, Soliman, Erasto's slain !
Bal. *Yet liveth Soliman to comfort thee.*
    Fair queen of beauty, let not favour die,   55
    But with a gracious eye behold his grief,
    That with Perseda's beauty is increas'd,
    If by Perseda grief be not releas'd.
Bel. *Tyrant, desist soliciting vain suits,*
    Relentless are mine ears to thy laments,   60
    As thy butcher is pitiless and base,
    Which seiz'd on my Erasto, harmless knight.
    Yet by thy power thou thinkest to command,
    And to thy power Perseda doth obey:

---

52. *Ay me,*] begins l. 53 in 1592.   58. *Perseda*] Manly; *Persedaes 1592;*
Perseda his Schick.

---

parts the actors are assuming (cf. Bradbrook, *Themes and Conventions,*
p. 102 n.).
    48. so love commandeth me] if it be so that . . . But the verb should be in
the subjunctive, so perhaps the meaning 'thus love commands me' is
preferable.

> *But were she able, thus she would revenge*   65
> *Thy treacheries on thee, ignoble prince:*   *Stab him.*
> *And on herself she would be thus reveng'd.*   *Stab herself.*

King. Well said, old Marshal, this was bravely done!

Hier. But Bel-imperia plays Perseda well.

Vice. Were this in earnest, Bel-imperia,   70
    You would be better to my son than so.

King. But now what follows for Hieronimo?

Hier. Marry, this follows for Hieronimo:
    Here break we off our sundry languages
    And thus conclude I in our vulgar tongue.   75
    Haply you think, but bootless are your thoughts,
    That this is fabulously counterfeit,
    And that we do as all tragedians do:
    To die today, for fashioning our scene,
    The death of Ajax, or some Roman peer,   80
    And in a minute starting up again,
    Revive to please tomorrow's audience.
    No, princes, know I am Hieronimo,
    The hopeless father of a hapless son,
    Whose tongue is tun'd to tell his latest tale,   85
    Not to excuse gross errors in the play.
    I see your looks urge instance of these words,
    Behold the reason urging me to this: *Shows his dead son.*

---

68. Well said, old] Well said olde *1592;* Well said!—old *Schick.*   79. for fashioning our scene,] for (fashioning our scene) *1592.*

---

68. *Well said*] well done; cf. *Titus Andronicus,* IV. iii. 63. Some edd. take the phrase in its modern sense, and punctuate the line to make it refer to Bel-imperia's speech; it is obviously part of the King's congratulations to Hieronimo.

77. *fabulously*] fictitiously.

84.] Cf. *Jew of Malta,* l. 557, 'the hopelesse daughter of a haplesse Iew' (Boas).

87. *instance*] evidence, a concrete example.

88.] With this revelation, compare Chettle's *Hoffman* (1602?), in the first lines of which the revenger 'strikes ope a curtaine where appeares a body', and Marston's *Antonio's Revenge* (1599?), l. 360, 'The Curtain's drawne, and the bodie of Feliche, stabd thick with wounds, appeares hung vp.'

See here my show, look on this spectacle:
Here lay my hope, and here my hope hath end: 90
Here lay my heart, and here my heart was slain:
Here lay my treasure, here my treasure lost:
Here lay my bliss, and here my bliss bereft:
But hope, heart, treasure, joy and bliss,
All fled, fail'd, died, yea, all decay'd with this.   95
From forth these wounds came breath that gave me life,
They murder'd me that made these fatal marks.
The cause was love, whence grew this mortal hate,
The hate, Lorenzo and young Balthazar,
The love, my son to Bel-imperia.   100
But night, the coverer of accursed crimes,
With pitchy silence hush'd these traitors' harms
And lent them leave, for they had sorted leisure
To take advantage in my garden plot
Upon my son, my dear Horatio: 105
There merciless they butcher'd up my boy,
In black dark night, to pale dim cruel death.
He shrieks, I heard, and yet methinks I hear,
His dismal outcry echo in the air:
With soonest speed I hasted to the noise,   110
Where hanging on a tree I found my son,
Through-girt with wounds, and slaughter'd as you see.
And griev'd I, think you, at this spectacle?
Speak, Portuguese, whose loss resembles mine:
If thou canst weep upon thy Balthazar,   115
'Tis like I wail'd for my Horatio.
And you, my lord, whose reconciled son
March'd in a net, and thought himself unseen,

---

103. *sorted*] selected, sought out.

112. *Through-girt*] pierced. 'Girt is here the past part. of "gird" =
"strike", which is to be distinguished from "gird" = "to encircle"' (Boas).

118. *March'd in a net*] a common phrase for palpable deceit and pretence
(Tilley N130), though 'dance in a net' is the usual form; e.g. Greene, 'a
nette wherein to daunce, and diuers shadowes to colour my knaueries
withall' (quoted in Mann's Deloney, p. 518). Cf. Nashe, III, 365.

And rated me for brainsick lunacy,
With 'God amend that mad Hieronimo!'—   120
How can you brook our play's catastrophe?
And here behold this bloody handkercher,
Which at Horatio's death I weeping dipp'd
Within the river of his bleeding wounds:
It as propitious, see, I have reserv'd,   125
And never hath it left my bloody heart,
Soliciting remembrance of my vow
With these, O these accursed murderers,
Which now perform'd, my heart is satisfied.
And to this end the bashaw I became   130
That might revenge me on Lorenzo's life,
Who therefore was appointed to the part
And was to represent the knight of Rhodes,
That I might kill him more conveniently.
So, Viceroy, was this Balthazar, thy son,   135
That Soliman which Bel-imperia
In person of Perseda murdered:
Solely appointed to that tragic part,
That she might slay him that offended her.
Poor Bel-imperia miss'd her part in this,   140
For though the story saith she should have died,
Yet I of kindness, and of care to her,
Did otherwise determine of her end:
But love of him whom they did hate too much
Did urge her resolution to be such.   145
And princes, now behold Hieronimo,
Author and actor in this tragedy,
Bearing his latest fortune in his fist:
And will as resolute conclude his part
As any of the actors gone before.   150
And gentles, thus I end my play:
Urge no more words, I have no more to say.

He runs to hang himself.

120. With ... Hieronimo!'] With God amend that mad *Hieronimo 1592;*
Which God amend that made *Hieronimo 1594.*

King. O hearken, Viceroy! Hold, Hieronimo!
    Brother, my nephew and thy son are slain!
Vice. We are betray'd! My Balthazar is slain!   155
    Break ope the doors, run, save Hieronimo!
              [*They break in, and hold* HIERONIMO.]
    Hieronimo, do but inform the king of these events,
    Upon mine honour thou shalt have no harm.
Hier. Viceroy, I will not trust thee with my life,
    Which I this day have offer'd to my son: 160
    Accursed wretch,
    Why stayest thou him that was resolv'd to die?
King. Speak, traitor: damned, bloody murderer, speak!
    For now I have thee I will make thee speak:
    Why hast thou done this undeserving deed?   165
Vice. Why hast thou murdered my Balthazar?
Cast. Why hast thou butcher'd both my children thus?
Hier. O good words!   [*Fifth Addition; see p.* 133]
    As dear to me was my Horatio
    As yours, or yours, or yours, my lord, to you.   170
    My guiltless son was by Lorenzo slain,
    And by Lorenzo and that Balthazar
    Am I at last revenged thoroughly,
    Upon whose souls may heavens be yet aveng'd

---

153. Hold, Hieronimo!] holde *Hieronimo, 1592.*   156.1. [*They* . . .
HIERONIMO.]] *1602; not in 1592.*   161. Accursed wretch,] *begins l. 162 in
1592.*   168. O good words!] *begins l. 169 in 1592.*

---

153. *Hold, Hieronimo!*] It is a question whether the King tells his train to
hold Hieronimo, or tells Hieronimo to 'hold', i.e., stop. I prefer the latter
explanation.

156.] Castile has obeyed Hieronimo (see IV. iii. 12–13) and they are
locked in. The revenger locks his victims in, in Chapman's *Revenge of
Bussy D'Ambois.*

156.1.] I insert *1602*'s direction, though at the risk of confusing the
original staging with that of a decade or more later. I take it that attendants
or guards 'break in' from off-stage and *run* to hold Hieronimo, who is
certainly guarded while the King addresses him.

165–7, 182.] Hieronimo has told everything, yet the King, etc. are
apparently still in ignorance and to their questions Hieronimo returns
nothing but an inexplicable refusal to speak. This extraordinary inconsistency is discussed in the Introduction, pp. xxxiv–xxxvi.

With greater far than these afflictions.   175
Cast. But who were thy confederates in this ?
Vice. That was thy daughter Bel-imperia,
      For by her hand my Balthazar was slain :
      I saw her stab him.
King.   Why speak'st thou not ?
Hier. What lesser liberty can kings afford   180
      Than harmless silence ? then afford it me :
      Sufficeth I may not, nor I will not tell thee.
King. Fetch forth the tortures.
      Traitor as thou art, I'll make thee tell.
Hier.   Indeed,
      Thou may'st torment me, as his wretched son   185
      Hath done in murdering my Horatio,
      But never shalt thou force me to reveal
      The thing which I have vow'd inviolate :
      And therefore, in despite of all thy threats,
      Pleas'd with their deaths, and eas'd with their revenge,   190
      First take my tongue, and afterwards my heart.
                          [*He bites out his tongue.*]
King. O monstrous resolution of a wretch !
      See, Viceroy, he hath bitten forth his tongue
      Rather than to reveal what we requir'd.
Cast. Yet can he write.   195
King. And if in this he satisfy us not,
      We will devise th' extremest kind of death
      That ever was invented for a wretch.
                    Then he makes signs for a knife to mend his pen.
Cast. Oh, he would have a knife to mend his pen.
Vice. Here, and advise thee that thou write the troth.   200
King. Look to my brother ! save Hieronimo.
                    He with a knife stabs the DUKE *and himself.*
      What age hath ever heard such monstrous deeds ?
      My brother, and the whole succeeding hope
      That Spain expected after my decease !

184–5. . . . Indeed, / Thou . . . son] Indeed . . . Sonne *1592.*   191.1. [*He
. . . tongue.*]] *1602; not in 1592.*   201. *King.*] Boas; *not in 1592.*

Go bear his body hence, that we may mourn   205
The loss of our beloved brother's death,
That he may be entomb'd whate'er befall:
I am the next, the nearest, last of all.
Vice. And thou, Don Pedro, do the like for us,
Take up our hapless son, untimely slain: 210
Set me with him, and he with woeful me,
Upon the mainmast of a ship unmann'd,
And let the wind and tide haul me along
To Scylla's barking and untamed gulf,
Or to the loathsome pool of Acheron,   215
To weep my want for my sweet Balthazar:
Spain hath no refuge for a Portingale.

The trumpets sound a dead march, the KING *of Spain mourning after his brother's body, and the* KING *of Portingale bearing the body of his son.*

[IV. v]
                    Ghost [*of* ANDREA] *and* REVENGE.

Andrea. Ay, now my hopes have end in their effects,
When blood and sorrow finish my desires:
Horatio murder'd in his father's bower,
Vild Serberine by Pedringano slain,
False Pedringano hang'd by quaint device,   5
Fair Isabella by herself misdone,
Prince Balthazar by Bel-imperia stabb'd,

---

213. haul] hall *1592;* hale *1594.*   214. gulf] *1623;* greefe *1592.*

IV. v. 0.1. Ghost . . . REVENGE] Enter *Ghoast* and *Reuenge. 1592.*   1.
Andrea.] *Ghoast. 1592 (and throughout).*

---

213. *haul*] Normal spelling in the 16th century was *hall* as in *1592;* the word is a variant form of *hale*, and *1594*'s emendation may be intended only as a regularizing of the spelling; but *1592* apparently makes a distinction between *hall* and *hale* (IV. v. 27) and it should be preserved; it is quite possible that *haul* was a nautical form for Kyd.

217.2–3. bearing the body of his son] The direction is inconsistent with the Viceroy's instruction to Don Pedro in ll. 209–10.

The Duke of Castile and his wicked son
Both done to death by old Hieronimo,
My Bel-imperia fall'n as Dido fell,   10
And good Hieronimo slain by himself:
Ay, these were spectacles to please my soul.
Now will I beg at lovely Proserpine,
That by the virtue of her princely doom
I may consort my friends in pleasing sort,   15
And on my foes work just and sharp revenge.
I'll lead my friend Horatio through those fields
Where never-dying wars are still inur'd:
I'll lead fair Isabella to that train
Where pity weeps but never feeleth pain: 20
I'll lead my Bel-imperia to those joys
That vestal virgins and fair queens possess:
I'll lead Hieronimo where Orpheus plays,
Adding sweet pleasure to eternal days.
But say, Revenge, for thou must help or none,   25
Against the rest how shall my hate be shown?
Revenge. This hand shall hale them down to deepest hell,
Where none but furies, bugs and tortures dwell.
Andrea. Then, sweet Revenge, do this at my request,
Let me be judge, and doom them to unrest.   30
Let loose poor Tityus from the vulture's gripe,
And let Don Cyprian supply his room:
Place Don Lorenzo on Ixion's wheel,
And let the lover's endless pains surcease
(Juno forgets old wrath and grants him ease):   35
Hang Balthazar about Chimaera's neck,
And let him there bewail his bloody love,

18. *inur'd*] practised, carried on (*O.E.D.*, 3).
19. *train*] way of life. A rather unusual usage: cf. *O.E.D.*, *sb.*¹, 12a.
28. *bugs*] bugbears, horrifying objects.
32.] Andrea, we recall, had reason to dislike Castile and wish him ill, as Hieronimo had not.
34. *the lover*] Ixion had tried to seduce Juno.
surcease] cease.

Repining at our joys that are above:
Let Serberine go roll the fatal stone,
And take from Sisyphus his endless moan: 40
False Pedringano, for his treachery,
Let him be dragg'd through boiling Acheron,
And there live, dying still in endless flames,
Blaspheming gods and all their holy names.
Revenge. Then haste we down to meet thy friends and foes,   45
To place thy friends in ease, the rest in woes:
For here though death hath end their misery,
I'll there begin their endless tragedy.   *Exeunt.*

Additional passages from the edition of 1602

FIRST ADDITION

(Between II. v. 45 and 46. See p. 43)

[*Isab.*] *For outrage fits our cursed wretchedness.*
    Ay me, Hieronimo, sweet husband speak.
Hier. He supp'd with us tonight, frolic and merry,
    And said he would go visit Balthazar
    At the duke's palace: there the prince doth lodge.
    He had no custom to stay out so late,   5
    He may be in his chamber, some go see.
    Roderigo, ho!

Enter PEDRO *and* JAQUES.

Isab. Ay me, he raves: sweet Hieronimo!
Hier. True, all Spain takes note of it.
    Besides, he is so generally belov'd,   10
    His Majesty the other day did grace him
    With waiting on his cup: these be favours
    Which do assure he cannot be short-liv'd.
Isab. Sweet Hieronimo!
Hier. I wonder how this fellow got his clothes: 15
    Sirrah, sirrah, I'll know the truth of all:
    Jaques, run to the Duke of Castile's presently,
    And bid my son Horatio to come home.

7. Roderigo, ho!] *ends l. 6 in 1602.*   13. he] *This ed.;* me *1602;* me he
1603; me that he *1618.*

13. *assure*] make certain, guarantee, ensure; cf. *O.E.D.*, 5; Schmidt, 2.
1603's emendation is generally accepted, but the line is made much
stronger if we assume that *me* was a careless mistake for *he*.

I and his mother have had strange dreams tonight.
Do ye hear me, sir ?

Jaques.   Ay, sir.

Hier.   Well sir, begone.   20
Pedro, come hither: knowest thou who this is ?

Ped. Too well, sir.

Hier. Too well, who ? who is it ? Peace, Isabella:
Nay, blush not, man.

Ped.   It is my lord Horatio.

Hier. Ha, ha! Saint James, but this doth make me laugh,   25
That there are more deluded than myself.

Ped. Deluded ?

Hier. Ay, I would have sworn myself within this hour
That this had been my son Horatio,
His garments are so like: Ha!   30
Are they not great persuasions ?

Isab. O would to God it were not so!

Hier. Were not, Isabella ? dost thou dream it is ?
Can thy soft bosom entertain a thought
That such a black deed of mischief should be done   35
On one so pure and spotless as our son ?
Away, I am ashamed.

Isab.   Dear Hieronimo,
Cast a more serious eye upon thy grief:
Weak apprehension gives but weak belief.

Hier. It was a man, sure, that was hang'd up here,   40
A youth, as I remember: I cut him down.
If it should prove my son now after all—
Say you ? say you ? Light! lend me a taper,
Let me look again. O God!
Confusion, mischief, torment, death and hell,   45
Drop all your stings at once in my cold bosom,
That now is stiff with horror: kill me quickly:
Be gracious to me, thou infective night,

20–4.] *as prose in 1602.*   30–1.] *one line in 1602.*   36. pure] *1615;* poore
1602.   37. Dear Hieronimo,] *begins l. 38 in 1602.*   44. O God!]
begins l. 45 in 1602.

N

And drop this deed of murder down on me:
Gird in my waste of grief with thy large darkness,   50
And let me not survive to see the light
May put me in the mind I had a son.
Isab. O sweet Horatio, O my dearest son!
Hier. How strangely had I lost my way to grief.
Sweet lovely rose, ill-pluck'd before thy time,

SECOND ADDITION

(Replacing Hieronimo's speech, III. ii. 65–6. See p. 54)

Lor. *Why so, Hieronimo? use me.*
Hier.   Who, you, my lord?
I reserve your favour for a greater honour:
This is a very toy, my lord, a toy.
Lor. All's one, Hieronimo, acquaint me with it.
Hier. I' faith, my lord, it is an idle thing,   5
I must confess: I ha' been too slack, too tardy,
Too remiss unto your honour.
Lor.   How now, Hieronimo?
Hier. In troth, my lord, it is a thing of nothing,
The murder of a son, or so:
A thing of nothing, my lord.   10
Lor.   *Why then, farewell.*

51. survive] *Dodsley;* suruiue, 1602.

SECOND ADDITION

5. it is] *Schick;* tis *1602.*   5–7. I' faith . . . thing, / I must . . . tardy, / Too
. . . Hieronimo?] *Manly; as prose 1602.*

THIRD ADDITION

(Between III. xi. 1 and 2. See p. 77)

1.   By your leave, sir.
Hier. 'Tis neither as you think, nor as you think,
     Nor as you think: you're wide all:
     These slippers are not mine, they were my son Horatio's.
     My son! and what's a son? A thing begot
     Within a pair of minutes, thereabout: 5
     A lump bred up in darkness, and doth serve
     To ballace these light creatures we call women:
     And at nine moneths' end, creeps forth to light.
     What is there yet in a son
     To make a father dote, rave or run mad?   10
     Being born, it pouts, cries and breeds teeth.
     What is there yet in a son? He must be fed,
     Be taught to go, and speak. Ay, or yet?
     Why might not a man love a calf as well?
     Or melt in passion o'er a frisking kid   15
     As for a son? Methinks a young bacon
     Or a fine little smooth horse-colt
     Should move a man as much as doth a son:
     For one of these in very little time
     Will grow to some good use, whereas a son,   20
     The more he grows in stature and in years,
     The more unsquar'd, unbevell'd, he appears,
     Reckons his parents among the rank of fools,
     Strikes care upon their heads with his mad riots,

---

4. A thing begot] *begins l. 5 in 1602.*   7. ballace] *1602;* ballance *1618.*
13. speak. Ay, or yet?] *Manly;* speake I, or yet. *1602;* speak. Ay or yet
Schick.

---

7. *ballace*] ballast. A variant form, partly through confusion with
balance, and partly through taking *ballast* = *ballass-ed* (*O.E.D.*).
    13. *Ay, or yet?*] The phrase is so obviously a shortened repetition of the
question 'What is there yet in a son?', that it is hard to understand why
some edd. have followed Schick in taking it as the beginning of the succeeding sentence.

Makes them look old before they meet with age: 25
This is a son:
And what a loss were this, consider'd truly?
Oh, but my Horatio
Grew out of reach of these insatiate humours:
He lov'd his loving parents,   30
He was my comfort, and his mother's joy,
The very arm that did hold up our house:
Our hopes were stored up in him,
None but a damned murderer could hate him.
He had not seen the back of nineteen year,   35
When his strong arm unhors'd the proud Prince Balthazar,
And his great mind, too full of honour,
Took him unto mercy,
That valiant but ignoble Portingale.
Well, heaven is heaven still,   40
And there is Nemesis and Furies,
And things call'd whips,
And they sometimes do meet with murderers:
They do not always scape, that's some comfort.
Ay, ay, ay, and then time steals on: 45
And steals, and steals, till violence leaps forth
Like thunder wrapp'd in a ball of fire,
And so doth bring confusion to them all.
Good leave have you, nay, I pray you go,

26–30. This . . . son: / And . . . truly? / Oh, . . . Horatio / Grew . . .
humours: / He . . . parents,] *Boas;* This . . . truly. / O . . . of these / Insatiate
. . . parents, *1602.*   38. unto] *Manly;* vs to *1602.*   38–9.] *one line 1602.*
45–7. Ay . . . on: / And . . . forth / Like . . . fire,] *Schick;* I, . . . steales, and
steales / Till . . . thunder / Wrapt . . . fire, *1602.*

---

42. *things call'd whips*] The phrase was probably taken from *2 Henry VI*,
II. i. 137: 'Have you not beadles in your town, and things called whips?'
Armin, *Nest of Ninnies*, 1608, p. 55, has, 'Ther are, as Hamlet saies, things
cald whips in store.' It is easier to believe that Armin meant Hieronimo
than that the phrase came from the old *Hamlet*; see Duthie, '*Bad*' *Quarto
of Hamlet*, p. 77. There is a parallel in Marston; see Appendix E.

FOURTH ADDITION

(Between III. xii and III. xiii, with final stage-direction replacing
III. xiii. 0.1. See p. 83)

Enter JAQUES *and* PEDRO.

Jaq. I wonder Pedro, why our master thus
    At midnight sends us with our torches' light,
    When man and bird and beast are all at rest,
    Save those that watch for rape and bloody murder?
Ped. O Jaques, know thou that our master's mind   5
    Is much distraught since his Horatio died,
    And, now his aged years should sleep in rest,
    His heart in quiet, like a desperate man,
    Grows lunatic and childish for his son:
    Sometimes, as he doth at his table sit,   10
    He speaks as if Horatio stood by him,
    Then starting in a rage, falls on the earth,
    Cries out, 'Horatio! Where is my Horatio?'
    So that with extreme grief and cutting sorrow,
    There is not left in him one inch of man: 15
    See where he comes.

Enter HIERONIMO.

Hier. I pry through every crevice of each wall,
    Look on each tree, and search through every brake,
    Beat at the bushes, stamp our grandam earth,
    Dive in the water, and stare up to heaven,   20
    Yet cannot I behold my son Horatio.
    How now? Who's there? Sprites? sprites?

17. crevice] *1610;* creuie *1602.*   22. Sprites? sprites?] sprits, sprits?
1602.

---

18. *brake*] thicket.
22. *Sprites?*] As *1602*'s *sprits* is only a spelling variant of the mono-
syllabic 'spirits', it matters little whether we read *spirits* or *sprites*. But the
latter perhaps better indicates to us the meaning of ghost or demon.

Ped.   We are your servants that attend you, sir.

Hier.   What make you with your torches in the dark?

Ped.   You bid us light them, and attend you here.   25

Hier.   No, no, you are deceiv'd: not I, you are deceiv'd:
     Was I so mad to bid you light your torches now?
     Light me your torches at the mid of noon,
     Whenas the sun-god rides in all his glory:
     Light me your torches then.

Ped.   Then we burn daylight.   30

Hier.   Let it be burnt: night is a murderous slut
     That would not have her treasons to be seen,
     And yonder pale-fac'd Hecate there, the moon,
     Doth give consent to that is done in darkness,
     And all those stars that gaze upon her face   35
     Are aglets on her sleeve, pins on her train:
     And those that should be powerful and divine,
     Do sleep in darkness when they most should shine.

Ped.   Provoke them not, fair sir, with tempting words:
     The heavens are gracious, and your miseries   40
     And sorrow makes you speak you know not what.

Hier.   Villain, thou liest, and thou doest naught
     But tell me I am mad: thou liest, I am not mad.
     I know thee to be Pedro, and he Jaques.
     I'll prove it to thee, and were I mad, how could I?   45
     Where was she that same night when my Horatio

---

33. Hecate] *Heccat 1623;* Hee-cat *1602.*   36. aglets] agglots *1610;* aggots
1602.   41. And sorrow] *ends l. 40 in 1602.*   44. Jaques.] *Iaques, 1602.*

---

     30. *burn daylight*] The phrase was commonly used to mean wasting time;
Tilley D123.

     33. *Hecate*] two syllables. There is, unfortunately, no chance that *1602*'s
Hee-cat is the correct reading: the personal pronouns in ll. 35–6 are femi-
nine.

     36. *aglets*] spangles or metallic ornaments; properly, the ornamental tags
of laces. The form *agglot* is noted in *O.E.D.*

     45. *prove it*] i.e., that the moon and the stars connived at the murder of
Horatio.

Was murder'd? She should have shone: search thou the
    book.
Had the moon shone, in my boy's face there was a kind of
    grace,
That I know, nay, I do know, had the murderer seen him,
His weapon would have fall'n and cut the earth,   50
Had he been fram'd of naught but blood and death.
Alack, when mischief doth it knows not what,
What shall we say to mischief?

Enter ISABELLA.

Isab. Dear Hieronimo, come in a-doors:
    O seek not means so to increase thy sorrow.   55
Hier. Indeed, Isabella, we do nothing here,
    I do not cry, ask Pedro and ask Jaques,
    Not I indeed, we are very merry, very merry.
Isab. How? be merry here, be merry here?
    Is not this the place, and this the very tree,   60
    Where my Horatio died, where he was murder'd?
Hier. Was—do not say what: let her weep it out.
    This was the tree, I set it of a kernel,
    And when our hot Spain could not let it grow,
    But that the infant and the human sap   65
    Began to wither, duly twice a morning
    Would I be sprinkling it with fountain water.
    At last it grew, and grew, and bore and bore,
    Till at the length
    It grew a gallows, and did bear our son.   70
    It bore thy fruit and mine: O wicked, wicked plant.

One knocks within at the door.

See who knock there.

---

47. Was murder'd?] *ends l. 46 in 1602.*   48–9. face . . . That I know,] face
(there was a kind of grace That I know) *1602.*   61. died] *1603;* hied
1602.   69. Till . . . length] *begins l. 70 in 1602.*   72. knock] *1602;*
knocks *1603.*

Ped.   It is a painter, sir.

Hier. Bid him come in, and paint some comfort,
          For surely there's none lives but painted comfort:
          Let him come in. One knows not what may chance,   75
          God's will that I should set this tree—But even so
          Masters ungrateful servants rear from naught,
          And then they hate them that did bring them up.

                      Enter the Painter.

Paint. God bless you, sir.

Hier. Wherefore ? Why, thou scornful villain,   80
          How, where, or by what means should I be bless'd ?

Isab. What wouldst thou have, good fellow ?

Paint. Justice, madam.

Hier. O ambitious beggar, wouldst thou have that
          That lives not in the world ?   85
          Why all the undelved mines cannot buy
          An ounce of justice, 'tis a jewel so inestimable:
          I tell thee,
          God hath engross'd all justice in his hands,
          And there is none, but what comes from him.   90

Paint. O then I see
          That God must right me for my murder'd son.

Hier. How, was thy son murdered ?

Paint. Ay, sir: no man did hold a son so dear.

Hier. What, not as thine ? That's a lie   95
          As massy as the earth: I had a son,

75. in.] *Manly;* in, *1602.* | 76. God's will that] Gods will, that *1602.*
But even so] *begins l. 77 in 1602.*   88. I tell thee,] *begins l. 89 in 1602.*
91. O then I see] *begins l. 92 in 1602.*

76-7.] It is not easy to perceive from the punctuation of *1602* what the
meaning is. It is possible that *God's will* is an imprecation and that *But even
so* is self-contained; we should then paraphrase: 'God, that I should set this
tree!—but let things be as they are.' The alternative reading, preferred
here, leaves much to be understood, i.e., 'One knows not what may chance:
it must have been God's will that I should set this tree, [can what has now
happened be God's will also ?]' And with *But even so* he attempts to console
himself with an analogy between the tree and ungrateful servants.

Whose least unvalu'd hair did weigh
A thousand of thy sons: and he was murder'd.
Paint. Alas, sir, I had no more but he.
Hier. Nor I, nor I: but this same one of mine   100
Was worth a legion: but all is one.
Pedro, Jaques, go in a-doors, Isabella go,
And this good fellow here and I
Will range this hideous orchard up and down,
Like to two lions reaved of their young.   105
Go in a-doors, I say.   *Exeunt* [ISABELLA, PEDRO, JAQUES].

The Painter *and he sits down.*

Come, let's talk wisely now. Was thy son murdered?
Paint. Ay, sir.
Hier. So was mine. How dost take it? Art thou not some-
times mad? Is there no tricks that comes before thine   110
eyes?
Paint. O Lord, yes sir.
Hier. Art a painter? Canst paint me a tear, or a wound, a
groan, or a sigh? canst paint me such a tree as this?
Paint. Sir, I am sure you have heard of my painting, my   115
name's Bazardo.
Hier. Bazardo! afore God, an excellent fellow! Look you sir,
do you see, I'd have you paint me in my gallery, in your
oil colours matted, and draw me five years younger than
I am—do you see, sir, let five years go, let them go like   120
the marshal of Spain—my wife Isabella standing by me,
with a speaking look to my son Horatio, which should

118. me in my] *Lamb;* me my *1602;* me for my *Schick.*

---

105. *reaved*] forcibly deprived, robbed (*O.E.D.*, *v.*[1], 3). The alternative
past form 'reft' would be more familiar.
107.] *1602* continues to print as verse up to the end of the scene, although
in Hieronimo's speeches (ll. 139–55) the 'lines' can be whole sentences in
length. Lineation is not recorded in the textual notes.
119. *matted*] made dull or matt. *O.E.D.*, s.v. *mat, v.*[2], cites this passage as
the earliest use of the word by 125 years, and 'matt' itself is very rare, even
in the 17th century. Is it possible that Boas was right in preferring 'set in a
mat or mount'?

intend to this or some such like purpose: 'God bless thee,
my sweet son,' and my hand leaning upon his head, thus
sir, do you see? May it be done?   125

Paint. Very well, sir.

Hier. Nay, I pray mark me, sir. Then sir, would I have you
paint me this tree, this very tree. Canst paint a doleful
cry?

Paint. Seemingly, sir.   130

Hier. Nay, it should cry: but all is one. Well sir, paint me a
youth, run through and through with villains' swords,
hanging upon this tree. Canst thou draw a murderer?

Paint. I'll warrant you, sir: I have the pattern of the most
notorious villains that ever lived in all Spain.   135

Hier. O let them be worse, worse: stretch thine art, and let
their beards be of Judas his own colour, and let their eye-
brows jutty over: in any case observe that. Then sir, after
some violent noise, bring me forth in my shirt, and my
gown under mine arm, with my torch in my hand, and   140
my sword reared up thus: and with these words:
    What noise is this? who calls Hieronimo?
May it be done?

Paint. Yea, sir.

Hier. Well sir, then bring me forth, bring me through alley   145
and alley, still with a distracted countenance going
along, and let my hair heave up my night-cap. Let the
clouds scowl, make the moon dark, the stars extinct, the
winds blowing, the bells tolling, the owl shrieking, the
toads croaking, the minutes jarring, and the clock strik-   150
ing twelve. And then at last, sir, starting, behold a man
hanging, and tottering and tottering, as you know the
wind will weave a man, and I with a trice to cut him down.

145. *Hier.*] *not in 1602.*   149. owl] *1602;* owls *1623.*   150. jarring]
iering *1602.*   153. weave] *1602;* wave *1603.*

---

137. *of Judas his own colour*] red.
138. *jutty*] project; cf. *Henry V*, III. i. 13.
150. *jarring*] ticking; *O.E.D.*, 2.
153. *weave*] sway from side to side. Cf. *O.E.D.*, *v.*², 1, which does

And looking upon him by the advantage of my torch,
find it to be my son Horatio. There you may show a pas- 155
sion, there you may show a passion. Draw me like old
Priam of Troy, crying, 'The house is a-fire, the house is
a-fire, as the torch over my head.' Make me curse, make
me rave, make me cry, make me mad, make me well
again, make me curse hell, invocate heaven, and in the 160
end, leave me in a trance—and so forth.

Paint. And is this the end?

Hier. O no, there is no end: the end is death and madness.
As I am never better than when I am mad, then methinks I am a brave fellow, then I do wonders: but reason 165
abuseth me, and there's the torment, there's the hell. At
the last, sir, bring me to one of the murderers: were he as
strong as Hector, thus would I tear and drag him up and
down.

He beats the Painter *in, then comes out again with a book
in his hand.*

FIFTH ADDITION

(Replacing IV. iv. 168–90, but incorporating lines 176–9 and
168–75. See p. 117)

Cast. *Why hast thou butcher'd both my children thus?*

Hier. But are you sure they are dead?

Cast. Ay, slave, too sure.

Hier. What, and yours too?

Vice. Ay, all are dead, not one of them survive.

Hier. Nay, then I care not, come, and we shall be friends:
Let us lay our heads together, 5
See here's a goodly noose will hold them all.

155. show] *Dodsley; not in 1602.*

---

not give this type of transitive use. Edd. have preferred *1603*'s *wave.*
with a trice] instantly; the same as 'in a trice'.

Vice. O damned devil, how secure he is.

Hier. Secure? why dost thou wonder at it?
> I tell thee Viceroy, this day I have seen revenge,
> And in that sight am grown a prouder monarch   10
> That ever sat under the crown of Spain:
> Had I as many lives as there be stars,
> As many heavens to go to as those lives,
> I'd give them all, ay, and my soul to boot,
> But I would see thee ride in this red pool.   15

Cast. Speak, who were thy confederates in this?

Vice. That was thy daughter Bel-Imperia,
> For by her hand my Balthazar was slain:
> I saw her stab him.

Hier.   O good words!
> As dear to me was my Horatio,   20
> As yours, or yours, or yours, my lord, to you.
> My guiltless son was by Lorenzo slain,
> And by Lorenzo and that Balthazar
> Am I at last revenged thoroughly,
> Upon whose souls may heavens be yet reveng'd   25
> With greater far than these afflictions.
> Methinks since I grew inward with revenge,
> I cannot look with scorn enough on death.

King. What, dost thou mock us, slave? Bring tortures forth!

Hier. Do, do, do, and meantime I'll torture you.   30
> You had a son, as I take it: and your son
> Should ha' been married to your daughter: ha, was't not so?
> You had a son too, he was my liege's nephew;
> He was proud and politic, had he liv'd,
> He might ha' come to wear the crown of Spain: 35
> I think 'twas so: 'twas I that killed him,

9. revenge] *Dodsley;* reueng'd *1602.*   19. O good words!] *begins l. 20 in 1602.*   35. ha'] a *1602.*

---

7. *secure*] arrogantly self-confident.

12–14.] From *Faustus,* ll. 337–8: 'Had I as many soules as there be starres, Ide giue them al for Mephastophilis.'

31–3.] Hieronimo turns from the Viceroy to Castile.

Look you, this same hand, 'twas it that stabb'd
His heart—do you see this hand ?—
For one Horatio, if you ever knew him,
A youth, one that they hang'd up in his father's garden,   40
One that did force your valiant son to yield,
While your more valiant son did take him prisoner.

Vice. Be deaf my senses, I can hear no more.
King. Fall heaven, and cover us with thy sad ruins.
Cast. Roll all the world within thy pitchy cloud.   45
Hier. Now do I applaud what I have acted.
            Nunc iners cadat manus.
Now to express the rupture of my part,
First take my tongue, and afterward my heart.
                         He bites out his tongue.

47. *iners cadat*] *Schick; mers cadæ 1602.*

_____

47.] 'Now let my hand fall idle!'

The Problem of Henslowe's Entries

(See p. xxi)

The relevant titles given by Henslowe in his records of performances at the Rose in the spring and early summer of 1592 are as follows (in chronological order of appearance and with the number of times each title is found):

spanes comodye donne oracoe	1
the comodey of doneoracio	1
Jeronymo [*various spellings*]	13
doneoracio	1
the comodey of Jeronymo	3
The comodey Jeronymo	1

After this first season, only 'Jeronimo' is found.

The variety of titles is no evidence that two plays existed: all the forms may be variants for the one play. Henslowe was interested in his receipts and not in whether a play was a tragedy or a comedy; if he could call *Titus Andronicus* 'Titus and ondronicus', he could certainly call 'doneoracio' the hero of *The Spanish Tragedy* (and it is significant that the entry in the Stationers' Register reads 'The Spanish Tragedy of Don Horatio and Bel-imperia'—see p. xxviii). It is not good argument to say that 'Jeronimo' is *The Spanish Tragedy* and that all other titles refer to some lost fore-piece or first part. One could just as well say that there were *three* plays, *The Comedy of Don Horatio*, *The Comedy of Jeronimo*, and *Jeronimo* or *The Spanish Tragedy*. But it is not nomenclature alone that has led to the belief that two plays are involved. There is also the strange fact that on three separate occasions, a performance of 'Jeronimo' was preceded by a performance on the day before of the play with one of the alternative titles.[1]

March 13	comodey of doneoracio
March 14	Jeronymo

[1] The General Editor has called my attention to a performance of *Jeronimo* on Monday, April 24, which was preceded by 'the comodey Jeronymo' on the Saturday before.

March 30	doneoracio
March 31	Jeronymo
May 21	comodey of Jeronymo
May 22	Jeronymo

Greg points out (Henslowe's *Diary*, II, 154) that there is 'hardly any instance of a play being repeated twice running' in Henslowe's records, but that there are examples of the first and second parts of two-part plays being performed on successive days. Discussion of the problem was confused in the past by the identification of Henslowe's comedy with *The First Part of Ieronimo*, published in 1605. But this play is clearly written after *The Spanish Tragedy* and based on it, and almost certainly intended as a burlesque. The problem as it now stands is, Which is more likely, that *The Spanish Tragedy* is a sequel to a now-lost play, or that the players broke their usual custom and occasionally played *The Spanish Tragedy* twice on consecutive days? I cannot find in *The Spanish Tragedy* anything to prove that it is a sequel; the many mentions of past events no more indicate a first part than similar mentions in *Cymbeline* or *Hamlet* indicate that those plays are the second halves of two-part wholes. The three occasions of performances on successive days are very strange, and one cannot dismiss the theory of a lost first part as untenable; yet it is possible to be sceptical and to demand more evidence than Henslowe provides. (It could, of course, be argued that the 'forepiece' was written *after* *The Spanish Tragedy*, because of the play's success, and that by 1592 it was occasionally played as a 'first part'.) But the problem of Henslowe's entries does not affect the inference that *The Spanish Tragedy* was being played at the Rose in early 1592.

APPENDIX B

The Kid in *Æsop*

(See p. xxiii)

It is now accepted that Nashe was thinking of the fable of the Kid in Spenser's *Shepheardes Calender* (the May eclogue, ll. 274–7) and not Aesop. McKerrow believes that Nashe is simply bringing in the Kid as a beast-fable analogy without the further purpose of referring to Thomas Kyd; though it is true that Kyd 'intermeddled with Italian translations' in translating Tasso's *Padre di Famiglia* in 1588, he was hardly the only translator from Italian. But Duthie is impressed by Oesterberg's view (see *R.E.S.*, xviii (1942), 389–91) that Nashe has clumsily twisted Spenser's fable in order to bring in an allusion to Kyd. Nashe says that his dramatists have exhausted their source, Seneca, 'which makes his famished followers to imitate the Kid in *Æsop*, who, enamoured with the Foxes newfangles, forsooke all hopes of life to leape into a newe occupation; and these men, renouncing all possibilities of credite or estimation, to intermeddle with Italian Translations'. Now Spenser's Kid was lost by his naivety, in being attracted by the glass which the disguised Fox showed him, and by his curiosity in reaching into the Fox's basket to take up a bell: the Fox swept him into his basket, and farewell Kid. Oesterberg says that there is no real parallel between Spenser's fable and the fate of the dramatists: Spenser's Kid does not 'forsake all hopes of life to leap into a new occupation'; in order to show that Thomas Kyd was one of the dramatists who gave up a barren profession and hopefully but fatally resorted to another, Nashe made use of an inappropriate fable to bring in the name 'Kid'.

I confess I find the argument most unconvincing. That Nashe is writing rapidly and carelessly is clear from his mistaken attribution of the fable to Aesop. He wanted a derogatory image for those who are attracted by some new gewgaw which proves fatal: the dramatists were attracted by Italian translations, the Kid by the glass and bell. That is the essential parallelism; the fact that the dramatists consciously change their lives and that the Kid does not seems to me to be of no significance. In any case, in E. K.'s gloss on Spenser's fable, the Kid resembles those who are attracted by 'the reliques and ragges of popish superstition', and are therefore damned for their weak-minded deviation; the Kid may well be said (allegorically speaking) to leap into a new occupation. It seems impossible to prove an allusion to Kyd from the weakness of the analogy between the Kid and the dramatists. Nashe may have had Kyd in mind as one of his dramatists, but the reference to the 'Kid in Aesop' does not prove it.

Kyd and *Tamburlaine*, Part 2

There is an interesting 'image-growth' in Kyd which suggests the possibility that when writing *The Spanish Tragedy* he had in mind *Tamburlaine*, Part 2 (?1588; published 1590). *The Spanish Tragedy*, I. ii. 52–61, gives a lurid description of a battlefield:

> Now while Bellona rageth here and there,
> Thick storms of bullets rain like winter's hail,
> And shiver'd lances dark the troubled air.
>
> .   .   .   .
>
> On every side drop captains to the ground,
> And soldiers, some ill-maim'd, some slain outright:
> Here falls a body scinder'd from his head,
> There legs and arms lie bleeding on the grass,
> Mingled with weapons and unbowell'd steeds.

Kyd took most of his suggestions from Garnier's *Cornélie*, and the third line is a conflation of two images in Garnier, one concerning splintered lances flying in the air like straw, and the other concerning the air being darkened and the sun paled by the dust of the battle (v. 136–40, 149–50). When Kyd later translated the whole of *Cornélie*, he recalled his previous image and, ignoring Garnier's straw, again suggested the impeded light:

> The shyuered Launces (ratling in the ayre)
> Fly forth as thicke as moates about the Sunne.
>
> (*Cornelia*, v. 170–1)

But in this transformed image of motes about the sun, Kyd has also been directly aided by a recollection of a passage in *2 Tamburlaine*, which also speaks in lurid terms of dismembered corpses on a battle-field:

> Hast thou beheld a peale of ordinance strike
> A ring of pikes, mingled with shot and horse,
> Whose shattered lims, being tost as high as heauen,
> *Hang in the aire as thick as sunny motes...?* (III. ii)

The question is, did Kyd know this passage when (with the help of Garnier) he was describing the battle in *The Spanish Tragedy*? It is certainly possible, for it looks as though the phrase in the second line of the Marlowe extract, 'mingled with shot and horse', has become (with the metonymy metabolized) Kyd's 'mingled with weapons and unbowell'd steeds' (last line of the Kyd extract). In using Garnier twice, in *The Spanish Tragedy* and in *Cornelia*, it is possible that on each occasion Kyd recalled a different part of a passage with the same theme from *2 Tamburlaine*. There are few other parallels with the play, but Kyd may be echoing one of Marlowe's uses of his favourite word 'glut' in 'Hath here been glutted with thy harmless blood' (II. v. 20), to be compared with 'We all are glutted with the Christian's blood' (*2 Tamburlaine*, I. i).

Watson's Elegy on Walsingham

There are some verbal resemblances between *The Spanish Tragedy* and an elegy on Walsingham which Thomas Watson published in 1590, an English rendering of his own Latin elegy *Melibœus*, published in the same year. Walsingham died on 6 April 1590. The resemblances are as follows (quotations from Arber's reprint, modernized):

(*a*) *Watson:*

> Stout Astrophel, *incens'd with sole remorse,*
> > Resolv'd to die, or see the slaughter ceas'd.

   Kyd (I. iv. 27–8):

> > Then, though too late, *incens'd with just remorse,*
> > I with my band set forth against the prince.

(*b*) *Watson:*

> > *Help to lament* great Melibœus' death:
> > *Let clouds of tears with sighs be turn'd to rain.*

   Kyd (II. v. 36 and 43–4):

> > Here Isabella, *help me to lament*

    ·   ·   ·   ·   ·

> > O gush out, tears, fountains and *floods of tears,*
> > *Blow, sighs, and raise an everlasting storm.*

(*c*) *Watson:*

> > His faith hath fram'd *his spirit holy wings*
> > > *To soar* with Astrophel *above the sun,*
> > And there he joys...

    ·   ·   [5 lines]   ·   ·   ·

> Our Melibœus lives where Seraphins
> > Do praise the highest in their glorious *flames,*
> Where flows the knowledge of wise *Cherubins...*

    ·   ·   [33 lines]   ·   ·   ·

> *Singing sweet hymns* for him whose soul is blest.

    ·   ·   [21 lines]   ·   ·   ·

> Diana, wondrous *mirror of our days...*

Kyd (III. viii. 15–22):

> *My soul* hath *silver wings*
> *That mounts* me up unto the highest heavens,
> To heaven, ay, there sits my Horatio,
> Back'd with a troop of *fiery cherubins*,
> Dancing about his newly-healed wounds,
> *Singing sweet hymns* and chanting heavenly notes,
> Rare harmony to greet his innocence,
> That died, ay, died, a *mirror in our days*.

Except for (*a*), the ideas and phrases shared by the two writers are not in the least uncommon, but the similarity seems more than accidental. If there is a dependence, it seems to be of Kyd on Watson, because (i) Watson is translating (though not word for word) from his own Latin, (ii) it is more likely in (*c*) that a borrower should compress an extended fancy, and bring in adjacent phrases, than that he should dilate, and (iii) the mythology of Isabella's speech in (*c*) is somewhat out of keeping with the Virgilian mythology of the rest of the play (though it is not unique, see p. lix).

Marston's Parodies of the 'Painter Scene'

(See p. lxv)

There are three parallels, the chief one being in Act V, Scene i of *Antonio and Mellida*. Balurdo talks with a Painter and the conversation includes such remarks as: 'I wold haue you paint mee, for my deuice, a good fat legge of ewe mutton, swimming in stewde broth of plummes . . . and the word shall be; *Holde my dishe, whilst I spill my pottage.*' 'Can you paint me a driueling reeling song, & let the word be, Vh . . . . . . It can not be done sir, but by a seeming kinde of drunkennesse.' In the previous scene, Levin points out (see p. lxii), Antonio's attempt to make his page express his grief by singing is like Hieronimo's attempt to make Bazardo express his grief by painting; for example:

> speake, groning like a bell,
> That towles departing soules.
> Breath me a point that may inforce me weepe,
> To wring my hands, to breake my cursed breast,
> Raue, and exclaime, lie groueling on the earth,
> Straight start vp frantick. . .
>
> .   .   .   .
>
> For looke thee boy, my griefe that hath no end. . .

Finally, in *Antonio's Revenge*, IV. i, there is a parallel with the lines in the Third Addition which run

> And there is Nemesis and Furies
> And things call'd whips.   (ll. 41–2)

Alberto is speaking:

> I, I am gone; but marke, *Piero*, this.
> There is a thing cald scourging *Nemesis*.

The King's Men and *The Spanish Tragedy*

There are some perplexing references to *The Spanish Tragedy* which raise the question whether the Admiral's Men maintained what would appear to be their original right in the play. First, there are two references to Richard Burbage, pillar of the Chamberlain's-King's Men, playing Hieronimo. One of these may perhaps be discounted: it is in the second *Return from Parnassus* and Burbage is instructing the young Studioso in acting (*Three Parnassus Plays*, ed. Leishman, p. 341):

> I thinke your voice would serue for *Hieronimo*, obserue how I act it and then imitate mee:
> > Who calls *Ieronimo* from his naked bedd?

Considering the authors' scorn for the public theatre and its ways (see Leishman, pp. 59–60), it is hardly likely that they would care whether Hieronimo was really one of Burbage's parts or not. The second reference is in one of the elegies on Burbage's death.[1]

> No more young Hamlett, ould Heironymoe
> Kind Leer, the Greued Moore, and more beside,
> That liued in him; have now for ever dy'de.

These lines are not found in one of the manuscript versions of the elegy; another, longer, version is recognized as spurious. Burbage could hardly have acted the plum part of Hieronimo when, as a youth, he was associated with the Strange's-Admiral's company (Nungezer, p. 68); the other plays mentioned, it is worth noticing, are all post-1600. It is a problem to think that Burbage had a name for acting the chief part in a play which did not belong to his company. But what significance is to be attached to Webster's Induction (1604) to Marston's *Malcontent*, which implies that *Jeronimo* was a King's Men's play that had been filched from the company by the Children of the Queen's Revels? Cundale is explaining how the King's Men come to be acting a play belonging to the children:

---

[1] *Shakespeare Allusion Book*, I, 272–3; Nungezer, *Dictionary of Actors*, p. 74; *Fliz. Stage*, II, 309.

Sly. I wonder you would play it, another company having interest
in it ?

Cundale. Why not Malevole in folio with us, as Jeronimo in Decimo
sexto with them ? They taught us a name for our play, wee call
it *One for another.*

The reference to 'folio' and 'decimo sexto' is of course to the size of
the actors. F. L. Lucas's gloss (Webster, *Works*, III, 307) runs, 'Why
should not our men's company retaliate, by acting *The Malcontent*,
for the pirating by the Children's company at Blackfriars of our
Jeronimo ?'

The usual explanation is that the *Jeronimo* play is *The First Part of
Jeronimo* (see Appendix A). But that play seems to be a children's
play to begin with, and we can hardly imagine Burbage winning fame
from acting the little Hieronimo—'As short my body, short shall be
my stay' (I. iii. 103). On the other hand, there could not possibly be
any righteous indignation among the King's Men at the theft from
them of *The Spanish Tragedy*, since it did not belong to them in the
first place. The only solution seems to be that the play mentioned by
Webster *is* the *First Part*, that it was adapted by the Children, when
they 'borrowed' it, into the form which we know, and that the references to Burbage as acting the *great* Hieronimo are mistakes.

Glossarial Index to the Commentary

This index lists words, phrases, names, tags, and selected proverbs which have required elucidation in the Commentary. It is neither a concordance nor a complete list of annotations. Words are normally cited in simple form (i.e., nouns in the singular, verbs in the infinitive), whatever the form in the text. When more than one line-reference is given, the word has been used in more than one sense. An asterisk before a word or a reference indicates that the meaning is not covered, or is only partly covered, by *O.E.D.*, or that a date given by *O.E.D.* is corrected.

Accident, III. vii. 54
action of the case, III. xiii. 61
advantage, III. xiii. 27–8, *III. xiv. 75
Aeacus, I. i. 33
aglet, Add. 4, 36
Alcides, III. xiii. 111
ambages, I. iv. 90
and if, III. iv. 73
apply, IV. i. 32
—— me to the time, III. ix. 13
approve, III. vi. 39
arbour, II. iv. 53
Ariadne, III. x. 89–90
*assure, Add. 1, 13
avail, *sb.*, IV. i. 47

Back, give, II. iii. 50
ballace, Add. 3, 7
ban, *vb*, III. vii. 65
band, III. xiii. 66
banquet, *sb.*, I. iv. 115.1
battle, *sb.*, I. ii. 32
*bear it out, IV. i. 24
beauty's thrall, II. i. 27
bend, *vb*, III. ix. 6
beside, sit, I. ii. 177
bewray, I. iii. 54
bower, II. iv. 53
brake, Add. 4, 18

*bring, be with thee to, III. xii. 22
bug, IV. v. 28
burn daylight, Add. 4, 30

Camp, *sb.*, I. ii. 1
can, *vb*, III. xiii. 118
care, *sb.*, IV. i. 39
case, if, II. i. 58
cast, *vb*, III. ii. 100
censure, *sb.*, I. ii. 175
centre of the earth, III. i. 23
chivalry, I. ii. 21
che le Ieron, III. ii. 94
circumstance, III. ii. 48
cite, IV. ii. 27
closely, III. iv. 62
coil, keep a, III. xiii. 45
colonel, I. ii. 40
colour, *vb*, III. i. 20
——s of device, I. ii. 27
commend, *sb.*, III. i. 68
companion, III. ii. 115
complot, III. ii. 100
conceit, *sb.*, I. iv. 82
——, *vb*, IV. i. 134
condescent, III. xiv. 17
condition, III. ii. 74
control, *vb*, I. ii. 139, II. iv. 7
convenient speed, II. iii. 38
conveyance, II. i. 47

149